Good Food from a Japanese Temple

introduction by Robert Farrar Capon

Good Food from a Japanese Temple

Soei Yoneda
Abbess, Sankō-in temple
with
Kōei Hoshino
and
Kim Schuefftan

Kodansha International
Tokyo, New York and San Francisco

distributed in the United States by Kodansha International/USA, Ltd., through Harper & Row, Publishers, Inc., 10 East 53rd Street, New York, New York 10022

published by Kodansha International Ltd., 12-21 Otowa 2-chome, Bunkyo-ku, Tokyo 112 and Kodansha International/USA, Ltd., 10 East 53rd Street, New York, New York 10022 and 44 Montgomery Street, San Francisco, California 94104

printed in Japan
first edition, 1982

LCC 82–80734
ISBN 0–87011–527–8
ISBN 4–7700–1024–9 (in Japan)

Library of Congress Cataloging in Publication Data
Yoneda, Soei.
Good food from a Japanese temple.
Includes index.
1. Vegetarian cookery. 2. Cookery, Japanese.
I. Hoshino, Kōei. II. Schuefftan, Kim. III. Title.
TX837.Y66 1982 641.5'636 82-80734
ISBN 0–87011–527–8 (U.S.)

CONTENTS

INTRODUCTION

By one of the manifold contradictions that underlie the attitude of Americans toward eating, cookbooks are now the hottest items on publisher's lists—and diet books run them a best-selling second. We are flailing about, it seems, for a golden mean but we come up only with extremes. On the one hand, we practically wolf down every new cuisine that finds its way into print; on the other, we harbor a deep suspicion that food is an enemy that must be dealt with only under the harshest of treaties.

Paradoxically, what all this frantic attention to food actually produces is inattention to the very things that make food enjoyable: sound cooking and gracious dining. We seem to have progressed, at both stove and table, from bad to bad without passing through anything even vaguely resembling good.

Take cooking, for example. If we were once a nation that boiled all the native goodness out of foods, we are now dedicated to the proposition that drowning them in alien flavors is the key to good cookery. It's not just that we put ketchup on too many things; it's that we act as if nothing at all is palatable until we make it so. Without ever seriously addressing the tastes and textures resident in our raw materials, we proceed straight to painting them over with thick coats of whatever seasonings happen to strike us as chic.

Or take dining. We went from the confining starchiness of formal sit-down dinners to the unbuttoned rootlessness of standup buffet suppers; yet nowhere along the line did we give either the food or the company a fair shake. And all this, mind you, from people who actually went to the bother of cooking and entertaining. Contrary to the usual alarms, it is not fast foods and convenience snacks that are our most serious problem. Such things have their places and they fill them tolerably enough. It's precisely in our deliberate attempts at notable cuisine that food worthy of gifted cooks and civilized diners is hard to find. Hence this book. Taken to heart and hand, it can go a long way toward putting that unhappy situation to rights.

My first experience of the cuisine presented here was at the small Buddhist temple, the *Sankō-in*, of which the author is Abbess. Tucked away in a suburb at the western edge of Tokyo, it is practically unnoticeable until you have walked the length of a nondescript driveway that deposits you suddenly—behind a pink apartment house, of all things—at the gate of the temple itself. Once inside though, both grounds and buildings become a tranquil island where the nagging question of *what time it is* simply does not arise and the things it is really *time for*—the food, the company, the simple grace of a tatami room, the changing, warming slant of afternoon sun through shoji screens—can be given full attention.

The outline of the meal follows a scheme of service that is a refreshing change from the usual western put-it-on-the-table-all-at-once approach: hot towels, whisked tea and a sweet bean cake by way of welcome; then a fascinating succession of vegetable dishes; and finally, soup, rice, pickled vegetables and green tea. With all but the first and last saké is served and, gently but firmly, it works its conversational magic. Indeed, the only major departure from Japanese cuisine is the fact that, in deference to Buddhist *shōjin* tradition, only vegetables—no meat, fish, eggs or dairy products—are served at the Sankō-in. It is a distinction *with* a difference, and a delightful one at that.

There is for example, a small plate of assorted cooked vegetables, beautifully arranged: a slice of mashed yam roll in *nori* seaweed, an arrow feather made of burdock root, a slice of lotus root tempura, a piece of simmered tofu and three lightly cooked snow peas. There is *rōbai*, a delicious concoction of deep-fried wheat gluten, softened in a soy-flavored stock and dressed with hot Japanese mustard. There is a mock "tofu" made of sesame "milk" and a *nori* roll filled with flavor-simmered spinach and served with a lemon-soy sauce. There is an altogether remarkable steamed savory cup in which grated turnip, chopped rice, ginkgo nuts, *shiitake* mushrooms, carrot slices, snow peas, fried waterchestnut balls and thickened *dashi* stock are turned into a delicate "custard" punctuated with an emphatic dot of *wasabi* horseradish. There is a starkly simple shredded ginger tempura, served crisp with mustard-soy for dipping. And there are clear soups and miso soups, and bamboo rice, vinegared turnips and pickled Chinese cabbage . . .

But enough. Clearly, from a cook's point of view the cuisine is mystery that cries out for investigation; and for a diner, it provides an experience not only of variety and finesse but also of great directness and simplicity. Every vegetable, however deftly or mysteriously sauced, tastes first of all like itself—even in dishes where several ingredients are combined. And every presentation, even the most artful (there isn't one that's not: even three bits of fried, shredded ginger on a plate are arranged so as to have a front and back) is worlds away from mere artiness. Everything looks like food meant to be relished by both eye and palate: the impression left upon guests is one of having comprehensively, finally and for good, *dined.*

In fairness, of course, it should be said that all elegant Japanese cooking and service produces the same sense of visual satisfaction. What is unique in this case, however, is not only that it is achieved by a menu consisting exclusively of vegetable dishes but also that the flavors of the dishes themselves remain memorable in a way that those of technique-dominated Japanese haute cuisine often do not. Indeed, so strong is the second impression, it is hard to keep in mind that the cuisine labored under any restrictions at all. The biblical writer who said "Better a dinner of herbs where love is, than a stalled ox and hatred therewith" should have tasted this food. He would have been sorely tempted to stop short at "Better a dinner of herbs. Period."

Dinners of herbs, however—as naturally and as gracefully as they may flow from this 600-year tradition of Zen temple cooking called *shōjin ryōri*—are hardly the American idea of a square meal. The vegetable kingdom has had an uphill job of it trying to conquer our dinner tables. As if it weren't bad enough that avowed enemies of vegetables have hindered that happy conquest, even purported friends stand forbiddingly in the way. For every child who hates spinach, there seem to be a dozen grain and legume lovers whose grim enthusiasms serve only to give brown rice and soy beans a bad name.

But that is to proceed too quickly. The history of the modern American use of vegetables is a vexed subject and a little time is required to do it justice. On the one hand, these delicious members of the humblest of the kingdoms of life have frequently been treated as less even than the dirt in which they grow. When we speak, for example, of the animal kingdom, we do its citizens the honor of recognizing, even of relishing their uniquenesses. It's rarely just "I want *meat* for supper." Far more likely it will be "How about beef, or lamb, or veal, or pork—or turkey, chicken, goose or duck?" But when it comes to vegetables we talk like the Archie Bunkers of comestibility, discriminating against them by the very indiscriminateness of our attention. "Children, eat your veggies" we say. "But I *hate* vegetables" they quickly learn to answer. To them—as to the prejudiced who learn early in life that all blacks look the same and that no Chinese waiter can be distinguished from any other—to them comes the insidious instruction that no artichoke, burdock, celeriac, dandelion or eggplant—nor any other fruit of the soil from fennel to zucchini—need ever be recognized as of *individual* interest. After all, they're only *vegetables.*

On the other hand—and in fairness to our ill-taught youths—it is not as if we gave them much reason to expect that any vegetables besides potatoes, carrots, peas and corn should exist. Oh, I know. Things are not quite that bad any more. They also know about celery and iceberg lettuce, I suppose. But the lack of imagination with which we approach even such a limited list is appalling. Plain boiled or plain raw is very nearly the full extent of our notion of preparation.

But however much those sins of defect may plague American kitchens, they hold no sway over the cookery in this book. To begin with, it uses the full range of vegetables. Some of them, no doubt, will be hard to come by in this country. But then, they are not the crucial thing. The *principles* of this cuisine are what matter most: if they are firmly grasped, the great variety of vegetables we do have but don't use can easily provide the resourceful cook with excellent substitutes. (Not to mention the fact that any cook who is also a gardener can grow practically all the so-called exotic ones in the back yard. American seed catalogues have, mercifully, been ahead of American tastes for years.)

It is the principles then—both of cooking and of presentation—that are the heart of this cuisine. More perhaps than with any other cookbook, you will find this not so much a collection of recipes (though it is indeed that, and a superb one) as it is a time-tested and brilliant way of coming at the whole subject of vegetable cookery. It requires no special equipment (not even a wok, though there may well be more unemployed ones in America than there are functioning ones in Japan). Indeed the only item it calls for that is not present in American kitchens is a sharp knife—and with this book's encouragement, even that national disgrace might become a thing of the past.

Better yet though, this cuisine does not require a vast array of seasonings and adjunct ingredients. True enough, it may tempt you, once you take it up, to scour the neighborhood for a well-stocked oriental grocery; but you can go a long way toward proficiency with little more than water, salt, sugar, saké and soy sauce (Japanese, please—Kikkoman is excellent and available everywhere) by way of basic seasonings. For of all the things it has to teach you, the principal one is *subtlety in the use of everything.*

As a matter of fact, it may even be an advantage to begin one's use of this book without the full armamentarium of exotica on hand. Americans, once they discover emphatic things like Japanese mustard and *wasabi* horseradish, are all too likely to use them in quantities gross enough to blow off the tops of skulls. And even with less aggressive ingredients such as soy sauce and the bean pastes called miso, they commonly apply them so ham-handedly that every dish tastes like a salt lick.

What the cuisine presented here has chiefly to offer therefore, is the chance to develop not only a discerning palate but a hand light enough to allow the natural flavors of vegetables to come through at their satisfying best. It has, of course, dozens of excellences beyond that, particularly when it comes to the elegance of its presentations. But if it could persuade even one cook per neighborhood of the virtue of subtlety, this country would be a better place to eat in. As it is now, our taste buds are practically deaf to any food that is not the gustatory equivalent of the last eight measures of a Beethoven symphony. How nice it would be if this book could teach us to admire food that knows how to lower its voice.

Alas, however, there is more to our problem with vegetables than under-use and over-seasoning. One would think, of course, that it would be quite sad enough that innocent creatures such as roots, tubers, stems, leaves, flowers, fruits and seeds should have to suffer the untender mercies of human beings who pay them no real mind. Indeed, in a world less far from its intended happy state than this one, we might expect that because of their very patience under insufficient attention, they would be excused from further abuse. We might logically suppose, might we not, that the last thing they would have to endure would be a paradoxical excess of attention—an exaltation by metaphysical hype which, while it goes on ignoring the right reasons for regarding them, praises them to the skies for all the wrong ones?

Well, we might; but we would suppose wrong. In addition to having their genuine merits paid not the least regard, vegetables have been cruelly saddled with ideological and spiritual virtues that bear no resemblance to their reality at all. Moreover, from a culinary point of view, this last super-exalted state of abuse is, if anything, worse than the first. More than any other comestible, vegetables have been made to *mean*. What they actually *are* is continually treated as subsidiary to what they are supposed to encapsulate, to effect, to express, to signify, to represent. In fact, so great is the load of spirituality placed upon them—so profound the reverence with which their almost redemptive qualities are regarded—that it is a wonder, not that their religionists cook them badly, but that they even dare to cook them at all.

It is widely held, for example, that with the exception of poisonous mushrooms, vegetables are not only *good for you*, but are the only foods that *cannot possibly be bad for you*. Meat may cause cancer, mackerel may be full of mercury, and eggs may plug your arteries with plaque; but veggies are an unqualified blessing. Quite obviously, of course, it does not take even a child of small intelligence and minimal experience very long to figure out that when a claim like that is made for a creature like spinach, a con job is in progress. Accordingly, and quite rightly, he reacts with scepticism: anything that needs significance spooned over it so liberally must be pretty poor stuff to start with. Popeye to the contrary notwithstanding, the only result of such oversell is the equation of spinach—and of vegetables generally—with the word "Bunk!"

But as if that were not enough, the merchants of meaning have felt obliged to endow vegetables with more immaterial qualities still. With great enthusiasm but with no manifest logic, they credit them not only with an inability to do you harm but with the power to do you good because they contain lesser amounts of a certain abstract entity. I have in mind, of course, calories. Vegetables, having fewer of them than, say, meat, are held to be positively slimming.

Of all the reasons for eating vegetables, that is the most egregiously mindless. To begin with, only non-eating can be positively slimming: no digestible food *per se* works by tearing down the human frame. If something is burned by my body at all, it yields up a certain number of calories of heat, thus making a deposit to my account, not a withdrawal from it. More than that though, calories themselves are not real beings. They are measurements, not things. They have no taste, texture, shape or smell; no human sense dedicated to the enjoyment of food has ever run into so much as a single one of them, let alone the herds in which they are said to run. As abstractions, of course—as a measure of the amount of heat given off during the combustion of anything—they have their uses. But in cooking? In dining? Admittedly, cabbage leaves yield up a certain amount of heat when burned in my body; but then, so would a suitable portion of the Declaration of Independence. We choose to cook the former and not the latter because ink and paper, even when they convey Thomas Jefferson's prose, have never been renowned for their flavor. Calories have nothing to do with the decision.

And as for the supposedly fewer calories that vegetables have, can there be anyone who does not realize that it all depends on what quantities you ingest? An ounce of beef suet has more calories than only a certain amount of any given vegetable. Eat ten pounds of spinach or one of potatoes and you'll find the contest goes the other way.

But as if even that was not enough, the claim is made that vegetables are positively good for you in a way that other foods are not. They constitute—all by themselves, it is asserted—the most beneficial of all possible diets. That, however, is a very tricky half-truth. And since it might easily be the case that readers could think this book intends to make common cause with everyone, however unbalanced, who makes such an assertion, a word is in order. It would be a shame to see this cuisine either embraced or dismissed for the wrong reasons.

Consider then. First, not every diet of vegetables alone is good for human beings: brown rice only has done people in permanently. Because the human body needs protein—and because no vegetable *by itself* has an amino acid profile comparable to the balanced ones of meat, fish and eggs—there are certain combinations of vegetables, notably that of grains and legumes, that are necessary to a sound diet.

Marvellously, every considerable cuisine with more than one or two hundred years' history under its belt has discovered that truth with no more help than it got from cooks and diners. The "rice and beans" syndrome, as it has been called, is universal; and it is represented in the cuisine of this book by the eminently balanced use of wheat, millet and rice on the one hand and of the omnipresent soy bean (in *tofu*, soy sauce) on the other.

The truth of the half-truth therefore is one that *shōjin* cooking admirably embodies: an all-vegetable diet, provided it is indeed a diet of *all* vegetables, is good for you. Just don't try to get by on turnip greens alone. The trouble with so much *principled* vegetarianism is that, for one reason or another, it frequently recommends just such follies.

But (and this, I promise, will be the last of these "buts") as if even *that* were not enough, the suppliers of significance have sometimes surpassed themselves and ascribed to a diet of vegetables—and almost even to vegetables as such—certain truly spiritual qualities. In fairness, that is not a half-truth like the proposition I accused them earlier of selling; rather it is a case of a very great truth indeed, separated by only a hair's breadth from the world's most dubious set of practical consequences.

First, the truth. Coming as I do from a Christian tradition that commends, as spiritual exercises, not only outright fasting but also abstinence from meat, I am far from questioning either the propriety or the value of such disciplines. We are not discarnate spirits. What we do, or omit to do, with our bodies has a great deal to do with our spiritual lives, however we see fit to conceive of them. *Shōjin* cuisine may come straight out of the Zen Buddhist tradition of abstinence from animal foods of all kinds; and no doubt the religious and philosophical assumptions on which that tradition operates are quite different from those of other faiths. The Armenian Lenten cuisine, for example, has its roots in a Christian world-view not instantly harmonizable with that of Buddhism. Nevertheless, both traditions not only arrived at versions of the same relentlessly vegetable and therefore ostensibly negative cuisine but also—and this is the crucial point of this introduction—*they arrived there in a marvellously positive frame of mind.*

Armenian vegetable cookery runs *shōjin* cuisine a close second for world honors. Neither tradition made the fatal error of thinking that abstinence from forbidden foods implied any obligation not to enjoy allowed ones; in both, asceticism with regard to meat was never interpreted as a license to treat vegetables badly. Spiritual masters may have prescribed the omissions from the diet; the inclusions, however, were subject only to the dictates of cooks.

It is essential to say this because while the present cloud of vegetarians that surrounds us may not consciously intend to cook badly, they more often than not do just that. This sad state of affairs is due mostly, I think, to the fact that, unlike the cooks of the cuisines just referred to, they have allowed their negativities to slop over into the kettle and spoil the food. There is an almost manichaean thrust to their monomaniacal assumptions: the fewer materialities you ingest, they seem to think, the more spiritual you will be; worse yet, in the case of materialities you must eat, that which tastes poorest will always be the best for you.

Admittedly, some of the feckless cooking of American vegetable enthusiasts comes from a circumstance that is both pardonable and remediable: they come out of one of the world's least attentive, and therefore least interesting traditions of cookery. For them to restrict themselves to vegetables only—when they cannot produce even a decent, rough-and-ready meat stew—is analogous to expecting that someone whose fiddle-playing is a disgrace even when hidden among the second violins will suddenly be able to distinguish himself by playing the Bach unaccompanied sonatas. Limitation demands greater artistry, not less; the work of compensating for the absence of a good half of the raw materials of cookery is not a job for half-cooks.

Interestingly, it is precisely when modern vegetarians try their hardest to do what *shōjin* cooking has always done with such apparent ease that the vast handicap under which they labor becomes manifest. Quite plainly, a good many Zen temple dishes bear a strong visual resemblance to prototypical meat, fish and egg presentations of Japanese cuisine. There are rice dishes that look for all the world like sushi but contain no seafood, custards that never saw an egg and, of course, tofu made to look like anything from shrimp balls to egg threads. Equally plainly, vegetable cooks here often strive to achieve just such resemblances, especially in their tofu "creations." The difference? Well, among other things, it is the difference between cooks who know from long experience with their materials just what will and will not work, and cooks who think any food can be forced into any mold. It is the difference between, on the one hand, the "pine cones" (*matsukasa*) in this book, which are deep-fried croquettes of mashed tofu studded with chopped soy-tinged *shiitake* mushrooms and dipped lightly in a ginger sauce—and which reveal, startlingly, that tofu does indeed have a taste; and, on the other hand, this item from a review of a vegetarian restaurant: Walnut-Tofu Burger, a mixture of walnuts, *tofu*, onions, peppers, garlic, bread crumbs, soy sauce, basil and oregano—which, it is claimed, tastes like ground sirloin. *O tempora! O mores!* Oh, well. I leave it to your native culinary sense not only to conclude that the second of those is mere puffery but also to suspect that the author of the review has never once in his life paid attention to the taste of plain beefsteak.

Once again though, enough. For the remainder of this preface, let me lay aside my philosophico-critical bag of tricks and tell you, as a plain stove-tender and dish-pusher, some of the happier things I have learned by experience with this cuisine.

Having first cooked from it during a gracious and incredibly rich day in the kitchen of the *Sankō-in*—under the watchful eye not only of that living repository of *shōjin ryōri*, the Abbess herself, but also of the vice-Abbess and four expert assistants—and having subsequently practiced it extensively in my own home, I can assure anyone who is even the least kind of cook that it is worth every minute devoted to it. Whether the dishes you prepare are just occasional experiments to be served at the family table, or a judicious sampling to be included as counterpoint to party fare from other cuisines, or a full assortment worthy of a formal Japanese dinner, both you and those you serve will be intrigued, delighted and, in the highest possible sense of the word, fed.

And since it is precisely the extensive, formal dinner that best raises all the questions of logistics that arise with this cuisine—and which seem, perhaps, more daunting in prospect than they are in practice—let me confine my comments to that alone. I have some assurances for you about what is actually required of the household cook who undertakes to prepare a not unreasonable eight or ten dishes from this book and to serve them to a party of, say, four, five or six.

I mention both cooking and serving because in American circumstances, except in certain rare or privileged cases, it is precisely the cook, frantically busy at the stove, who must also by some alchemy double as the host or hostess serenely seated at the table. For your comfort, even though the artfulness of this cookery may make it seem ambitious, it is nevertheless eminently doable once you get right down to it: it lends itself, as certain other cuisines do not, to considerable advance preparation. A good many of its concoctions are, or can be, served at room temperature. The apparent necessity of having to run to the kitchen every five minutes to make the next dish need not necessarily be a problem at all. With judicious menu-planning, more than half the items for a dinner can be not only cooked but arranged on plates, ready to serve, before the meal even begins. I have myself, on at least one triumphant occasion, done fourteen dishes, managed to have all of them served separately—and still contrived to restrict my role-conflicts as host and cook to a mere two absences in the kitchen. (The secret is to have a partner who will do absolutely all the serving: the cook does whatever last-minute kitchen work may be necessary before a given course, arranges the food on plates, returns to his or her place as host, refreshes everybody's saké—and then looks on imperially while the partner rises, clears, and serves.)

I mention the separate presentation of dishes, by the way, because while the food in this book can indeed be served homestyle and all at once, I would not willingly leave anyone to assume that an attempt at formal Japanese service is either impossible or profitless. I am, as you know by now, the last person to sprinkle spiritual snow over the marvellously earthy business of eating. But I am not, for all that, ready to maintain that there is no earthly reason for deliberate and gracious service. There is in fact every such reason: our very nature, overwound to the snapping point by the inhuman demands of clock time, cries out to be slowed and gentled at the table. We may live our days by fits and starts, but it serves no human purpose to let the pandemic hubbub invade our evening meals as well. Be bold about it then. Your guests may find the first few miniscule, leisurely courses of their *shōjin* dinner a violation of every ticking body-clock they have. But by the end of the meal they will have entered that vast, high time—known only to the very foolish and the very wise, the very young and the very old—outside of which the world only mourns how little time it has.

Whatever style of service you choose, however, the deep sense of satisfaction this cuisine affords will remain with you long after logistics have been left behind. The ancient Greeks had a word for the things they considered most worthy of attention. Happiness, they believed, could be achieved only when *ta kalakagatha*—the beautiful and the good—were the objects of constant regard. In that respect, *shōjin ryōri* is nothing less than a paragon of culinary wisdom. Beauty and goodness go hand in hand throughout this book; eye and palate—and therefore mind and spirit—will find delights on every page. I can wish you no more genuine happiness than that of letting its truly human attentiveness inform your own. You have a superb guide right in your hand. Take it, read it, and *cook*.

Robert Farrar Capon

Shelter Island, New York
May 1982

THE VERSE OF THE THREE MORSELS OF FOOD

The first morsel is to destroy
all evils,

The second morsel is to practice
all good deeds,

The third morsel is to save
all sentient beings—

May we all attain the Path of Buddhahood.

Japanese vegetables

1, 2, pumpkins; 3. mountain yam (*Yamato imo* type); 4. mountain yam (*naga imo* type); 5. lotus root; 6. burdock root; 7. bamboo shoot; 8. daikon radish; 9. rape blossoms; 10. cucumbers; 11. eggplants; 12. fava beans; 13. spinach; 14. raw and boiled fiddlehead ferns; 15. *shimeji* mushrooms; 16. ripe and green *yuzu* citrons; 17. young *sansho* leaf sprigs (*kinome*); 18. chrysanthemum leaves; 19. *enokidake* mushrooms; 10. *shiitake* mushrooms (fresh); 21. shelled and unshelled ginkgo nuts; 22. green *shiso* leaves.

Spring Tray Setting

(*clockwise from back left*) Vinegared Sea Greens and Turnip (page 103); dish containing Fiddlehead Ferns (page 101), Simmered *Fuki* (substitute celery or asparagus, cut as shown), and Simmered *Ganmodoki* (substitute thick deep-fried tofu); clear soup with wheel gluten (*kuruma fu*) and parboiled greens; Herb Rice (substitute any leafy green for perilla in Perilla Rice, page 75)

Summer Tray Setting

(*clockwise from back right*) dish containing pickled ginger shoots (available bottled), Braised *Shiitake* Mushrooms (page 144), and Jade Nuggets (page 136); Cold Sōmen Noodles and Dipping Sauce (page 125); Simmered Okra (use okra instead of eggplant, page 119); pickles: Cucumbers in Miso (page 90) and Nara Pickle (available commercially)

Autumn Tray Setting

(*clockwise from back right*) dish containing Braised *Shiitake* Mushrooms (page 144), Dried-Frozen Tofu Tempura (page 183), Simmered Japanese Pumpkin (page 131), Ginkgo Nuts (skewered), Saké-Braised Asparagus (substitute asparagus cut as shown in Saké-Braised Spinach Crowns, page 179); Chestnut Rice (page 77); Vinegared Cucumbers (page 116); Pressed and Vinegared Cucumbers (page 117)

Winter Tray Setting

(*clockwise from back right*) dish containing Simmered Burdock (cut as shown and simmer as in Arrow Feathers, page 157), parboiled snow peas, Deep-Fried Millet *Fu* (skewer as shown but do not wrap in *nori*, page 188), maple-leaf *fu* (commercial preparation); clear soup with sheet *fu* cut into julienne strips, snow peas, and *yuzu* citron garnish; Rice Bales (page 80) and Shiba Pickle (available commercially); Deep-Fried Waterchestnut and *Nori* Squares (page 165)

Spring

Konbu Kelp and Bamboo Shoots (page 99)

Bamboo Sushi (page 97)

Chrysanthemum Leaf Roll (page 105)

Sansho Pods and *Konbu* Kelp Relish (page 108)

Horsetail Rice "Balls" (page 74)

Fava Beans with Sea Greens (page 103)

Quick *Oden* (page 107)

Savory Dried Horsetails (page 96)

Fiddlehead Ferns (page 101)

Rape Blossoms with Mustard-Miso Dressing (page 93)

Konbu Kelp Sushi Rolls (page 104)

Summer

Whole Simmered Eggplants (page 119)

Light Vinegared Eggplant (page 120)

Eggplant and Fava Beans (page 122)

Eggplant with Miso Sauce (page 123)

Eggplant Purple (page 123)

Green Beans with Sesame Dressing (page 113)

Simmered Japanese Pumpkin (page 131)

Pressed and Vinegared Cucumbers (page 117)

Cucumber Rolls (page 118)

Junsai (page 124)

Simmered Plums (page 111)

Autumn

Saké-Braised *Enokidake* Mushrooms (page 144)

Pine Cones (page 150)

Mountain Yam and Mushroom Croquettes (page 141)

Ginkgo Nuts in Thick Sauce (page 148)

Braised *Shiitake* Mushrooms (page 144)

Jade Nuggets (page 136)

Mountain Yam Rolls (page 139)

Vinegared Gourd Ribbons (page 151)

Sweet Potato and Mountain Yam Balls (page 154)

Chestnut, Persimmon, and
Ginkgo Nut Tempura (page 149)

Turnips Above and Below (page 158)

Crisp Turnip with Sesame-Mi
Dressing (page 158)

Turnip Chrysanthemums (page 160)

Turnip and Apricot Salad (page 172)

Daikon with Miso Sauce (page 170)

Bright and Crunchy Daikon Rolls (page 168)

Winter

Arrow Feathers (page 157)

Lotus Root with Lemon Syrup (page 176)

Burdock with Spicy Sesame Dressing (page 156)

Sweet Bean-Stuffed Lotus Root (page 174)

Saké-Braised Spinach Crowns (page 179)

Fried and Simmered Dried *Yuba* (page 196)

Konnyaku Tempura (page 185)

Deep-Fried Dried *Yuba* (page 195)

Konnyaku Lumps (page 184)

Simmered Dried-Frozen Tofu (page 182)

Rōbai (page 192)

All Season

Konbu Puffs (page 186)

Salad with White Dressing (page 206)

Apricot and Agar-Agar Salad (page 223)

Sōmen Noodle *Nori* Roll (page 204)

Rice Patties (page 205)

Sesame "Tofu" (page 196)

Beet "Tofu" (page 201)

Tangerine "Tofu" (page 202)

Konbu Kelp "Tofu" (page 200)

Savory Raw Sugar "Tofu" (page 200)

Deep-Fried Millet *Fu* (page 188)

Deep-Fried Waterchestnut and *Nori* Squares (winter, page 165)

Deep-Fried Mountain Yam Nuggets (autumn, page 140)

Rice (pages 72-81)

January—Flower Petals

February—Bean Rice

March—Ginger Rice

April—Cherry Blossom Rice

May—Green Pea Rice

June—Unohana Rice

July—Perilla Rice

August—Thick-Rolled Sushi

September—Chestnut Rice

October—Ginkgo Nut Rice

November—*Shimeji* Mushroom Rice

December—Hot *Sōmen* Noodles

Nori-Wrapped,
Triangular Rice "Balls"

"Rice Bales"

Miso-Flavored,
Circular Rice "Balls"

Green Pea Rice Spheres

Shōjin food is excellent party and buffet fare because much of it is served at room temperature and can be prepared in advance. This festive spread was photographed at the Sankō-in temple. Other than the colorful fresh wheat gluten (*nama fu*) miniature confections, all the food pictured is included in the recipes in this book. The background screen shows a series of Zen ink paintings, and the blue pattern on the sliding doors is the crest of the temple.

ABOUT ZEN TEMPLE FOOD

WHAT IS SHŌJIN COOKING?

When Kodansha International came to us with the idea of producing a book in English on the *shōjin* cuisine prepared in Zen Buddhist temples, we resolved to apply our long experience in the *shōjin* cooking tradition to the task, and after one and a half years the work has been completed. I personally hope that with the publication of *Good Food from a Japanese Temple,* a new audience will be introduced to a culinary art fully understood by very few Japanese and at present all but unknown in other countries. Our efforts will have been rewarded if this book leads to a greater awareness, wider application, and increased enjoyment of this art and contributes to the health, pleasure, and longevity of everyone who cooks and eats this food.

Shōjin cooking is vegetarian, which, in Japan, includes certain sea plants. The word *shōjin* is composed of the characters for "spirit" and "to progress" and originally had the meaning of zeal or assiduity in progressing along the path to salvation. In concrete terms, *shōjin* cooking is a discipline meant to improve one's training in and practice of the Buddhist faith through the consumption of only the simplest foods.

Another type of Japanese cooking, and one better known to those outside Japan, is *kaiseki* cookery, linked with that quintessentially Japanese art, the tea ceremony. But *kaiseki* cooking originally was incorporated into the "Way of Tea" from Buddhist culinary traditions and was likewise meant to contribute to spiritual development. It is an offshoot of *shōjin* cooking.

There are two main reasons why *shōjin* cooking is based on vegetables and sea plants. The first relates to the geography and topography of the Japanese islands and the second to the Buddhist religion. Generally, it is easier to grow vegetables in Japan than to raise animals on a paying basis. Of course animal husbandry is possible, but it is more difficult and expensive than agriculture.

To this fact was added the dictates of the Buddhist religion, which reached Japan in about 530 A.D. The religion sets forth five proscriptions: thou shalt not kill (*fusesshō*), not steal (*fuchūtō*), not commit adultery (*fujain*), not lie (*fumōgo*), and not drink alcohol (*fuinsha*). The first of these proscriptions, "thou shalt not kill," applies not only to human beings, but to cattle and swine as well as to birds and even insects. It thus effectively denies meat products to believers. This is particularly true for monks, who must engage in strenuous ascetic practices. Those who break these rules are expelled from their monasteries. The scriptures also teach that monks who have fallen from the way will themselves be reborn as cattle in the next life.

Various Buddhist sects reached Japan over subsequent centuries. And from the new sects that appeared in the Nara, Heian, and Kamakura periods, further subsects were formed as well. The *shōjin* cooking in this book is that of the Zen sect, established in Japan in the last of the three above-mentioned historical periods, the Kamakura (1185–1333). To be more precise, it is the cooking of the Rinzai branch of Zen, as practiced at a nunnery of a certain kind. This is explained below.

Of course the proscription against killing living things applied to the other sects as well, such as the Pure Land (*Jōdo*), Nichiren, and Shingon, and the monks of these sects, too, eat in the *shōjin* style. But it is only the Zen sect that has maintained the strict *shōjin* techniques to the present. The reason that only the Zen monks stubbornly continue to base their cuisine on *shōjin* dictates must be ascribed to the close relationship in that sect between culinary practice and ascetic discipline.

The Zen sect began in Japan in 1168 with the establishment of Rinzai Zen by the monk Eisai (or Yōsai). Soon thereafter, another cleric, Dōgen, founded a separate branch of the Zen sect, Sōtō, in 1225. A third branch, Ōbaku Zen, was established by the Chinese monk Yinyuan (Ingen) in 1654. The three branches use completely different methods to transmit the Zen teachings. Rinzai, centered in metropolitan areas, made massive contributions to Japanese culture in scholarship, architecture, and the arts in the medieval (1185–1600) and Edo (1600–1868) periods. By contrast, the Sōtō sect developed a close relationship with the lower classes and provided them with strong spiritual sustenance. This intimate connection with the masses was further strengthened by the newest of the three sects, the Ōbaku, which provided support for those lacking the strength to attain salvation on their own.

We at the Sankō-in are affiliated with the Rinzai sect. The Sankō-in, however, is not a monastery but a nunnery, and as such provides women with a place to pursue a religious vocation.

The group-oriented way of life of Zen temples, where monks undergo study and training in the Zen teachings imported from China, is explained in detail in a book entitled *Hyakujō seiki*. It sets forth a strict code of dress, correct salutation, and prayer. To enter the gates of Zen temples, where these rules are still followed and all efforts are focused on religious discipline, is to enter a place very different from a modern city. It becomes clear immediately how much the Zen institution has a different sense of time.

Zen is based on seated, silent meditation and aims at attaining the state of Void (*mu*). But it also recognizes the absolute need for people to go on living, and this spirit is carefully cultivated in the practices surrounding *shōjin* cooking. The choice of ingredients, their preparation, and even the ways of conducting oneself while dining are all based on religious discipline and carried out every day with no exceptions.

Though the spirit underlying this discipline is discussed below, I would like at this point to introduce the fundamental principles behind the *shōjin* techniques I myself was taught. From an early age we in monasteries and nunneries are instructed in great detail about the reasons for eating the *shōjin* way. At the foundation of this teaching is the principle of causation (*innen*), the phenomenon given rise by man's cycle of birth, death, and rebirth. The concept is explained in the Lankāvatāra Sutra (*Ryōgakyō* in Japanese).

Among the teachings of this work is a detailed explanation of why meat is not used in *shōjin* cuisine. This sutra is my life-blood, and even now when I put my hand on my heart I can vividly empathize with the earlier monks and nuns who incorporated *shōjin* techniques into their religious discipline. The Lankāvatāra Sutra can be read on various levels and is difficult to grasp at the first, superficial reading. Repeated efforts gradually make clear the nature of this writing and the reasons why the eating of meat runs counter to Buddhist ideas.

Nevertheless, Buddhist teachings do not state that all people must desist from eating meat. For those of the faith, "in some cases" eating meat is condoned, but only if certain conditions are observed. These special cases include times of major illness.

The *shōjin* cookery of the Zen sect thus developed from the prohibition against killing any living being. In its use of vegetables and sea plants, which were created to support human life, it still today serves the purpose for which it was designed.

THE TENZO

Because of *shōjin* cooking's exclusively vegetarian makeup, it lacks the protein-rich flavor of fish, poultry, and other meats. For this reason, *shōjin* food is constantly varied to take advantage of seasonal ingredients and to exploit the possibilities of various food combinations. This outlook is expressed in our motto, "cooking with love" (*chōri ni kometa aijō*).

One of the books that has stood me in particularly good stead in my own *shōjin* cookery is *Tenzo kyōkun*, by Dōgen, the founder of the Sōtō sect of Zen. In the *Tenzo kyōkun*, Dōgen describes the way the *tenzo*, the cook in a Zen establishment, should prepare food for monks involved in practices of religious discipline. He first points out that "Tenzo duty is awarded only to those of manifest excellence—who exhibit deep faith in the Buddhist teachings, have a wealth of experience, and possess a righteous and benevolent heart. This is because *tenzo* duty involves the whole person." He then goes on to say that "If one without true Buddhist spirit was to perform the *tenzo* duties, he would commit errors of judgment and inconvenience many, thus ultimately resulting in much loss." The *tenzo* takes care not to waste a single grain of rice or cutting from a vegetable, and his orderly and reasoned approach to the culinary arts has much in it worthy of emulation by moderns in their own kitchens.

Similar emphasis on care in food preparation is found in the *Zen'en seiki*, the text on which Dōgen's *Tenzo kyōkun* is based. "In the preparation of meals, constantly be of moral spirit. Take care to choose the produce of the four seasons. Determine the manner of preparation proper to the ingredients. Introduce variation in cooking techniques. Make every effort to enable the monastic community to eat with enjoyment."

The monk on *tenzo* duty wakes earlier than the others and prepares the morning meal, then in the evening must before retiring make the preparations for the following day. As instructed in the *Zen'en seiki*, he is constantly concerned with how best to enable the other monks to eat with enjoyment and peace of mind. In sum, the choice of ingredients, their preparation, and their consumption all pertain to the fundamental concept of "cultivation of the self by means of *shōjin* cuisine."

Also included in the principle of true *shōjin* cooking as transmitted by the Zen sect is the concept that love and gratitude should be offered up to the Buddha by the *shōjin* cooks in the performance of their duties. The preparation and consumption of meals, therefore, has deep religious significance and is conceived of as a discipline rather than as an end in itself. This ethos is expressed by the other names used to refer to *shōjin* cooking. One is *yukuseki*, a word meaning "medicine." Another is *onjaku*, which means "warm stone," referring to the disciplinary practice in Zen temples wherein one would fast at night and stave off hunger and cold with a warm stone held to the stomach. It, too, later came to mean "medicine." As mentioned above, *shōjin* cooking was also incorporated into the tea ceremony, where it is known as *kaiseki* cooking, a term meaning "breast stone" and having much the same connotations as *onjaku*. These alternative names for *shōjin* cooking point out another important aspect of Buddhist cooking theory—that food is a medicine to protect the body from decay and death. The Buddhist canons state that "to hunger and thirst is to suffer. From hunger and thirst develop all diseases. Eating is thus to be considered a medical treatment and as a way to cure disease." The monks therefore say that "food is medicine" and think of this spirit in the following way: "Monks in the Buddhist faith are meant to discipline themselves and suffer in pursuit of the Buddha's teachings, while receiving support from the laity. Concentrating on rectifying the delusions of the mind requires a person to eat the smallest amount of food possible and still survive. And in the act of eating one must not be selective on the basis of one's own likes and dislikes. Nor must the amount of food be varied to suit personal tasts. Fending off hunger and thirst with the smallest amount of food possible to support the life process is the same as a bee taking nectar from a flower—it takes the nectar only and ignores the appearance of the flower and its aroma."

But at the foundation of *shōjin* techniques is the desire to save people from the suffering depicted in the Buddhist teachings, to contribute to their happiness, and to enable them to make contributions as healthy members of society. But it is through discipline and unlimited continuation of strict training that this kind of individual character is realized. With the unrestrained consumption of meats, the entire body loses its toughness and, in consequence, its capacity for discipline. But even with *shōjin* food, one is not to eat until sated. One should instead consider food as medicine and eat only enough to ensure health. Interestingly, a Chinese book on the subject makes a similar statement: "Food, when seen as medicine for preserving life, has no deleterious side effects." It continues, "Therefore, if one falls sick, one should first examine one's diet, then choose well, chew carefully, and give thanks. In this way, the curative powers of nature, with which mankind is blessed, are given full rein to act, and nearly all diseases are conquered."

At this point it becomes necessary to discuss the rigid discipline to which the *tenzo* adheres in the preparation of *shōjin* cuisine. After the meals of the day are ended, the *tenzo* goes to the temple kitchens. There, he discusses the next day's menu with the five monks who oversee temple affairs—the superintendent (*sōkantoku*), head of general affairs (*sōmu*), treasurer (*kaikei*), head of personnel (*jinji*), and head of repairs (*shūri*).

"What do you think we should prepare for tomorrow?"

"What side dishes would be appropriate?"

"How shall we prepare the rice gruel (*okayu*)?"

They exchange opinions, and their conversation itself becomes another of the many disciplines performed at the temple.

When consensus is reached, the menu for the following day is posted on bulletin boards outside the abbot's quarters and the dormitory. When this is done, the *tenzo* and his assistants begin their preparations. It is imperative for the *tenzo* to actively involve himself personally in both the selection and the preparation of ingredients. He puts himself into his work heart and soul, looking to the smallest details of his task and allowing not a moment's negligence. He respects the ingredients he handles and selects them as if he were planning to serve them to a king. This attitude he retains both when washing the food and cooking it. As expressed in the Buddhist proverb "Even tiny drops accumulate into a great sea," the repetition of good acts brings one each time a step closer to the Way of the Buddha.

The *tenzo* also inspects the rice as it is washed in order to ensure the absence of sand or grit. This he carefully discards, but not without being on constant guard for even one grain of rice that might be mistakenly wasted. He at no time lets his mind wander as he cleans the rice. The *tenzo* also concerns himself with the "six tastes" and the "three virtues" (*rokumi santoku*). The six tastes are bitter, sour, sweet, hot, salty, and "delicate" (*awai*), and the *tenzo* works to balance these effectively, while also incorporating the three virtues of lightness and softness, cleanliness and freshness, and precision and care. In so doing, he expresses the spirit of *shōjin* cookery. A balance of the six tastes and the three virtues happens naturally when, in the cleaning of the rice, the washing of the vegetables, the boiling in the pot, and in all the other aspects of the cooking process, the *tenzo* commits himself totally and directs his attention to nothing else but the work at hand.

But the six tastes are by no means easy to achieve. Those of past generations used to say of the process that "Nine minutes is too little and ten, too much" to show the delicate balance called for and the difficulty of achieving it. Moreover, in order to further improve taste, the *tenzo* must concentrate on the degree of warmness or coldness, the presence or absence of aroma, and the texture of the food.

Another important aspect of the preparation of *shōjin* cooking is seasonal variation. To realize this, the *tenzo* looks to the "five methods" (*gohō*) and the "five colors" (*goshiki*). The "five methods" refer to the different ways food can be cooked and comprise boiling, grilling, deep-frying, steaming, and serving raw. The five colors are green, yellow, red, white, and black (that is, purple). A balance of these variables makes light, vegetarian meals delicious and interesting.

Zen master Dōgen gives a simple summary of the difficult art of perfecting flavor as follows: "When washing rice, focus attention on the washing and let no distraction enter." He summarized this practice as *tōmai sanmai*, or "rice-washing *samādhi* (contemplation)." I am convinced that this spiritual attitude toward cooking—being totally present to what you are doing and allowing no distractions—is valid anywhere in the world and that its application will bring any cooking to perfection.

But the work of the *tenzo* is not limited to choosing ingredients and cooking them. In this work, he is accompanied by another monk who is undergoing religious discipline. This monk (*shugyōja*) recites sutras at the hearth and offers prayers to the deities and Buddhas.

Aside from preparing the main course, the *tenzo* must choose various side dishes and soups. The important point in this process is not to question the amount of the ingredients received from the person in charge of the kitchen, but rather to simply prepare them with all of one's self directed to the task. The *tenzo* is never to frown at the amount or quality of the ingredients, or become annoyed, or utter words of blame. Day and night the *tenzo* must concern himself with what type of flavor to bring out of the ingredients with which he is working, while uniting mind and body in a deeply sincere culinary effort.

When the results of his labors are brought to the table, it is customary in Zen temples to utter five phrases before eating. They are known as the *gokan no ge* or the "five reflections."

> I reflect on the work that brings this food before me; let me see whence this food comes.
>
> I reflect on my imperfections, on whether I am deserving of this offering of food.
>
> Let me hold my mind free from preferences and greed.
>
> I take this food as an effective medicine to keep my body in good health.
>
> I accept this food so that I will fulfill my task of enlightenment.

In this way, before eating the food that was prepared with such loving care, the monks ponder these five phrases and cultivate a spirit of gratitude. This is a kind of grace of the Zen temple.

In my own case, at age four I entered the tutelage of Jikō Asukai, a woman of noble lineage and the twenty-ninth abbess of Kyoto's "Bamboo Palace," the Donke-in nunnery. The "Bamboo Palace" is a nickname given by an emperor to the Donke-in temple sometime in the seventeenth century. At age seven, I myself took the tonsure and began my life of monastic discipline at the Donke-in. Though I have served as the abbess of the Sankō-in in Tokyo since my twenty-eighth year, my knowledge of *shōjin* cooking is based on the teachings of those at the Donke-in. I have, however, added to these teachings certain ideas of my own and investigated new tofu, sushi, and vegetable possibilities. Moreover, after the Second World War, when commerce increased between Japan and the West, I began to experiment with adding to *shōjin* cuisine vegetables imported from other countries. Steaming or boiling ingredients hitherto unknown to Japanese, such as Italian vegetables and potatoes from America, and incorporating them into *shōjin* meals has led *shōjin* food as a whole to take on a different aspect from that of previous years.

Due to my long years of involvement in *shōjin* cookery, I have reached the point where at the moment I start to prepare food, I immediately start thinking of ways to vary the taste of my ingredients. This is because I remain faithful to Dōgen's principle of "rice-washing contemplation" (*tōmai sanmai*), wherein all thoughts unrelated to the meal at hand are purged. And no matter what new types of *shōjin* cooking I create, I continue to recite the "five reflections" before each meal.

THE SANKŌ-IN

We at the Sankō-in refer to our *shōjin* cooking as being in the style of the "Bamboo Palace." Of the many different Zen temple cooking styles, our method has been handed down through the years in a nonostentatious and pure manner, rather, we like to think, like a quiet stream running through a valley hidden deep within the mountains. The word "palace" (*gosho*) in the name refers to a residence of a member of Japan's imperial family. "Bamboo Palace" (*Take no Gosho*), however, is a "nun's palace" (*bikuni gosho*), also commonly called a *ni monzeki* or "nunnery for a member of the imperial family." It is to such establishments that imperial princesses retired or were made to retire to the religious life as a princess-abbess. The *shōjin* food made here has the gentle, elegant, and refined nuances of the cuisine served to the imperial family, plus the directness and simplicity of Zen religious life.

There are, generally speaking, three types of Zen institutions. One is specifically for the practice of religious discipline. Another is the more general type of Zen temple. And the third is the nunnery. There are only a few of the Zen *ni monzeki* type of nunnery, to which daughters of the imperial family were sent. Zen does not have *monzeki* monasteries that housed male members of the imperial family as prince-abbots, but other Buddhist sects do have such monasteries that acted as recepticles for male imperial offspring. Despite the fact that most lands of the nobility were gradually appropriated by others through the centuries, the *ni monzeki* type of nunnery was always sedulously protected by those who held power. The practice of the numerous offspring of an emperor retiring to a religious life started at a quite early date. Later, during the Edo period (1600–1868), it was official policy of the shogunate that all imperial offspring were forcibly retired to Buddhist nunneries and monasteries. In these *monzeki* nunneries and monasteries, Buddhist culture and courtly culture were amalgamated, and both survive intact there at the present day.

The Donke-in temple, the Bamboo Palace in Kyoto's Sagano district, where I took my first instruction in the Way of Zen, is one of the nunneries that is part of this long *ni monzeki* tradition. The abbess of the Donke-in was a devout individual who came to her position as the head of the establishment at the age of sixteen. While upholding the long traditions of the temple, she also diligently worked to instruct apprentices.

The deaconess of a *ni monzeki* nunnery is called the *ichirō* or "elder." At the Donke-in, the office was filled by the nun Sōmei Yoshimura, who devoted the more than eighty years of her life to the day-to-day operation of the temple. It was she who taught me with great thoroughness the elements of cooking as well as of cleaning, sewing, and other essential aspects of temple life. At the Donke-in, the nuns are involved morning and night in this kind of work, as well as in the study of the Buddhist canon.

Deaconess Sōmei was very strict in her instructions on how to carry out the work of the temple. If the cleaning was not done correctly, it had to be done again until perfect. But she was also kind hearted, sensitive, and polite. I cherish my memories of the times in my youth I enjoyed by the temple azaleas and cherry blossoms the lunches she so carefully prepared. I even look back fondly on the times I was made to work until late at night making Bamboo Sushi, rubbing my tired eyes and being scolded as I worked. It was because of this severe training that we at the Sankō-in are still able to provide authentic *shōjin* cuisine. I also think back with pleasure on the boat rides we took every year in close-by Arashiyama. While enjoying the reflection on the water of the deep-green trees, and listening to the sound of the boatman's bamboo pole as we moved along the river, we would eat with glad gusto the *shōjin* lunches so lovingly prepared for us. We enjoyed such moments often, despite the religious training and the daily work that occupied us morning and evening, and my heart becomes full even today when I recall them.

Later I was assigned to Tokyo, to the suburb of Koganei, and became abbess of the Sankō-in temple there. The type of *shōjin* cooking we prepare at the Sankō-in, though, is the same as I was taught at the Bamboo Palace. As mentioned earlier, however, we at the Sankō-in have added a number of new techniques to this foundation. We are always careful, though, to carry on the Bamboo Palace cooking tradition, and we make every effort to produce food of the highest quality.

We began offering our *shōjin* cuisine to the public seventeen years ago. Because of my inexperience in worldly matters, approximately twenty-three thousand square meters of temple land had been sold without my knowledge, and the financial reserves of the temple had disappeared as well. It seemed at one point that the Sankō-in could no longer continue to operate. The fact that we still do so is due to the inspiration of the assistant abbess, Kōei, to support the Sankō-in by offering our own *shōjin* dishes to the public. We could in that way continue to exist and also propagate the teachings of Buddhism through our cooking.

Fortunately, due to the benevolent protection of the deities and Buddhas, the *shōjin* dishes of the Sankō-in have met with favorable public response. I am thankful that we have been able to complete repairs on the main gate structure and carry out other needed improvements.

Our temple regimen begins at five o'clock in the morning. After cleaning the main hall and weeding the garden, we read the sutras. Breakfast of rice gruel follows, and then the assistant abbess, Kōei, and I divide the work of making offerings to the Buddha and seeing that food is prepared.

Next we begin making the *shōjin* dishes for the day's patrons. Because we are a nunnery, we do not have people come for overnight stays and observe religious disciplines as is the case at other temples. But we are able, I think, to introduce visitors to another aspect of Zen by the food we serve and to show them how *shōjin* cooking fits into temple life. We have two sittings daily (except Thursdays)—at 12:00 noon and at 2:00 P.M. Reservations must be made in advance, and in the last two years, we have been booked a month or more in advance in spring and autumn, when the weather is at its best. We can serve a maximum of about forty people each day. The cooking is done by local women who wish to experience and learn *shōjin* cookery. Their experience includes other aspects of Zen temple routine as well as kitchen work.

At Zen monasteries, the monks arise at three o'clock in the morning. They hear a sermon then read sutras and worship in front of an image of the Buddha. Thereafter they take their morning meal. When the *tenzo* has prepared the dishes and set them out, he summons the monks by striking a cloud-shaped board with a mallet. In answer, a fish-shaped board at the monks' quarters is struck. At this signal the monks file into the dining hall and one after another salute the server with their hands in the attitude of prayer, after which they receive their portions.

By contrast, monks undergoing religious discipline go out into the street with a begging bowl. They walk through residential districts, pausing in front of individual homes or shops to pray for the happiness and prosperity of those within, and then receive rice or coins by way of thanks. These monks are known as *unsui*, and they eat two full meals a day. In the morning they eat rice gruel, sesame salt, and pickled daikon radish (*takuan*). At noon they have boiled barley with rice, miso soup, and a small amount of boiled vegetables and pickled daikon. Though the monks are ostensibly supposed to eat only twice, a light snack is also provided after the evening sutra reading. The monks then retire at about eight o'clock.

Like monks' meals, our own meals at the Sankō-in are quite simple, with one soup and one vegetable. If there is some boiled dish left over from the day before, we give thanks and eat it. Since we discard nothing, we will, in the case of a cancellation of a *shōjin* meal by a group of patrons, reheat and eat it ourselves for two or three days. The same is true if too much soup remains in the pot after the last customer leaves.

At the Sankō-in we also have our own philosophy about how to cut and arrange food, following the Bamboo Palace style *shōjin* cuisine. We cut the vegetables a bit smaller than bite-sized and serve them with an eye toward the colors of the current season. All seem to enjoy these "feminine touches" in our *shōjin* cuisine. Our patrons also delight in the charming tableware we use. Atop black-lacquered trays we place bowls whose motifs—autumn foliage, peonies, chrysanthemums, maple leaves, and the like—relate to the season at hand. We serve only those ingredients in keeping with tradition, and our patrons appreciate this emphasis on the genuine.

A number of years ago I was told of a restaurant in Tokyo that supposedly served *shōjin* cooking, and I was invited for a meal there. But although the owners advertised their cooking as *shōjin* style, the soup stock (*dashi*) was made in the conventional manner, with dried bonito shavings. In true *shōjin* cooking the soup stock is made with *konbu* kelp only in conjunction with the "six tastes and three virtues." Because of the existence of these imitations, we at the Sankō-in make special efforts to preserve the character of *shōjin* cooking as handed down at the Donke-in. In fact, whenever I set out to prepare a *shōjin* meal, I recall my upbringing at the Donke-in in far-off Kyoto as I stand in the kitchen. In this way, both my sad and my happy memories from my days at the Donke-in accompany my *shōjin* preparations, and they have sustained me until today. In times of war and of peace, sickness and health, I have for over seventy years thrived on *shōjin* cooking.

SHŌJIN CUISINE AND HEALTH

Fifteen years ago last summer, while I was weeding in the garden of the Sankō-in, I was suddenly struck with chest pains and had difficulty breathing. I could not lie down and was forced to sit for some time without moving. It was my first heart attack. On the advice of my doctor, I went to a hospital for tests and was told that I had to remain hospitalized for some time. I was informed that my heart had sustained major damage, and that I had only a half-year to live.

The assistant abbess, my student Kōei, cared for me following the directions of my doctor. Since I was somewhat heavy, I was first told to lose weight, and when I reached the goal established for me, I began to feel somewhat better.

The testimony of many famous and virtuous monks shows that the Buddha, too, said that "when one falls ill, one must grapple with the illness with one's whole spirit." He thought of nothing but assiduous effort (*shōjin*) to overcome disease. No one becomes ill just by willing it. And living in the face of a disease so severe it could end in death at any time requires great effort and perseverance. It was my good fortune to have been trained to persevere at the Bamboo Palace since the age of seven, disciplining myself to work hard and train my body and mind. By virtue of this I was able to endure the strict dietary regimen and over twenty stays in the hospital. I saw the promised half year of life stretch to fifteen years. But the dietary regimen I mentioned required in itself severe practice in self-discipline. Since my heart disease was caused by diabetes, I was required to renounce the sweets that I had indulged in. Treatment for diseases that usually strike older people also often require a limited diet of animal products. Happily this proved no problem for me, because since the age of four, when I first entered a Zen nunnery, I had been trained to live on vegetarian *shōjin* cooking.

After my heart attack, I carefully followed the advice of my doctor and persevered in my dietary restrictions. As a result, I completely regained my health and am now enjoying every day of my seventy-fifth year. That I have been able to live to this age is thanks to my life-long *shōjin* diet. My longevity has shown me once again how beneficial a diet based on vegetables is in toughening the body. The fact that through *shōjin* cooking I was able to live so long and recover from illness with relatively little suffering also made me want to share my happiness with as many people as I could and to present an example for those who presently suffer from disease.

But having experienced serious illness, I am also convinced that, more than following doctor's orders and applying oneself after becoming ill, it is important to do all one can to avoid falling ill in the first place. To do so I recommend paying attention to diet. I have given some thought after my own fashion to why *shōjin* cuisine seems an effective program. I have also consulted the physician who treated my heart disease, Dr. Teruo Ōta, assistant head of a hospital devoted to heart research, and asked him about the relationship between the body and a diet of vegetables. Dr. Ōta supports *shōjin* cooking and he stresses that a *shōjin* diet can maintain health and prevent diseases of older people. The medical explanations he provided me have been of great help.

Japan's agricultural traditions, derived from those of Southeast Asia, have combined with the Buddhist proscription on the killing of animals to give rise to *shōjin* cooking, which, though including no fish, meat, or even eggs, sustains the health of monks. That this diet is sufficient in nutrition is underscored by the fact that through the centuries most monks have lived long and healthy lives.

But for those who are not living in monastic communities, the establishment of a balanced vegetarian diet requires effort and perseverance. An unplanned, yet completely vegetarian life style can in fact have deleterious effects, such as an increased susceptibility to renal insufficiencies and to infectious disease. Nevertheless, for moderns, prone to overconsuming meat products and avoiding vegetable fiber, the introduction of the essence of *shōjin* cooking and the advantages of vegetarianism cannot help but lead to an increased resistance to disease.

THE SPIRIT OF THE KITCHEN

I completely agree with the saying "flavor comes from the heart." Preparing food is training for the spirit, and taking care to make food as delicious and beautifully arranged as possible cultivates our aesthetic sensitivity. There is no more splendid form of training.

It is in the kitchen where this work is carried out. When the kitchen is kept clean, fresh, and easy to work in, the vegetables, sea plants, and other ingredients, chosen according to the season, take on an added luster. We must always keep in mind, though, that no matter how far the world progresses, these ingredients remain the blessings of nature. We must also be aware that natural disaster and want can occur at any moment. It is vitally important to be prepared for such calamities by eliminating waste and pursuing with humility and respect the "spirit of the kitchen." Nor should we abandon a culinary project when we have forgotten one of the ingredients. A sensitivity toward how to make the best of what is on hand will allow unexpected success. And the happiness of cooks when this happens is something that only they can know.

Furthermore, use the pots and pans you are used to. Surrounded by familiar kitchen implements, the cook is like a symphony conductor, ready to draw forth beautiful music from the instruments at his fingertips.

A meal reflects the gentle nature and warm heart of the cook. Of course, some of us are more clever with our hands than others. But if one does the best one can, a fine meal results, almost as if by divine grace.

Though our modern lives are full of comfort, we have gradually become distant from our natural environment. Living in homes with heaters and air conditioners isolates us from the changes in the four seasons. We tend to forget the gentle breeze in the tree tops and the warm rays of the sun. *Shōjin* cooking emphasizes rather than hides the delights of the seasons and seasonal changes. As the world progresses, this ideal becomes more and more difficult to realize. But *shōjin* cooking melts into nature. On a cold and snowy day in winter, one sits hunched over, warming the tips of one's fingers on a Steamed Savory Cup (page 161). And in the summer's heat there are cold noodles (*sōmen*) on a bed of ice and deep green leaves. Or one can enjoy cold, white tofu as it floats in clear water.

People are naturally attracted to gorgeous and expensive cuisine. But after a hard day's work, the simple yet delicious taste of a bowl of rice gruel (*okayu*) with a pickled plum (*umeboshi*) and pickled daikon radishes (*takuan*) is unforgettable, just as is the flavor of rice just off the stove accompanied by miso soup. After fatiguing labor one does not long for rare delicacies. A contented heart makes even the simplest food delicious. Conversely, those who live in sloth cannot really enjoy even the finest cooking, no matter how carefully and lovingly it is prepared.

"Flavor comes from the heart" implies both cooking with one's whole soul and giving thought to the right atmosphere in which to serve the results. When care is paid not only to placing the dishes on the table but to the cleanliness and neatness of the room, the floral settings, and the arrangement of food on the plates, the meal tastes twice as good. And again, a spirit of gratitude is essential. Without giving thanks to those who eat our food, as well as to those who provided the ingredients and those who prepared them, we can never fully appreciate the spirit of *shōjin* cooking.

I would like to express my heartfelt gratitude to the assistant abbess, Kōei Hoshino, without whose efforts and energy this book would never have been realized. My profound thanks also go to Kim Schuefftan of Kodansha International for his enthusiasm and for capturing things unstated as well as translating the stated; to Katsuhiko Sakiyama of Kodansha International for holding things together; and to Reiko Tsunemi, Shizu Omori, Yumi Ōta, and the others who studied *shōjin* cooking under my guidance for their generous assistance.

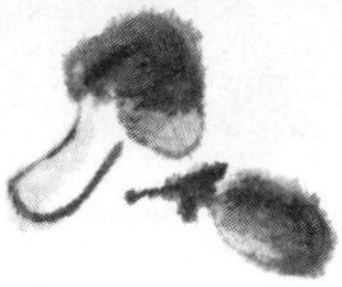

INGREDIENTS

azuki beans (often romanized *adzuki*). These small red beans are now grown extensively in the United States and Europe and are available at some supermarkets, many health food stores, and oriental groceries. To cook: 1. Soak beans in water overnight. Drain. 2. Bring to boil quickly in ample water. Drain. Add fresh water and again bring to a boil quickly. 3. Reduce heat to medium-low and simmer, covered, until quite soft. Add cold water twice to the boiling beans when the volume decreases somewhat. This is known as "surprise water" in Japanese; it acts to reduce cooking time. Do not add any other ingredient or flavoring to the beans until after they are completely boiled or the cooking time will be greatly prolonged.

Sweet azuki bean paste is known as *an* (also *anko*). The usual formula for making *an* is equal amounts by volume of boiled azuki and sugar with a pinch salt. Simmer this mixture over low heat, stirring frequently, until it becomes thick and glossy. For chunky bean paste, simply stir with a wooden spoon, mashing beans to obtain the texture you like. Pureed *an* is made by whirring the sweet, cooked paste in a processor or blender then returning it to the saucepan and cooking until thick over low heat, stirring almost constantly. This is the simple way of making pureed *an*. The professional method involves getting rid of the bean skins and squeezing the sweet paste through muslin bags, etc.—fussy and overrefined according to some opinions.

Canned boiled azuki and *an* are available and convenient, but the flavor of homemade is better.

bamboo shoots (*takenoko*). The season for bamboo shoots in Japan is April and May. Preparing the raw shoots is complicated and need not concern us here. Whole, half, and sliced shoots are available canned and in water packs the year round.

Since there is usually a bamboo grove in temple precincts, it is only natural that bamboo shoots are part of *shōjin* cooking. Various temples may have their own special bamboo dishes, such as the Bamboo Sushi (page 97) of the Donke-in temple. The virtue of bamboo shoots is in the texture as well as the flavor.

burdock root (*gobō*; *Arctium lappa*). These roots are harvested twice a year—from May to September and from October to February. Good-quality roots are firm, have an unblemished skin, and are straight. The best are without the hole in the center that forms when roots get thick. The skin is the best part of the root, so do not scrape, but, rather, scrub with a stiff brush to clean.

Burdock turns dark very quickly upon being cut, therefore immediately put cut burdock into water or water with a touch of vinegar in it to avoid discoloration.

chrysanthemum leaves (*shungiku; kikuna; Chrysanthemum coronarium*). There are two yearly harvests of this leafy vegetable—in spring (when it is known as *shungiku*) and autumn (when it is *kikuna*)—in fact, it can be harvested any time but midsummer, but is at its best in March and November. It is part of the chrysanthemum family, but only the

leaves are used as a vegetable. The best quality chrysanthemum is sold with root attached.

The fragrance of these leaves is likened to temple incense. It is thought to expel badness in one's heart.

chrysanthemum petals (*kigiku*) are sold both fresh and dried in Japan. The bright yellow dried petals are available year round in large or small packages of pressed sheets. This packaged type is often available in oriental markets. The petals must be reconstituted briefly in hot or tepid water.

cucumbers (*kyūri*). The cucumber season in Japan is from June to October, but these vegetables are available year round because they are easily cultivated in hothouses.

The Japanese cucumber is about the same length but about half the thickness of the American cucumber. It is crisper, less watery, and more tender. The skin is also thinner and not as bitter as the American variety. The recipes here are for the Japanese variety,

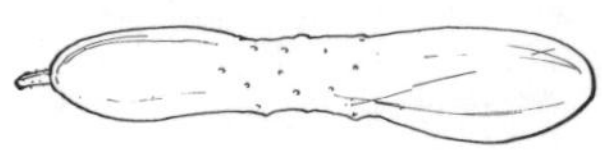

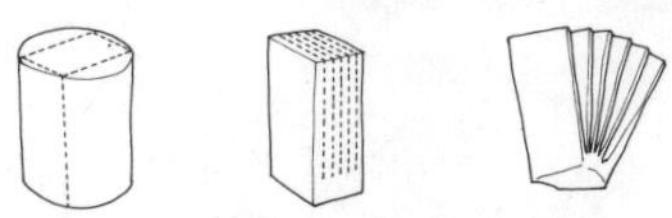

cucumber fan shape

so some small compensations have to be made in some cases. Try to buy Japanese cucumbers if available and not too expensive. If unavailable, buy the youngest cucumbers you can find. It may be necessary to peel and seed large American cucumbers.

daikon radish (*Raphanus sativus*). Midwinter is the daikon radish season, when these large white root vegetables are at their largest and juiciest. The summer daikon is wizened and harsh in flavor in comparison. Generally, the daikon sold in North American supermakets are smaller than those available in Japan.

Daikon is ubiquitous in Japanese cooking, but there are many varieties, from large globes to ones that grow in sinuous curves. The best quality are large, firm, and succulent. If the skin is wrinkled or soft, the radish is old and of poor quality.

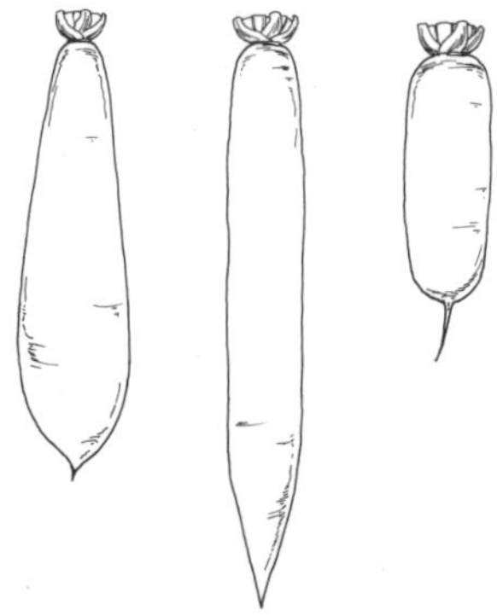

Daikon also comes in dried form; the most common is *kiriboshi daikon*, long, dried strips or ribbons, which resemble brown twine. This dried form should be reconstituted in warm water.

Pickled daikon is also important in Japanese food, the most famous daikon pickle being the odoriferous *takuan*.

eggplant (*nasu*). Japanese eggplants come in a number of sizes and shapes, all of them smaller than the eggplants sold in American markets. The average Japanese eggplant, if one can average so many types, is about 4 inches (10 cm) long. For the purposes of the recipes here, by all means try to buy Japanese eggplants—or even grow your own. The Japanese variety has firmer flesh and is sweeter and less watery than the large American type.

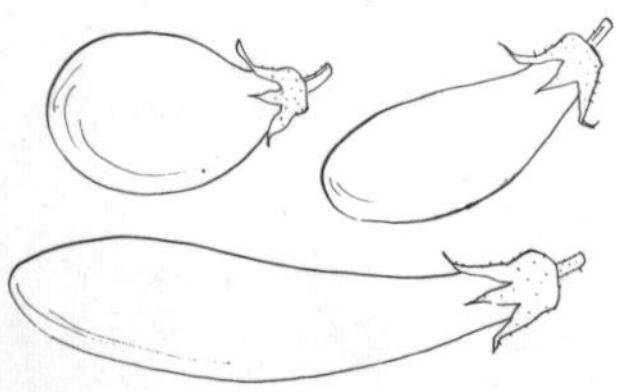

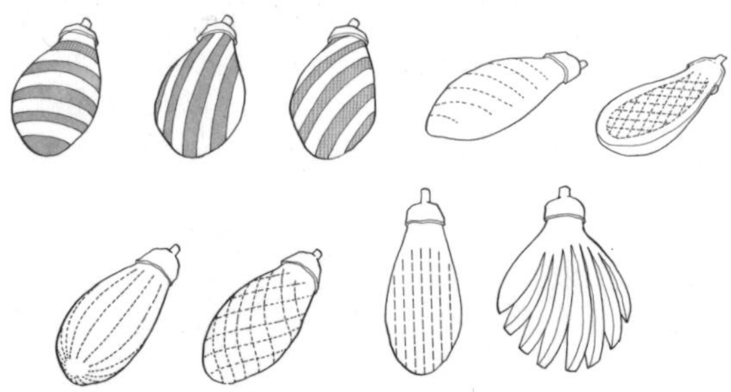

some eggplant peeling and cutting methods
(not included in recipes)

Look for eggplants with firm, shiny, plump flesh and a deep purple color; the cut end of the stem is a whitish green on the freshest ones. Do not buy ones that are wrinkled, soft, and tired. It is not necessary to eliminate acridity by sprinkling with salt or soaking in water for most types of Japanese eggplant, though it is a good idea to place cut eggplant in water to avoid discoloration if you cut it some time before cooking. In fact, in temple cooking, the slight acridity of eggplant is considered part of the deliciousness of this vegetable and is fully utilized (as in Eggplant Purple, page 123).

***enokidake* mushrooms** (*Flammulina velutipes*). These mushrooms are now widely cultivated and available year round in Japan. The cultivation of these attractive and delicious mushrooms has spread to the United States, where they are sold in some oriental food shops and gourmet markets. Naturally grown *enokidake* are brown; the cultivated ones have long stems and are cream colored.

Good-quality *enokidake* are delicate and crisp. When they get old, the caps discolor, the stems sag, and the package smells like something fermenting. Buy only fresh *enokidake*. Cut off the spongy base before using.

fiddlehead ferns (*warabi*; *zenmai*). There are two types of fiddlehead fern eaten in Japan—*warabi* (common bracken) and *zenmai* (*Osmunda japonica* and *O. cinnamomea*). *Zenmai* is probably not found in North America. The recipes in this book are for *warabi*

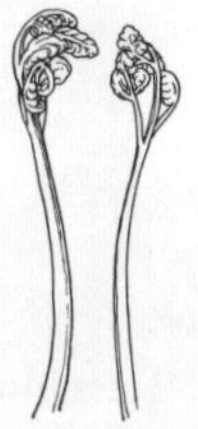

that has already been cooked; this is available bottled and in water packs. Do not eat raw *warabi*. It contains a mild toxin—thiaminase—the same as in horsetails, which breaks down when cooked.

fu, see wheat gluten

ginger (*shōga*). The fresh rhizome is now appearing more and more in American markets and should always be available at oriental food shops. Ginger should be peeled before using (though you can leave it unpeeled when making ginger juice, if you like). Keeps well refrigerated in plastic wrap. The knobs should be firm, the skin unwrinkled and an even tan color. Ginger with wrinkled or puckered and discolored skin is too old and should not be bought.

Make ginger juice by finely grating fresh ginger, with or without skin. Just be careful that the ginger you grate is well washed and has no dirt in crevices. Squeeze juice from grated ginger, either with your fingers or in a cloth napkin or piece of cheesecloth. Discard pulp.

Powdered ginger, dried ginger, and crystallized ginger are *not* substitutes for the fresh root.

ginkgo nuts (*ginnan*). Fresh ginkgo nuts may be available in the United States, but good canned nuts are on the market in tiny cans. Check oriental groceries for either the fresh or canned. Obviously the flavor of the fresh is superior.

If buying fresh nuts, choose the whitest and largest; avoid shells that are brownish or discolored. (See page 148 for shelling procedure.) Canned nuts should be plump and a pastel green; dry, cracked, whitish nuts are not usable.

gourd ribbons, see *kampyō*

***hijiki* seaweed** (*Hizikia fusiformis*). This seaweed is sold dried and packaged and is widely available in oriental markets and health food stores. Choose black *hijiki*—there should be no brown strands.

Reconstitute for about 30 minutes in cold water. The volume of this dried seaweed increases greatly when reconstituted, so use an ample volume of water.

horsetails (*tsukushi*; *Equisetum arvense*). Only the firm heads of young shoots should be gathered, and the stem sheath beneath the head should be removed. Horsetails contain

the same mild toxic protein, thiaminase, as fiddlehead ferns, which is destroyed by heat. Do not eat them raw.

Wild vegetables (*sansai*, lit. "mountain vegetables") are hardly used in *shōjin* cooking. They are generally considered very luxurious. Horsetails, especially, can be gathered for only a very brief period (perhaps 2 weeks), and dishes using this ingredient are the height of luxury.

junsai (watershield; *Brasenia schreberi*). The immature leaves are surrounded by a gelatinous sheath, and the plant grows only in deep, old ponds whose water is pure and

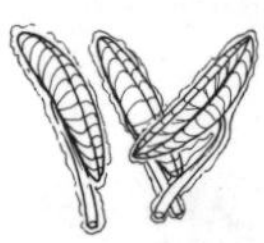

clear. *Junsai* grows in North America and Australia as well as in West Africa and Asia; it comes in bottled form from Japan and China and, naturally, is quite costly. Strictly a luxury food.

kampyō (gourd ribbons). The botanical dictionaries give the English name of this plant as "white flower gourd"; the botanical name is *Lagenaria siceraria.* These globular gourds are about the size of a large pumpkin. The ribbons used in Japanese cooking are shaved

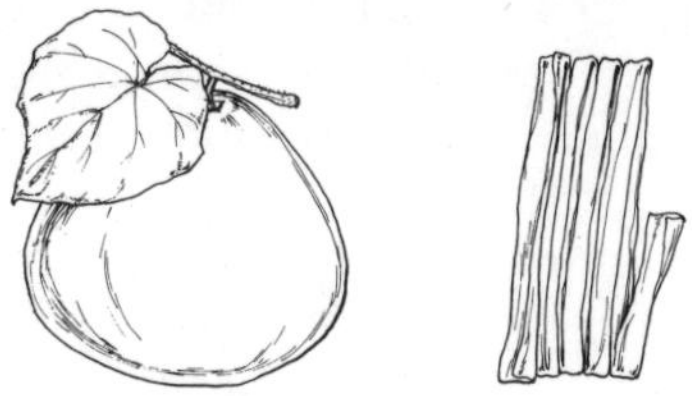

from the thick flesh and dried. Good-quality *kampyō* is flat, white, and slightly spongy. Avoid *kampyō* that is yellowish, wrinkled, and stiff and dry. It comes in plastic packages, and, since it is used in certain kinds of sushi, should be available in Japanese or oriental markets.

Reconstitute by sprinkling with salt, scrubbing briefly (like scrubbing socks), rinsing off salt in running water, then soaking for 5 minutes in water.

katakuriko, see potato starch

***konbu* kelp** (genus *Laminaria*). The best-quality *konbu* (also pronounced *kobu*) comes from small islands in the frigid seas off Hokkaido. When buying *konbu*, look for flat leaves that are a midnight brownish black in color (often dusted with a fine white bloom) and as thick as possible. Wrinkled, thin, green kelp is of poor quality. Wipe surface of *konbu* with a damp cloth before using. Keep *konbu* in an airtight container.

There are a number of processed *konbu* varieties; the ones used in this book are *tororo konbu* and *kizami konbu. Tororo konbu* is made by softening the *konbu* with a weak acetic acid solution then drying and scraping the kelp with a special tool. *Kizami konbu* is so rare that most Japanese are not aware that it exists. It is finely shredded *konbu* of a special type (*mitsuishi konbu*) and is made at only one or two places in Kyoto (see page 186).

konnyaku. This thick, gelatinous substance is made from the root of the devil's tongue plant (*Amorphophallus konjac*), the main ingredient of which is mannan. *Konnyaku* is bland in flavor and comes in a number of forms, of which the cake (*ita konnyaku*) is the most common. In Japan this measures $6 \times 2\frac{1}{2} \times 1\frac{1}{4}$ inches ($15\frac{1}{2} \times 6\frac{1}{2} \times 3$ cm). *Konnyaku* filaments are known as *shirataki* and come in small bundles packed in water. *Ito konnyaku* (do not confuse with *ita konnyaku* above) are threads somewhat thicker than the filament form; filaments and shreds are often confused, and local terminology is unclear.

***kuzu* starch**. The *kuzu* (often romanized *kudzu*) vine (*Pueraria hirsuta*) has a starchy root from which this excellent starch is made. Good-quality *kuzu* comes in powdery lumps, is milky white, and has a very slight sheen. The lumps can easily be rendered into powder by pounding with a pestle or by whirring in a food processor or blender. This starch gives foods a strong elasticity and is ideal for such things as Sesame "Tofu" (page 196) and the other flavored "tofus." It is also known for its medicinal qualities, especially for upset stomach. Today true *kuzu* starch is quite expensive, because the vine only grows wild.

The cheap varieties of starch labeled "*kuzu*" are potato starch or a mixture of *kuzu* and potato starches. The potato starch known as *katakuriko* (see entry under potato starch) is a good substitute. Cornstarch is not a substitute.

lily root (*yurine*). Even the root of the lily is flower shaped. This is an expensive food and appears only in special dishes and at New Year. It should be creamy white and without blemish. The texture is somewhat mealy and the flavor sweet. Used mainly in Kyoto cooking.

lotus root (*renkon; hasu*). These roots grow in sausagelike links deep in mud and are harvested in autumn and winter. Their size varies greatly, but a medium diameter is about 2 inches (5 cm). High-quality roots have thick flesh, are creamy or grayish white, and should have no discoloration or blemishes. The inside surfaces of the holes should not be dark.

Lotus root discolors immediately when cut, so place in water containing a touch of vinegar as soon as sliced or scraped.

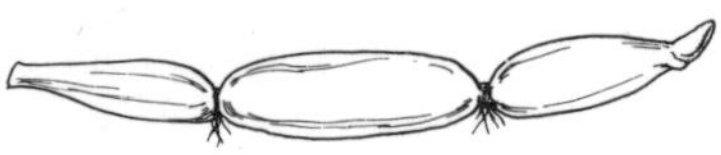

***matsutake* mushrooms** (*Trichloma matsutake*). September and October is the season for these mushrooms that cannot be cultivated. The immediate response of most Japanese to the word *matsutake* is "expensive." The best *matsutake* have thick, short stems, and the cap is tightly curled under, not spread open. The aroma should be compelling. Do not wash these mushrooms well or the aroma will disappear; just wash quickly in lightly salted water and pat dry immediately.

millet gluten (*awa fu*). This confection is made of a mixture of pounded cooked millet and fresh wheat gluten (see page 66). The color is yellowish, and in Japan it comes in long sticks or thin loaves, which are cut as desired.

miso. There are three basic miso types: sweet, medium salty, and salty. In general, white miso is sweet, dark miso is salty. Buddhist nunneries in Kyoto usually prefer the sweet white miso known as *saikyō* miso, though this term does not seem to be known much in the Tokyo area. There are other sweet white misos, and sugar may be added to them to approximate the flavor of *saikyō* miso, which is the sweetest of all.

Saikyō miso does not keep very well compared to other misos with a greater salt content. Store this miso in a well-sealed plastic bag or airtight container in the refrigerator. Since miso becomes saltier with time, if your uses of it are not great, it is best to buy only small amounts of *saikyō* or other sweet miso and use it as quickly as possible.

Various kinds of miso are now being exported to or are being made in the United States. Ask your oriental grocer for the appropriate type for your needs.

mochi. This is made from glutinous rice that has been steamed and then pounded. It is sold in sheets and in either round (mainly in Western Japan) or square pieces. Formerly *mochi* was a winter food; today it largely still is, but it comes also vacuum packed in plastic and is available year round. Fresh, soft, just-made *mochi* tastes best.

Mochi is grilled. It will expand and puff up, somewhat like a marshmallow, and also like the latter will burn if the heat is too hot. Grill *mochi* over a heat source or under an oven broiler.

mushrooms, see *enokidake, matsutake, shiitake, shimeji*

mustard. True Japanese mustard (*wagarashi*) is a preparation made of brown mustard (*Brassica juncea*) and involves a complex series of steps. For this reason, it is rare today. Today's basic Japanese mustard mix, then, is powdered hot mustard mixed with a few drops of hot water (hot water is better, it is said) until a thick paste is formed. This is usually done in a small saké cup, and the cup is inverted for 30 minutes or so to allow the mustard flavor to mature. Any hot powdered mustard will do; just be sure that it is hot, not the mild mustard popular in America.

nattō. This is a fermented soy bean preparation made by the action of a special bacterium (named, appropriately, *Baccilus natto*). It has a rich cheeselike flavor and a sticky, somewhat slimy consistency that is not appreciated by everyone. With good *nattō*, the sticky "threads" formed when mixing should be strong and stubborn and the beans should be moist. Since this food is the result of bacterial action, no preservative can be used. Thus, *nattō* should be eaten as soon as possible.

***nori* seaweed.** *Nori* comes in standard-sized sheets measuring 7×8 inches (18×20 cm). Half-sheets, quarter-sheets, and various other smaller sizes are also packaged and sold. In *shōjin* cooking, generally *nori* is not toasted, as it is in conventional Japanese cooking, except for special purposes, such as preparation for crumbling it finely. Keep *nori* dry in an airtight container.

oil, vegetable. Japanese oils are excellent. They are odorless and tasteless, light, and take a high temperature if used for deep-frying. The usual oils are a blend—generally of soy bean, rice, rape seed, and corn oils. Sesame oil has special uses, mainly as a seasoning and to give a mild background flavor to certain frying oils; it is not used in this book. Buy the best vegetable oils available, choosing ones without flavor and odor. The result is worth a little extra expense. Cottonseed, safflower, and sunflower oils are also excellent. Peanut oil has a distinct flavor, which limits its practicality for *shōjin* cooking.

okara. The solid residue left when boiled soy beans have been ground and strained in the tofu-making process is *okara* (the liquid is the soy milk from which tofu is made). Though still one of Japan's cheapest foods, *okara* has been neglected by cooks in recent years. It is mainly used as animal feed today and is only available from the neighborhood tofu maker, not at food shops. It goes bad very quickly and is sold only in the mornings.

Though *okara* has little flavor of its own, it absorbs other flavors well. A little oil in *okara* dishes brings it to life. *Okara* is known by the euphemism *unohana*, which is a type of white wildflower, and the mélange made with *okara* and finely chopped *shiitake* mushrooms, burdock, carrots, etc. etc. is also known as *unohana* (see page 187).

onions. No onion of any kind (or garlic) is used in the Donke-in temple *shōjin* cooking. This is an ancient tradition.

perilla (*shiso*; *Perilla frutescens*). These minty, aromatic leaves come in green and red varieties. Both types are in season in June and July, but the green is cultivated for use the year round, while the red is available during its season only and is mainly used to make *umeboshi* (see plums).

persimmons (*kaki*; *Diospyros kaki*). Oriental persimmons are ripe while still firm. There are many varieties of these persimmons, and they are in season from late September through November.

plums, fresh and pickled (*ume*, *umeboshi*, and *bainiku*). Japanese *ume* (*Prunus mume*) actually are not plums, but a type of apricot. Suffice it to call them plums because custom has decreed it. *Umeboshi* are made by soaking *ume* in brine for a month or so, weighted; they are then sun-dried and returned to the brine many times. Red *umeboshi* get their color from red perilla (*shiso*) leaves, which are pickled with the *ume*. The flesh of *umeboshi* is known as *bainiku* (literally, "plum flesh"). *Umeboshi* are ubiquitous in Japan and can be found in every kitchen cupboard. They are reputed to have many properties, among them the ability to stop food from going bad (thus their inclusion in lunch boxes) and efficacy as a stomach medicine.

potato starch (*katakuriko*). This is the most common household starch in Japan. Originally, the starch of this name was made from dogtooth violet (*katakuri*) root. Today it is made of sweet potato or white potato starch. *Katakuriko* is about 50 percent stronger than cornstarch (that is, it takes 1.5 units of cornstarch to do the job of 1 unit of *katakuriko*). Its virtue is that it has little flavor and can make clear, thick sauces that catch light and seem to have a deep glow. Its defect is that it leaks water in time and is thus not good for foods that will be eaten the next day (such as lemon pie, etc.).

pumpkins, Japanese (*kabocha*; *Cucurbita moschata*). The small Japanese pumpkin is a different species of *Cucurbita* than the European pumpkin (*C. pepo*) and winter squash (*C. maxima*). There are a number of varieties, all of which are similar in flavor. The

Japanese pumpkin is sweet in flavor, with orange flesh and (usually) green skin, and is about 6–7 inches (15–17 cm) in diameter on the average.

rape blossoms (*na-no-hana* or *aburana; Brassica campestris*). The season for this green vegetable with yellow flowers is March and April. It is best before the flowers have opened. The plant has a long history; it was first brought to Japan from China for its oil-yielding seeds.

rice, glutinous (*mochi-gome*). This variety of short-grain rice is sticky and must be cooked by washing, soaking in water (at least 2 hours before cooking, but usually overnight), then *steaming*, not boiling. It may be boiled, but the result is unsatisfactory. Various starches are made from glutinous rice. *Mochiko* is just ground glutinous rice; *shiratamako* is glutinous rice that has been ground and highly refined. Both these starch powders make forms of *mochi* (see *mochi* entry) when mixed with water and cooked in various ways.

Shiratamako is sold in powdery lumps, which, like *kuzu* starch, may be reduced to powder easily by pounding in a mortar or whirring in a food processor or blender.

rice, short-grain (*okome*). The rice used in Japan is the short-grain variety, which is somewhat stickier and moister than long-grain rice. It also absorbs less water in cooking than long-grain rice. The latter is not appropriate for Japanese food and should be avoided. Short-grain rice is always available in oriental food stores, and many conventional markets now stock it. (See also rice cooking methods, pages 71–72.)

saké. Saké is made by the action of a type of yeastlike mold (*koji; Aspergillus oryzae*) on rice. Of course, saké is the ideal accompaniment to *shōjin* cooking, but it also is an ingredient that acts to tenderize and enhance the flavor of foods. Some people prefer to simmer out the alcohol in saké before using it in cooking, but this is a matter of personal taste. The amounts of saké given in the recipes are conservative. Since saké may be used in cooking much more freely than soy sauce and salt, by all means increase the amounts given if you like.

saké lees (*saké kasu*). This is the pulpy residue that remains from saké brewing. These lees find a few uses in Japanese cooking, largely in pickling and in the recipes included in this book. *Saké kasu* is sold in packaged, pressed sheets or in paste form. In either form it must be dissolved in water or liquid just before using. The easiest way to do this is to soak the lees overnight then whirr in a processor or blender or mash with a fork, crushing all small lumps with your fingers until totally dissolved. Saké lees keep a long time in the refrigerator and indefinitely in the freezer.

sansho (*Zanthoxylum piperitum*). This aromatic plant is referred to as Japanese pepper or prickly ash in dictionaries. It is not pepper, and prickly ash conveys as much meaning as "*sansho*," so why not use the Japanese word? Both the leaves and seed pods are used. The young leaf sprigs are known as *kinome* and are in season in late April and early May, until they reach a length of about 2 inches (5 cm) or so. *Kinome* are mainly used to garnish foods (but see Quick Oden, page 107). *Sansho* pods are pickled in miso or salt when still green, as well as being simmered with *konbu* kelp (see page 108). They are used as a spice when dried, either whole or powdered. Sichuan pepper is the same as *sansho*, with but a small difference in flavor.

sea greens (*wakame; Undaria pinnatifida*). This type of seaweed is sold in fresh, salt-preserved, and dried forms. The fresh probably is not sold abroad. Salt-preserved sea greens need only be rinsed free of salt and soaked in water 5 minutes or so. The dry *wakame* expands greatly and should be reconstituted in ample water. Just let it soak until soft and fully expanded—10 minutes or so, depending on various conditions. You may wish to cut off the rib or vein if it is tough.

seaweed, see *hijiki, konbu* kelp, *nori* seaweed, and sea greens

sesame seeds (*goma*). There are both white and black types of sesame. The black is not a parched form of the white, but is a different variety with a slightly stronger flavor and somewhat less oil than the white seeds. If a recipe does not specify black sesame, use white. When using sesame as a garnish, use the color that looks best—black on green vegetables; either white or black on rice, etc.

Sesame is sold in raw (*arai goma*) and toasted (*iri goma*) forms. (There is also a toasted and ground form, which is best avoided.) Keep seeds in an airtight container free from moisture. The oil in sesame seeds gets rancid after some time. Taste seeds before using. If they are rancid, throw them away; the flavor cannot be corrected.

seven-flavor spice (*shichimi tōgarashi*). This aromatic spice mixture is composed of red pepper flakes, dried mandarin orange peel, white poppy seed, sesame seed, powdered *sansho*, hemp seed, and perilla (*shiso*) or green *nori* seaweed.

***shiitake* mushrooms** (*Lentinus edodes*). This versatile brown mushroom is available in both fresh and dried forms. The fresh is now being cultivated and sold in some markets in the United States, and the dried is widely available in oriental food stores. Black Chinese mushrooms are a good substitute and may, in fact, be the same thing, though

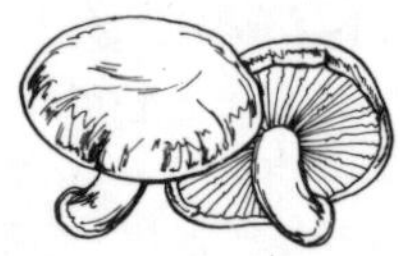

reference books are vague. Ordinary white mushrooms are totally different in flavor and aroma, but will do if nothing else is available.

In buying fresh *shiitake*, look for caps that are curled under, not opened out. The underside of the caps should be whitish. Brown or mottled undersides indicate old mushrooms. The thicker the mushroom, the better. Some get so thick that the top of the caps split and crack. These are the best quality. There are spring and fall crops—the spring mushrooms are better, with thicker flesh and stronger aroma.

Dried mushrooms are sold whole, cut into strips, and in crumbled or powdered forms. Thick flesh and good aroma (you can usually sniff and tell if the aroma is good even if packaged in clear plastic) are the criteria for good dried *shiitake*. Reconstitute in tepid water until soft. Reconstitution time will vary greatly with thickness and size of mushrooms, but calculate 2–3 hours for good mushrooms. A shorter soaking time is possible if the *shiitake* are to be used in simmered foods.

Unlike white mushrooms, the stems of *shiitake* are tough and must be removed with both fresh and dried mushrooms. Reserve these for soup stock if you wish.

***shimeji* mushrooms** (*Lyophyllum aggregatum*). The season for these mushrooms is October and November. Fresh *shimeji* should be delicate-crisp, rather like *enokidake* in texture. Stems should be short and plump, and the flesh should be white. White mushrooms will do as a substitute if *shimeji* are not available.

shiratamako, see glutinous rice

shiso, see perilla

***sōmen* noodles**. There are many types of noodles in Japan, but only the very fine type (*sōmen*) is traditionally used in *shōjin* cooking, particularly in the cooking of nunneries housing an imperial princess-abbess. It is worth spending a little more and getting the hand-stretched (*tenobe*) *sōmen*, not the machine stretched; the latter retains an unpleasant oily odor.

Boil *sōmen* in ample water (*not* lightly salted). The boiling time is short, but varies a bit with the type of *sōmen*. Noodles are done when a piece thrown against a wall sticks and does not fall off. Rinse in cold water. Types of *sōmen* include egg *sōmen* and green tea *sōmen* as well as other flavors, some of which are probably recent inventions.

soy sauce (*shōyū*). This condiment is made by fermentation of boiled and salted soy beans and wheat. There are three main types of soy sauce—*koikuchi*, *usukuchi*, and *tamari*. *Koikuchi* is the ordinary, dark sauce and the only kind used in this book. *Usukuchi* is lighter in color than *koikuchi* but has a higher salt content. *Tamari* is a problem. Some sources say it is a crude type of soy sauce; some say it is the liquid that remains in soy sauce fermentation after the usual sauce is removed; and some say it is made with different ingredients and brewed by a different process.

Important. Use only the Japanese type of soy sauce for Japanese cooking. The soy sauces used in Chinese cooking are totally different and are not appropriate. Kikkoman makes an excellent product that we use exclusively in the Sankō-in kitchen. It is also made in the United States and is available almost anywhere there. This is the only commercial endorsement in this book, and it is made happily, without qualification. The Kikkoman people produce a product that has set a standard for Japanese soy sauce in North America. Rely on it.

spinach (*hōrensō*). Japanese spinach has flat, pointed leaves and is sweeter, more tender, and less acrid than the spinach variety grown and marketed in North America. Buy the youngest spinach you can find, unless the Japanese variety is available.

Spinach root crowns—the rosy-colored place where leaf stems and root join—is a marvelous vegetable in its own right. The spinach crown recipes (pages 177–79) can also be used for spinach leaves or other greens such as beet tops and chard.

starches, see *kuzu*, potato starch. Cornstarch really is not a good substitute for Japanese starches because it has a powdery flavor. Try to find and use the traditional starches called for if possible.

tofu. The size of a tofu cake in Tokyo is roughly 5 ½×2 ¾×1 ½ inches (14×7×3 ½ cm). The sizes of tofu cakes in the United States apparently vary. All the references to tofu cakes in the recipes here are to the Tokyo size. Please compensate if necessary.

The various types of tofu are:

regular or "cotton" (*momen*)
"silk" (*kinu*)
grilled (*yakidōfu*)
deep-fried tofu of different kinds (see *usuage* entry)

Regular tofu is made by straining the whey from soy milk curd in a cotton cloth. "Silk" tofu has a much finer and more delicate texture than the regular, but, in fact, it is tofu that is simply unstrained, coagulated soy milk. Grilled tofu is regular tofu that has been pressed then grilled to make the surface firm.

tofu, frozen and dried (*Kōya-dōfu*). This form of dried tofu comes packaged in standard-sized cakes and is known as *Kōya-dōfu, kōri-dōfu, shimi-dōfu,* and *kogori-dōfu*—all the same thing. It is almost pure vegetable protein.

Reconstitute it by soaking in cold water until it swells and becomes spongy. Then repeatedly press it firmly but gently between the palms of both hands under running water until the milky emission ceases.

Choose freeze-dried tofu that is firm and a uniform tan color. It turns brown with age.

ume, see plums

usuage (thin deep-fried tofu). You cannot make this at home because it is a special type of tofu which is cut thin, pressed to rid it of water, and then double-fried, first in low-temperature then in high-temperature oil. The size of *usuage* sheets in Japan varies, but about 5×3 inches (12 ½×7 ½ cm) can be considered average. *Usuage* should almost always have excess oil removed by pouring boiling water over it. Do this before cutting or slicing. For cutting into julienne strips, first cut in half lengthwise, stack halves, and cut stack into strips.

vinegar, rice. The delicate flavor of rice vinegar lends itself best to *shōjin* cooking. Western vinegars are too harsh and should be avoided. Most supermarkets stock rice vinegar.

wakame, see sea greens

wasabi horseradish, powdered. The fresh *wasabi* root may be available abroad, but it is very expensive even in Japan. All the recipes here call for the powdered type of *wasabi*, which is available in oriental markets. This is not true *wasabi*, but is made of horseradish mixed with some *wasabi* and something else perhaps. The powder has the same flavor as the fresh, but is sharper. This sharpness is better for the recipes included in this book.

Prepare powdered *wasabi* by mixing a few drops of hot water with the powder until a thick paste is formed. Place this in a saké cup or shot glass and turn the glass upside down for about 10 minutes to allow the "bite" and flavor to mature. Make only as much as you need. It does not keep.

wheat gluten (*fu*). There are two forms of wheat gluten—fresh and dry. The procedure to make the fresh, raw gluten is described on pages 65ff. This fresh gluten is often combined with other starches and fashioned into colorful miniature forms, similar to the tiny fantasies made of marzipan, or into sticks that become leaf or flower shapes when sliced. (This colorful use of wheat gluten can be seen in the buffet photograph on page 32.) Generally, such forms are used in clear soups and in simmered dishes, or they are eaten as sweets.

Dry gluten is made by mixing fresh *fu* with flour or glutinous rice powder and then drying or grilling this mixture. It is also made in a wide variety of forms and sizes (see page 83) and is used in clear soups, simmered dishes, and vinegared dishes.

yams, mountain (*yama no imo; Yamato imo*). There are a number of varieties of mountain yam, all of which are species of *Dioscorea*. The type best suited to the recipes in this book is called, variously, *Yamato imo, itchō imo, te imo, Busshō imo* (botanical: *Dioscorea*

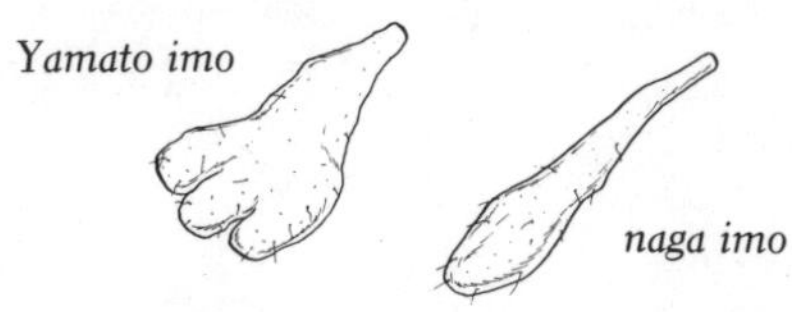

esculenta), etc. This is shaped like a large hand or ginkgo leaf and has less water, a more powdery texture, and a sweeter flavor than the other types. It is also somewhat harder to find and a little more expensive than, say, the long yam (*naga imo; D. batatas*).

The sweet reddish tuber called a yam in the United States is a type of sweet potato and is not a substitute.

yams, field or taro (*sato imo, ko imo*, etc.; *Colocasia antiquorum*). This appears only in passing in this book. The thick skin must be peeled and then the yams boiled. The small ones are considered best.

***yuba*, fresh and dried.** When soy milk is heated, a film or skin forms on its surface, just the same as cow's milk. This skin is *yuba*. Fresh *yuba* is used extensively in *shōjin* cooking, but does not appear in this book because it was feared that this fresh form might not be available abroad. Dried *yuba*, which comes packaged in sheet form (also in small rolls and pieces of various shape) is available at oriental food stores. For deep-frying, dried *yuba* does not need to be reconstituted. For soups and other uses, reconstitute by wetting quickly and placing on a clean kitchen towel to soften.

***yuzu* citron** (*Citrus junos*). The fragrant citrus fruit appears also in Chinese and Korean cooking. Generally the peel or zest only is used; the pulp may be squeezed for its sour juice, but there is not much of it. The season is autumn and early winter, when the fruit

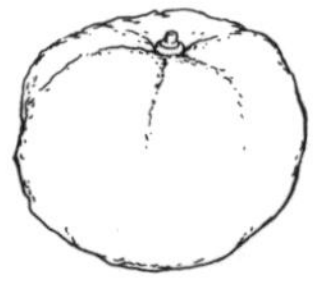

becomes the size of a small tangerine and ripens to a yellow orange color. The skin is thick but delicate and loose over the pulp. Immature, green *yuzu* are used for cooking purposes from midsummer, but the green fruit is not as good as the ripe.

The delightful fragrance of the peel is like that of no other citrus fruit. It would lend itself well to many uses in Western cooking. Lemon or lime peel or zest will substitute, though neither is similar.

BASICS

Though the life in a Buddhist temple (a monastery or nunnery) is highly structured and ordered, there seem to be fewer rules regarding the serving of *shōjin* food than there are in the world of secular Japanese haute cuisine. It would be interesting to trace the reasons for this in the history of Japanese food. For instance, there is no "soup and three" (*ichijū sansai*; soup and three dishes cooked in different ways, considered to form the basic, minimum meal) principle in *shōjin* cooking. Rather, custom and tradition—the custom of various sects and temples that have a tradition of cooking--are respected. Thus, cooking at the Sankō-in follows the tradition and custom of the Donke-in temple in Kyoto, where I spent the early years of my life.

But the main purpose of this food is pleasure and enjoyment, and the purpose of this book is to be practical. This chapter outlines basic equipment and procedures that help the cook in the kitchen, and the next chapter explores seasonal variations of basic Japanese dishes—rice, miso soup, clear soup, and pickles. This latter may seem like extravagance, but a sensitivity towards what the seasons and months of the year offer us is at the heart of this cooking. Serving frozen green peas in December is the extravagance—made possible only through technology and market demand. Enjoying Green Pea Rice when the peas are young, tender, and fresh in May is a basic pleasure, made more intense by the fact that *fresh* young peas are not available in December.

EQUIPMENT

You do not need any special kitchen equipment for cooking *shōjin* food. There are, however, a handful of Japanese tools that are designed to do certain jobs and that will save you time and energy.

Graters (oroshi-gane). The most useful Japanese kitchen tool for the purpose of this book is the grater. This produces a very fine grate of a pulplike consistency, not little shreds. All the references in this book to finely grated ingredients refer to the results of using the Japanese grater.

There are two kinds of graters. The traditional one is a flat surface (usually metal or

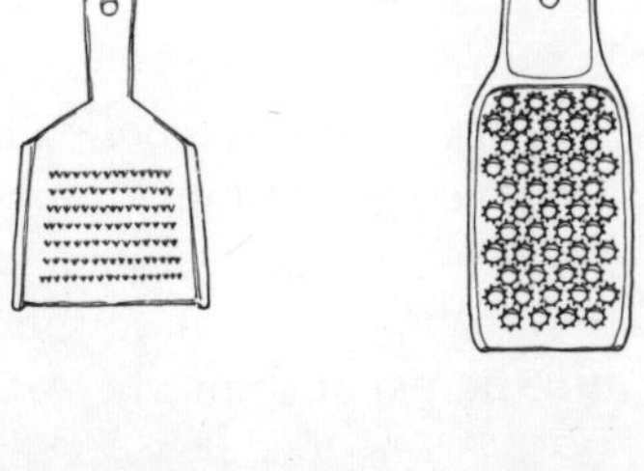

ceramic) punctuated by raised spikes. Professional cooks use tinned copper graters of this type, but it is also made in aluminum and stainless steel. Ceramic graters are usually in dish form.

A certain amount of food remains caught in the spikes of the traditional grater. The best way to remove this is with a small whisk of clean twigs or with a Japanese tea whisk.

The other, new, type is metal or plastic and is a flat surface perforated by round holes around whose circumferences are tiny spikes. (This grater design is used for the fine grating wheel that accompanies food processors.) This type comes in a number of different styles. One of the most convenient is a grater plate that fits as a lid into a plastic box, which catches the gratings.

These tools do a specific job well and are also very convenient for Western cooking.

Grinding bowl (suribachi). The Japanese mortar has the advantage of having a serrated or

grooved inner surface. This *suribachi* is particularly useful for grinding toasted sesame and nuts. A standard mortar and pestle can be substituted, but the *suribachi* is the more efficient tool for some uses.

Food is caught in the grooves of the *suribachi,* but such loss can be minimized by using a small bundle of toothpicks to clean the grooves, or adroit use of a rubber spatula (for some foods), or by adding a liquid to the ground solid in the *suribachi,* as is done with sesame dressing.

Suribachi come in a few sizes. It is convenient to have both a large and small one, but obtain the large one first, then buy a small one if you think it necessary.

Bamboo rolling mat (maki-su). There are a number of rolled dishes in this book. A Japanese rolling mat is a convenient tool to make these, but a clean, folded kitchen towel can be used just as well (see also page 64).

Drop lid(s) (otoshi-buta). Drop-lids are used only a few times in the recipes here. Their

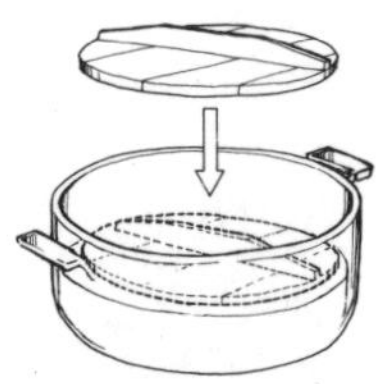

function is to inhibit the roiling movement of a simmering liquid (and thus of the ingredients being simmered) and to shorten cooking time. If drop-lids are not available, either ignore the direction to use one or improvise one from glacine paper or baking parchment cut a little larger than the diameter of the saucepan, so the paper bends up the sides of the pan, with a small vent cut into the paper somewhere.

Container or basin for making sushi rice. A (shallow) basin with a wide diameter of a nonmetallic material is best for tossing hot rice while adding the vinegar mixture to make

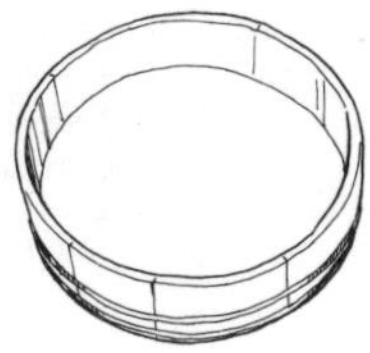

sushi rice. In Japan, the traditional container for this purpose is made of cypress and is called a *hangiri*. It is fashioned in the same manner as a barrel and is a beautiful object by itself, commonly being banded with gleaming copper. Unfortunately, the price is high. Still, it is the best tool for the job and is a pleasure to own and use. It can double as a serving tray, if you find it difficult to rationalize this expensive purchase just for an occasional fling at making sushi rice. However, a large plastic or enameled wash basin will do just as well.

Chopsticks (ohashi). There are many styles of Japanese chopsticks. *Shōjin* food is elegant and is best served to guests with simple, not ornate, lacquered chopsticks. But lacquered chopsticks are slippery, and many people do not care to use them for this reason.

The plain wooden chopstick to use for guests, then, is that known as the Rikyū style. It is made of straight-grained, unadorned cedar and is simple and elegant of line. It also comes in inexpensive forms.

For your everyday use, ordinary disposable chopsticks—the bamboo type is preferable to pine—are satisfactory.

Long cooking chopsticks are excellent in the kitchen, especially for deep-frying and ar-

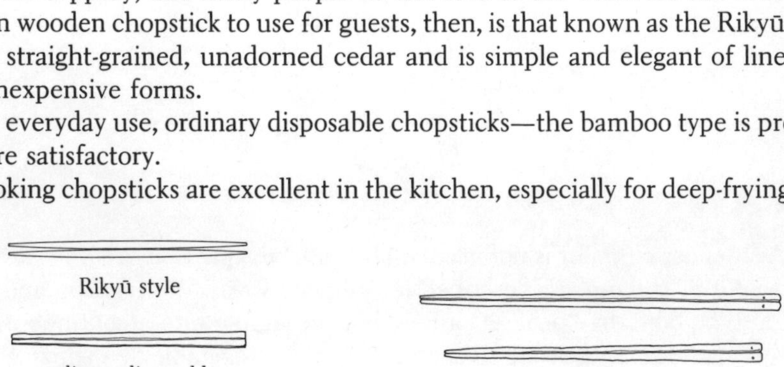

ranging foods on dishes. If you cannot find cooking chopsticks, simply go out and cut yourself some long, straight twigs, peel and dry them thoroughly, taper the ends, and finish them to convenient length and smoothness.

Colanders. Bamboo baskets have been the traditional colanders in Japan. Besides deep ones, there is a very convenient slightly convex flat shape. This can be used for draining foods in a single layer, not a mound, as happens with deep colanders. It is also very convenient for sun-drying foods. It is worth having one or two flat draining baskets (of whatever provenance) in the kitchen.

Knives. By all means have Japanese knives in your kitchen. They can be used for any type of cooking. A vegetable cutter (*nakiri-bōchō* or the professional type known as *usuba*) is a good first purchase. That alone should be sufficient for *shōjin* cooking. But a *deba-bōchō* (like a cleaver with a point) and a "willow-leaf" slicer (*yanagi-ba bōchō*) will complete your set of Japanese knives and allow you to do anything.

But whatever kind of knives you have, KEEP THEM SHARP!

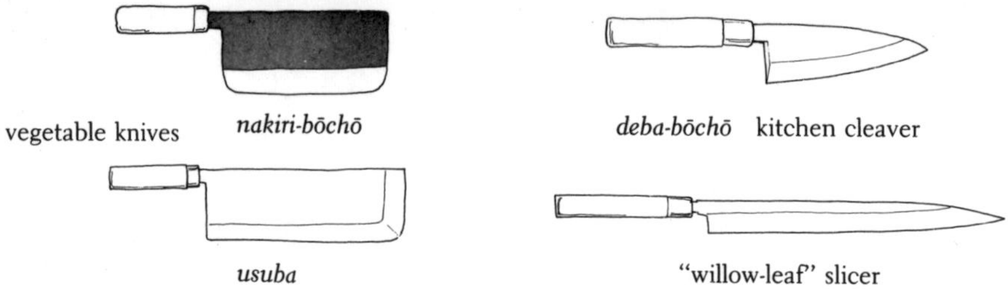

CUTTING

Slices. Cut vegetable into the desired lengths, then cut lengths into slices with the grain (i.e., lengthwise). You might find it useful to cut off one slice of a cylindrical shape and use this cut surface to stabilize the vegetable on the work surface.

Julienne strips: Arrange slices in small vertical stacks or staggered stacks and cut the slices into the degree of fineness you desire—do not make the stack of slices too large, or the cutting becomes sloppy.

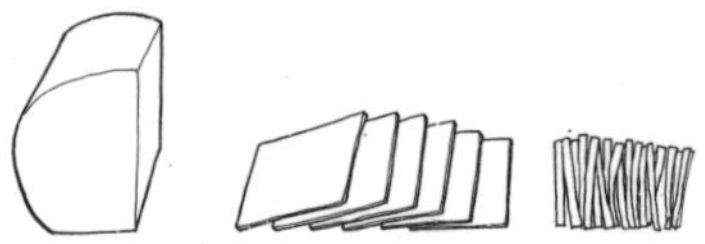

Shreds. A shredder or grater is not used in Japanese cooking to make fine shreds. Rather, shreds are cut by the process described for julienne strips. With daikon and cucumber, this can also be done by "peeling" a length of vegetable into a continuous paper-thin sheet, working from the outside to the center of the vegetable in a spiral, then cutting this sheet into fine shreds. This is a professional's trick, however, and is mentioned here because it is interesting, not because it is practical (at first).

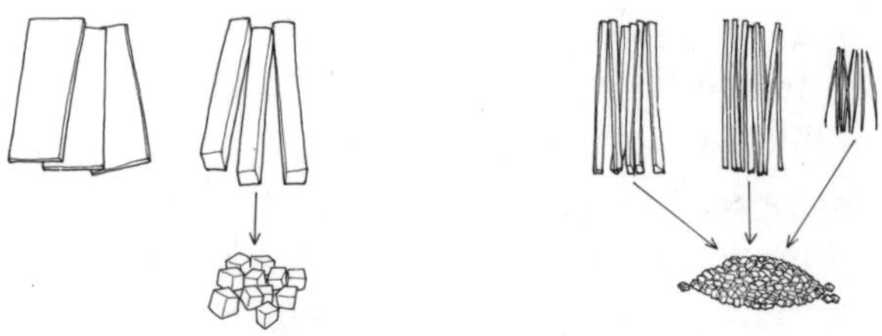

Dicing and fine-chopping. Cut thick slices into long blocks, then cut across these to produce dice. For fine chopping, cut thin slices into julienne strips or shreds and cut across these to produce a mince.

Diagonal slices. Japanese cooking often uses slices cut on the diagonal from a cylindrical vegetable.

Rounds and half-moons. This technique (cutting a cylinder crosswise) is self-evident. Cucumber rings for soups may be made by peeling a cucumber, hollowing out the seeds with a chopstick, then cutting crosswise into rings.

Wedges and chunks. Rotate cylindrical vegetables while cutting at an angle to produce wedge-shaped chunks.

Slivers. Shave burdock and carrot as you would to sharpen a pencil to produce thin slivers—good for stews and simmered dishes.

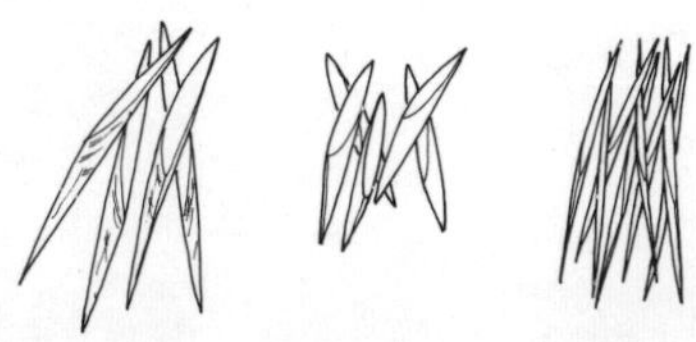

Beveling. The sharp, cut edges of pumpkin and daikon may be beveled to keep such edges from crumbling after simmering.

Leaf and decorative shapes. Small metal cutters are sold in Japan for punching out decorative leaf and flower shapes from carrot and other vegetable slices. Another way to obtain such slices is to sculpt or notch a length of vegetable into the desired shape and cut this into slices (see sketches).

leaf-shaped cutter

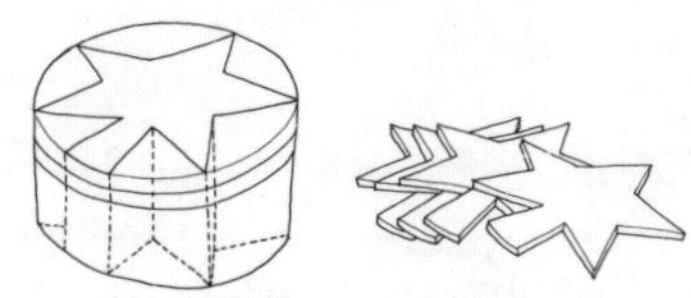

making leaf shapes

PARBOILING GREEN VEGETABLES

In general, vegetables should be subject to high heat for a short period. This principle applies to parboiling vegetables as well. Bring an ample amount of lightly salted water to a rolling boil over high heat. Add vegetables and boil, uncovered, just until the color deepens or they just start to cook. Plunge immediately into cold water or rinse under cold water in a colander. A cold rinse halts the cooking process and fixes the color. (There are some exceptions to this rinsing rule.)

Be sure that stems of leafy vegetables have roughly the same cooking time as the leaves. If stems are hard or thick, cut them off and discard or parboil them separated from the leaves. Or, place them in the boiling water first, then add the leaves, as is done with chrysanthemum leaves (page 105).

MAKING NORI (AND OTHER) ROLLS

There are a number of rolled dishes in this book. The rolling technique is the same for each and employs a device—a bamboo rolling mat or a folded kitchen towel to help make the roll even and firm. Rolls may be made without such a device, but the results will be messy unless you have acquired the knack.

The rolling technique is better explained by pictures than by words. In general, after spreading whatever is to be rolled on the rolling mat or folded kitchen towel, slip your thumbs under the near edge of the mat (or towel) and pick it up. Use the mat to lift the near edge of the *nori* seaweed or whatever food you are rolling and bring it over to form a firm roll. Be sure the mat does not tuck under with the food, but is used to surround the roll. The mat is also used to exert even pressure on the roll to keep it firm, but do not squeeze too hard.

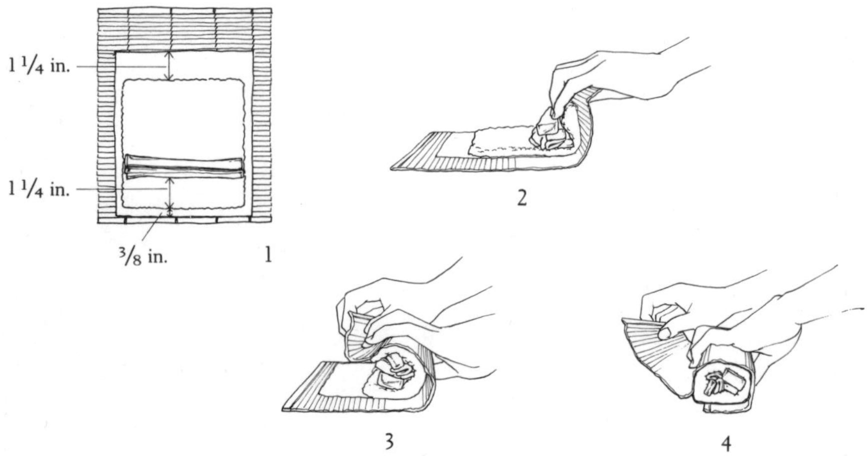

DEEP-FRYING

The best temperature for deep-frying any vegetable is the one that allows the fastest cooking, without, of course, scorching or change of flavor. In this book, medium temperature oil (345°F/170°C) is generally recommended because it is safe for the vegetables available in Japan. In some cases, a somewhat higher temperature might get better results.

It is recommended that you adjust your deep-frying temperatures to the vegetables available. In the United States, where vegetables are generally larger, thicker, and more fibrous than in Japan, it is a good idea to test-fry a vegetable to determine the oil temperature best suited to it. The temperatures in this book are best used as a general guide rather than as dogma.

VINEGAR DRESSINGS

The type of vinegar dressings favored at the Sankō-in are generally sweet, though there are a few in this book that are not so and are referred to as "flavor vinegars." The conventional categories of *nihaizu* and *sanbaizu* vinegar dressings found in Japanese cuisine do not apply to Sankō-in food. That is, there are no formulas for vinegar dressings; each dressing is made to complement the recipe. Generally, however, sweet vinegars use 1 part sugar to 3 parts rice vinegar. Salt, saké, soy sauce, etc. may be used to modify this base.

Another general rule is, when eliminating moisture from parboiled or water-rinsed vegetables, avoid squeezing out too much moisture. Squeeze things gently. Soft, somewhat moist (not soggy wet, however) vegetables taste best.

PIQUANT SOY SAUCE COMBINATIONS

Soy sauce flavored by something else is used in two ways: as a dip only and as a sauce as well as a dip.

In this book, the first category is represented by mustard-soy sauce and *wasabi* horseradish-soy sauce. In general, the piquant ingredient should enhance the flavors of other foods, not dominate them. Do not use large quantities of either mustard or *wasabi* horseradish to mix with soy sauce.

The second category is represented by ginger-soy sauce and *yuzu* citron (or lemon)-soy sauce. In this case, the ginger (juice) and acid juice flavors should be vigorous (but again, not dominating). The strength depends on the dish, but the restraint used for dips only need not be observed.

SESAME TOASTING AND GRINDING

Toasted sesame is sold under the name *iri goma* in Japan and in the United States. This need only be ground. For that matter, pretoasted and ground sesame is also packaged and sold. The former is convenient in a pinch. As for the latter, though "wood-eating saint" (*mokujiki shōnin*) was a nickname given to Buddhist priests of certain aescetic persuasions, it is difficult to recommend this packaged sawdust to readers.

Make toasted and ground sesame from scratch with raw sesame seeds. The reward in aroma and flavor is worth the small effort.

Toasting: Heat a small dry frying pan or saucepan over medium heat, reduce heat to low and add sesame seeds. Stir seeds constantly while toasting. When seeds pop twice, shake pan, keeping seeds in motion until there are seven loud pops (you may want to cover pan to stop seeds from popping out). Remove from heat immediately!

Sesame seeds are very easy to burn. The flavor gets bitter before the color darkens perceptibly, so toast them carefully. It only takes a few seconds to ruin a batch; in fact, expect to ruin a batch or two before getting the knack.

Put hot sesame seeds in a *suribachi* bowl or mortar and grind until the oil forms an aromatic, flaky paste. The aroma of freshly toasted sesame seeds being ground is one of the delights of Japanese cooking.

WHEAT GLUTEN

Raw wheat gluten is easy to make at home—about like making bread. Japanese commercial bakery bread flour (possibly Canadian wheat) yields about 30 percent gluten by weight. High gluten content flour is called "strong" or "bread" flour. Do not use cake flour.

Add just enough water to bread flour to make a very firm dough. The amount of water varies with the flour.

Knead dough about 20–30 minutes. Long kneading activates the gluten, but 20 minutes is probably sufficient. A food processor, though it can only handle small quantities of dough, is efficient, and here is a use for that plastic mixer blade. You will loose some gluten with a processor, however, because it sticks.

Cover dough with a damp cloth and let rest at least 30 minutes.

Place dough in a bowl of water under a running faucet and knead and wash out the starch. Continue until the water is clear—or nearly so. A food processor can do this, but the result is a terrible mess. It is best done by hand. You can also feel the starch leave the dough as you wash it—the mass becomes elastic and rubbery.

The wheat gluten at this point is not yet smooth in texture. Knead it on a dry work surface until it becomes smooth and homogeneous. While kneading, add 1 Tbsp *shiratamako* (glutinous rice powder) for every 1/4 lb of wheat gluten. A food processor is handy for this step of incorporating the dry and lumpy *shiratamako* into the gluten dough. Let the gluten rest at least 30 minutes before using.

When the gluten is deep-fried, it expands and bubbles. Without *shiratamako*, it will deflate. However, its flavor is not affected, and the gluten may be used without the addition of *shiratamako*, though it will be somewhat more gluey in texture.

After a long afternoon of testing and experimentation with various homemade wheat gluten mixtures and the *Rōbai* (page 192) recipe at the Sankō-in, we came to the conclusion that this form of protein tastes good regardless of its texture and that one need not be afraid of just using it as is. But the addition of *shiratamako* does improve the texture.

Raw wheat gluten keeps about 5 days refrigerated. It will loose its rubberiness as it goes bad. However, *Rōbai* I (crisp fried) freezes well and is easy to store.

USES FOR POT LIQUORS

The flavored pot liquors remaining after simmering an ingredient need not be thrown away. The following uses are only a few possibilities. Since they are flavored mainly by soy sauce, salt, and saké, pot liquors keep for at least a day or two in the refrigerator.

1. As flavor-simmering liquid for dried-frozen tofu (*Kōya-dōfu*)—reconstituted and whole or reconstituted and pounded (or processed) into fine crumbs.
2. As simmering liquid to make gruel from leftover cooked rice, or as addition to a rice gruel.
3. As flavor-simmering liquid for *okara* (tofu lees). Add finely chopped cooked or parboiled vegetables if desired.
4. As flavor-simmering liquid for potatoes.
5. As flavor-simmering liquid for *cooked* burdock.
6. As cooking liquid for leaf vegetables, which should first be cut into manageable sizes.
7. As flavor-simmering liquid for eggplant, sliced or cut in appropriate sizes.
8. As flavoring in stir-fried dishes.
9. Carefully strained, as a flavoring in aspics.

Where a pot liquor is used to simmer vegetables, this simmering liquid should be eaten together with the cooked vegetable. That is, the vegetable is not drained but is served with an ample portion of the pot liquor in which it is simmered. Use of pot liquors can be very creative, and one pot liquor can be used repeatedly, becoming richer in flavor with each use.

TABLEWARE AND SIZE OF SERVINGS

It is too much to expect readers to make entire *shōjin* meals at first, or that you will zip out and buy an entire set of Japanese dishes. Yet, since the purpose of this book is to present a type of cooking with a strong and long tradition, the servings in the recipes are Japanese, not Western, portions. These are small and may seem too small at first, but a Japanese meal is composed of small quantities of many things, while a modern Western meal is a lot of a few things. Further, the rice and soup bowls used at temples housing an imperial princess-abbess are smaller than the conventional Japanese sizes. If you wish to double the recipes, simply double the ingredient quantities. (In some cases, simmering liquids need not be doubled in volume, but this is no problem and is easily handled with a little practice.)

Japanese dishes—tableware—are designed for small individual portions. Included here are some sizes and shapes of typical Japanese dishes to give at least some pointers about how you can improvise with what you have or what to buy, if you want to do so. Purchases may be made in small steps—one or two types of dish may be bought rather than an entire "set." Japanese dish sets of one pattern do exist, but it is proper as well as fun and interesting to build an entire Japanese service with different yet complementary and harmonizing dishes. A study of the color photos will give some pointers. The dishes in the photographs were all chosen by the author. They are the dishes used to serve food to paying guests at the Sankō-in temple. None is either expensive or precious, but every one was carefully chosen and clearly reflects the taste and choice of one person.

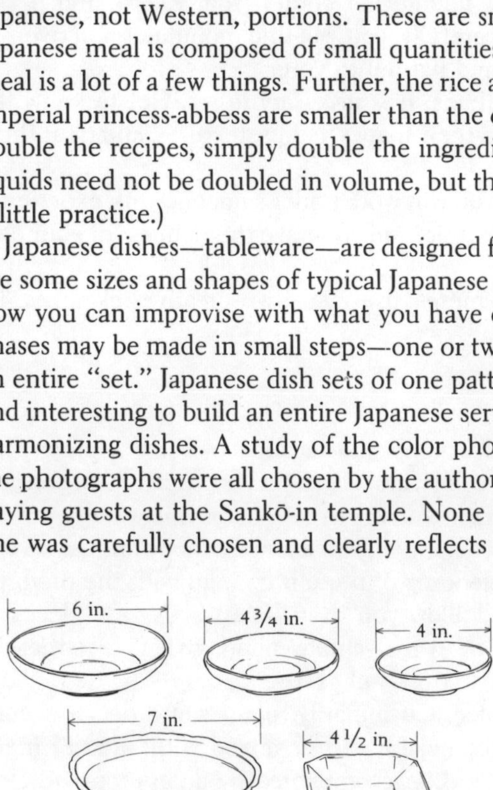

plates (*hirazara*)

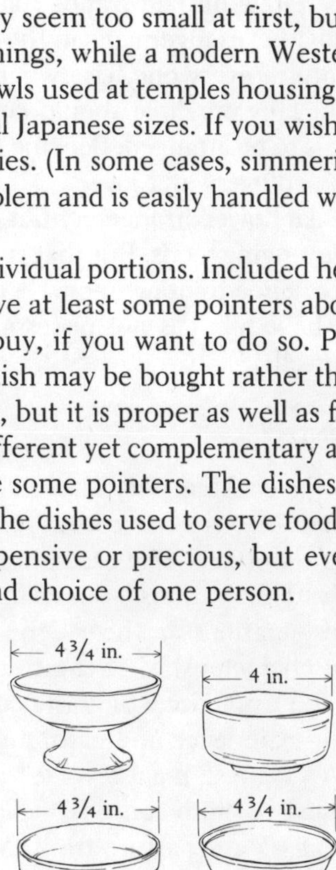

dishes (*fukazara*)

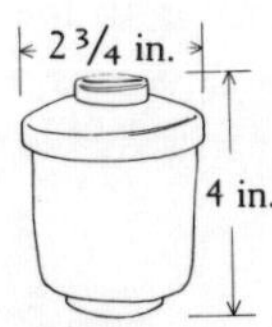

lidded cup for steaming (*chawan mushi*; p. 161)

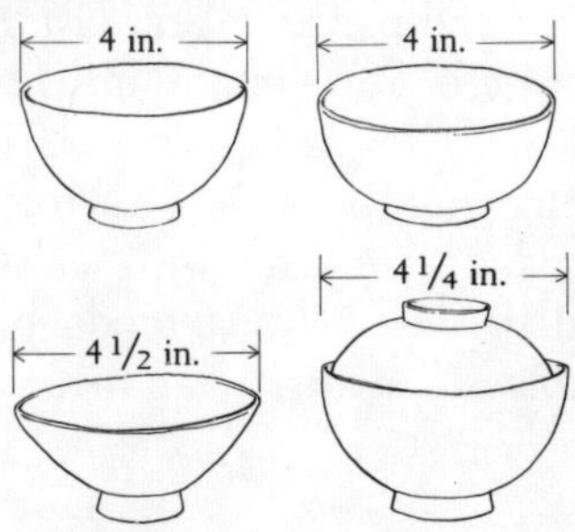

soup and rice bowls

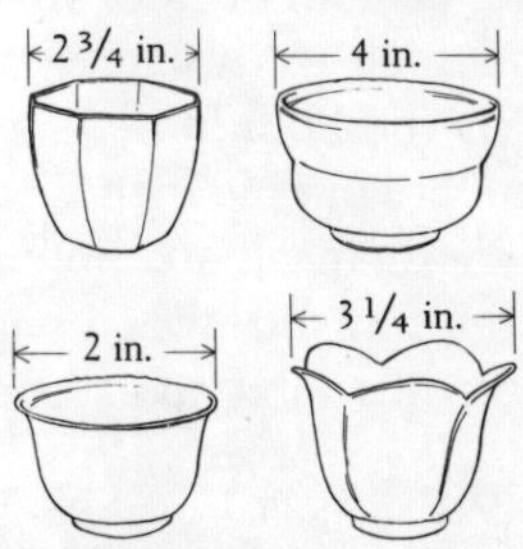

deep dishes (*otsubo*)

FOOD ARRANGEMENT

There is nothing magic or mysterious about the way food is arranged in Japan, though many foreign visitors are impressed with such arrangements. It is likely, however, that without much experience and practice, you will not be able to arrange food in a true Japanese manner. What you can do, and do well, is arrange food as *you* would arrange it.

In *shōjin* cooking, there are a few basic rules, the rest is you.

1. Food is arranged like a landscape on a plate. Such a landscape includes mountains, a river, riverbanks, bridge, fields, roads—whatever.
2. The landscape should reflect the season. For instance, in summer, mountains are blue; in autumn, red; in winter, brown; in spring, flowery.
3. Draw on landscapes that you know. The author comes from Kyoto, and if you study the arrangements in the color pages carefully, you will find mountains and rivers of Kyoto in every one. Use what is familiar and natural to you.
4. This principle should come first, perhaps. *It is necessary to see.* Get to know the foods to be arranged. Become intimate with their shapes, colors, textures, and treat them with courtesy and love.

Like flower arrangement, it is helpful if you can work under someone with experience in arranging foods. But that is next to impossible, and you have the richness of your own experience to draw upon.

Above all, it is not necessary to be Japanese—use your own creative resources. Be yourself.

MENUS

Shōjin cooking puts importance on the harmony and balance of a few simple principles—i.e., the five cooking methods, five colors, and six tastes (see page 37). In contrast to the world of Japanese haute cuisine, there are no rules of order or proper sequence for serving the various types of food in *shōjin* cooking. Balance and harmony are the pivotal considerations. In theory, the successful blending of these principles with the products and characteristics of the four seasons will allow you to make attractive and delicious food. In practice, study the color plates, look at the sample menus that follow, then let your experience and natural good sense take over and do the rest.

A Japanese meal revolves around the rice. Customarily, plain white rice is accompanied by miso soup. A "color rice"—rice cooked with or mixed with another ingredient—is a departure from everyday fare and is accompanied by an appropriate clear soup and pickle. The various dishes of the meal are chosen to harmonize with the rice, the soup, and the accompanying pickle.

Also, custom decrees that rice, soup, and pickle appear last at a full Japanese meal. The reasons for this are not important here. More important is to serve a meal that will nourish you both in body and spirit.

Here are sample menus for the twelve months of the year that should give an idea of what *shōjin* meals are. Some liberties have been taken with seasonal dishes, as was done with the tray settings on pages 18 and 19. The seasonal model presented in this book is very flexible—if a good food is available and it fits, by all means use it.

January
Zen Temple *Ozōni* (page 86)

onishime (plate with a variety of foods—like an antipasto)
Burdock with Spicy Sesame Dressing (page 156)
Saké-Braised Snow Peas (page 109)
Mountain Yam Balls (with *wasabi* horseradish) (page 154)
Sweet Simmered Kumquats (page 167)
Vinegared Lotus Root (use lotus root preparation in Sweet Bean-Stuffed Lotus Root, page 174, and slice lotus)
pickle: Burdock in Sweet Vinegar (page 89)

February
rice: Bean Rice (page 73)
clear soup: Grilled Tofu in Thick Broth (add cubes of grilled tofu to the broth in Zucchini in Thick Clear Soup, page 129, eliminating zucchini)
Rōbai (page 192)
Deep-Fried Waterchestnut and *Nori* Squares (page 165)
Crisp Turnip with Sesame-Miso Dressing (page 158)
pickle: Dried Daikon Strips in Sweet Vinegar (page 90)

March
rice: Golden Shred Sushi (page 211)
clear soup: Deep-Fried Dried *Yuba* (page 195) and a parboiled green
Simmered *Hijiki* (page 108)
Chrysanthemum Leaves with Sesame Dressing (page 106)
pickle: Whole Turnips in Miso (page 90)

April
rice: Bamboo Sushi (page 97)
clear soup: Parboiled Fiddlehead Ferns and Tofu
Quick *Oden* (page 107)
Chrysanthemum Leaf Roll (page 105)
pickle: Tofu in Miso (page 90)

May
rice: New Tea Rice (page 74)
clear soup: Chrysanthemum Tofu (page 85)
Fava Beans with Sea Greens (page 103)
Mountain Yam with Plum Dressing (page 138)
pickle: Okra in Miso (page 90)

June
rice: Rice Bales (page 80)
clear soup: *Junsai* (page 84)
Sesame "Tofu" (page 196)
Eggplant and Fava Beans (page 122)
pickle: Cucumbers in Miso (page 90)

July
rice: Cold *Sōmen* Noodles in Dipping Sauce (page 125)
Dried-Frozen Tofu Tempura (page 183)
Vinegared Cucumbers (page 116)

pickle: Three-Minute Eggplant Pickle (page 91)

August
rice: Perilla Rice (page 75)
clear soup: Zucchini in Chilled Thick Clear Soup (page 129)
Eggplant Purple (page 123)
Simmered Japanese Pumpkin (page 131)
Simmered Dried-Frozen Tofu (page 182)
Pressed and Vinegared Cucumbers (page 117)
pickle: Celery in Miso (page 91)

September
rice: Chestnut Rice (page 77)
clear soup: Sesame "Tofu" in Broth (page 198)
Deep-Fried Mountain Yam Nuggets (page 140)
Braised *Shiitake* Mushrooms (page 144)
Vinegared Gourd Ribbons (page 151)
pickle: Egglant in Miso (page 90)

October
rice: *Shimeji* Mushroom Rice (page 78)
soup: *Kenchin Jiru* (page 85)
Piquant Waterchestnut Balls (page 166)
Turnip Chrysanthemums (page 160)
pickle: *Shiitake* Mushrooms in Sweet Miso (page 91)

November
rice: Ginkgo Nut Rice (page 77)
clear soup: *Matsutake* mushroom (page 137), parboiled green, and *yuzu* citron
Rōbai Simmered with *Konbu* Kelp (variation of *Konbu* Kelp and Bamboo Shoots, page 99, using *Rōbai* instead of bamboo shoots)
Salad with White Dressing (page 206)
pickle: *Shimeji* Mushrooms in Saké Lees (page 91)

December
rice: Temple Gruel (page 79)
Karamono (page 167)
Pine Cones (page 150)
Spinach with Walnut Dressing (page 176)
Bright and Crunchy Daikon Rolls (page 168)
Deep-Fried Dried *Yuba* (page 195)
pickle: Cabbage in Miso (page 91)

RICE, SOUPS, PICKLES

RICE

There are probably as many ways to cook rice in Japan as there are people who cook. This may seem surprising for what appears to be a simple, cut-and-dried procedure. Certainly the same thing cannot be said for boiling potatoes. In fact, the statement is false, because today most Japanese households have automatic rice cookers (gas or electric), and young cooks of either sex have no experience of cooking rice in a saucepan or pot on a stove.

The mnemonic for cooking rice on wood-burning stoves is *ato saki soro-soro, naka pa-pa*, which means low heat at beginning and end and strong heat in the middle. The interpretation of this simple rule varies considerably.

Three methods of cooking rice are included here to allow readers to find the way that gets the best flavor for the kind of rice available. The variety of short-grain rice, whether its cultivation is wet or dry, its storage age—all these factors affect the flavor and the cooking method. Most people have no source for such esoteric information. So—just cook the rice and enjoy. If you wish to experiment, try these cooking methods or make up your own. The first is the author's, who is from Kyoto; the second is that of a woman who rigorously tests various cooking methods. The third is that of an eighty-three-year-old mother of seven and grandmother of nine, a native of Tokyo.

Washing: Before cooking begins, the rice must be washed—very well. Stir the rice vigorously in the saucepan you will cook it in, changing water repeatedly until the water is as clear as it will get. There should be no powder in the rice to cloud the water. This milky water can be used to parboil acrid or bitter vegetables such as bamboo shoots or to nourish your garden, etc.

Water: After washing rice, add 10 percent more water than volume of dry rice and let rice stand in water in the saucepan or rice cooker for 30 minutes to 1 hour.

Style I: Cover pan and cook over low heat until boiling. Check by lifting lid.

Increase heat to medium-high and keep lid slightly ajar until foam rises in pot (about 4 minutes).

Place lid on securely and reduce heat to low until rice is cooked and all water absorbed—roughly 10 minutes. Taste the rice. If it needs more cooking, then do so.

Style II: Bring rice to a boil over high heat in covered pan.

Remove lid and reduce heat to medium-high. Cook until liquid gets very foamy and holes are formed in surface of rice. You cannot see the rice surface, but most of the foaming occurs above these holes.

Cover pan, reduce heat to low, and cook until all liquid is absorbed—about 9–10 minutes.

Style III: Cover pan and bring to a boil over high heat. Do not remove lid at any time during cooking (unless some extra ingredient is added near end).

When lid begins to dance, reduce heat to low and cook until all liquid absorbed—about 15–20 minutes.

Raise heat to high for 30–40 seconds; turn off heat, and let stand for 5 minutes.

If you have an enameled cast iron pot with a snug fitting lid to cook rice in, then you are lucky. If your rice-cooking pot does not come up to this ideal, make friends with it and find out the best way to meet its requirements for making good rice.

Finally—what is good rice? The rice you think most delicious is *it*; or if you cook for a family, what consensus decrees. There are no rules of deliciousness, regardless of what "experts" say. However, the more experience you have with rice, the more you will come to favor a certain kind of cooking or, conversely, the more you will savor every kind of cooked rice for its unique virtue.

In temple cooking, variations of rice dishes are known as "color rice." Such variations are, naturally, seasonal and once played an important role in the diet of temples housing an imperial princess-abbess. Apparently at one time such or similar variations were more common in the general Japanese diet, at least for those who ate rice regularly.

Here are some "color rice" variations for the twelve months. In fact, two of them are not rice, but *mochi* and noodles. Some months have more than one variation. Feel free to create any "color rice" you like, using the freshest seasonal ingredients.

For 4 servings, use 1 ⅔ cups dry rice (400 mL) and 10 percent more water by volume, which amounts to 1 ⅔ cups plus 3 Tbsps (440 mL). These amounts are constant in the following recipes unless otherwise indicated. Never refrigerate cooked short-grain rice—it gets hard quickly. The one exception to this rule is Rice Patties (page 205).

January FLOWER PETALS *(Ohanabira)*

In its original form this was imperial palace food, eaten at New Year as a substitute for the traditional *ozōni* soup.

At the Donke-in temple, it was eaten on January 3. The original version was a round of *mochi* topped by a thin diamond-shaped piece of millet *mochi*, which was topped, in turn, by burdock. This combination was then rolled. The present version eliminates the millet *mochi* and can be easily made at home. Square pieces of *mochi* may be used as well as round; the latter are more attractive.

16-inch (40-cm) length burdock root (gobō), *scrubbed with a stiff brush, split lengthwise into fourths or sixths (depending on thickness), and cut into 4-inch (10-cm) lengths*
2 ½ cups water
8 Tbsps sweet white Kyoto (saikyō) *miso*
8 Tbsps saké
8 round (or square) pieces mochi

Bring burdock and water to a boil quickly. Reduce heat to medium, place pot lid ajar, and simmer 1 ½ hours, until burdock is soft. Drain and cool. Mix miso and saké in a small saucepan and simmer 5 minutes over low heat. Place miso mixture in a bowl, add cooked burdock, and marinate overnight.

Moisten and wring out a cloth napkin.

Grill a piece of *mochi* on one side only, just until soft throughout. (Be careful it does not puff up too much and get hard to handle.) Place soft *mochi* on damp cloth and spread with fingers until about 4 inches (10 cm) wide or in diameter.

Place 4–6 burdock pieces in middle of *mochi* and fold over so edges meet. Repeat for each piece of *mochi*. Eat hot! Two pieces is a single portion. Does not keep.

February BEAN RICE *(Mame Gohan)*

Black bean rice is associated with the festival for the deity Daikoku in November, while soy bean rice is associated with the Setsubun Festival (Demon Expelling) in February. The word for beans is used in Japanese sayings as a pun meaning good health (in winter). This dish is likely a very old way of preparing rice, but it is almost unknown to the Japanese public today.

3 Tbsps dried yellow soy beans (daizu)
1 2/3 cups short-grain rice
1 2/3 cups water
1 Tbsp saké
1 1/2 tsps salt

Parch beans in a small saucepan over medium heat, shaking pan and letting it rest on heat for *alternate* 5 seconds for a total of about 3 minutes. The beans will crackle, become fragrant, and will scorch in spots. Cool beans on a plate or flat basket.

Place cooled beans in a clean towel, fold towel over beans so they are loosely contained, then roll with a rolling pin with hard pressure. This is to remove skins and break some beans in half. Continue until no more skins break off and there is no further significant change. Spread beans on towel or newspaper and pick out meat. Discard skins.

Place rice in a saucepan, add beans and other ingredients, and cook in the conventional manner (page 71).

May be eaten hot or at room temperature, as rice "balls."

March GINGER RICE *(Shōga no Sakura Gohan)*

short-grain rice and water for 4 servings
1 tsp soy sauce
1/6 tsp salt
1 tsp saké
2 1/2-inch (30-gm) knob fresh ginger, thinly sliced then cut into very fine ("needle") shreds

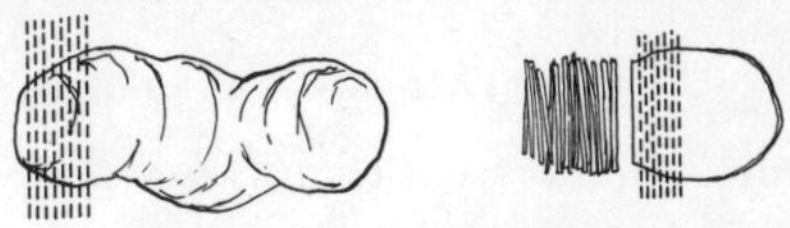

Mix rice with all ingredients and cook in any conventional manner (page 71). Eat hot or at room temperature as rice "balls."

April (1) CHERRY BLOSSOM RICE *(Sakura Gohan)* (4 very small servings)

This is one of the most luxurious rice variations, distinctive for its fragrance of cherry trees in bloom. The salt-preserved double cherry blossoms come in bottled form.

1 cup short-grain rice
1 cup plus 2 Tbsps water
16 salt-preserved cherry blossoms

Cook rice in the conventional way (see page 71).

Tear salt-preserved cherry blossoms (including stems) into small pieces with your fingers. Do not chop with knife. Toss with hot rice and serve immediately. May also be eaten at room temperature in the form of rice "balls." Does not keep.

April (2) FIDDLEHEAD FERN RICE *(Warabi Gohan)*

1/4 lb (115 gm) water-packed (or canned) fiddlehead ferns (warabi), *cut into 1 1/4-inch (3-cm) lengths*

FOR FLAVORING FIDDLEHEAD FERNS

7 Tbsps dashi
1 tsp soy sauce
1 tsp saké
pinch salt

short-grain rice and water for 4 servings
1 tsp salt
1 Tbsp saké

Place fiddlehead ferns in flavoring liquid and simmer over low heat for 5 minutes. Combine rice, water, 1 tsp salt, and 1 Tbsp saké and cook rice in conventional way (see page 71). When rice is cooked, toss with fiddlehead ferns and serve hot. May also be eaten at room temperature in the form of rice "balls." Keeps 2 days.

May (1) GREEN PEA RICE *(Endō Gohan)*

1 scant tsp salt
3/4 cup boiling water
3/4 cup green peas (frozen OK)
1/2 tsp salt
1 2/3 cups short-grain rice

Dissolve 1 scant tsp salt in 3/4 cup boiling water. Add green peas and simmer over medium heat until cooked. Pour pot liquor into a measuring cup and add enough water to make 1 2/3 cups plus 3 Tbsps liquid (440 mL; i.e., 10 percent more liquid than volume of rice). Reserve peas. Add 1/2 tsp salt to liquid, then use this to cook rice in the conventional way (page 71). When rice is done, add green peas and toss. Serve hot or at room temperature in the form of rice "balls." Keeps 8 hours.

May (2) HORSETAIL RICE *(Tsukushi no Gohan)*

1 cup raw field horsetail sprouts (see page 48)
short-grain rice and water for 4 servings
1 Tbsp soy sauce
1/2 tsp salt
1 Tbsp saké

Pick horsetail sprouts about 4 inches (10 cm) long. Remove sheath, then break at the nodes. Heads plus stem segments should equal 1 cup. Combine all ingredients and cook rice in the conventional manner (see page 71). Eat hot or at room temperature. Makes excellent rice "balls."

May (3) NEW TEA RICE *(Shincha Gohan)*

Kyoto devotees of the *sencha* type of tea ceremony are fond of this elegant manner of preparing rice. New tea appears on the market when the young leaves are picked in early summer, and this rice embodies the essence of that season.

short-grain rice and water for 4 servings
1 tsp salt

1 ½ *tsps new tea* (shincha), gyokuro *type (available year-round in vacuum sealed packets)*

Cook rice in the conventional way (see page 71). On a totally dry cutting board, chop tea very fine. Mix with salt. Mix tea-salt mixture into hot rice *just before eating.* Eat hot! Does not keep.

June UNOHANA RICE *(Unohana Gohan)*

short-grain rice and water for 4 servings
½ *cup Fried* Unohana, *page 189*

Cook rice in the conventional way (see page 71). Add hot *unohana* to hot cooked rice and toss to mix well. Eat hot or at room temperature. Keeps 1 day.

July PERILLA RICE *(Shiso Gohan)* (4 very small servings)

Perilla (*shiso*) is in season from May to October. These delicate, aromatic leaves have become known in the United States because of their inclusion in some types of sushi.

1 cup short-grain rice
1 cup plus 2 Tbsps water
4 small green perilla (shiso) *leaves, stems removed, washed, and patted dry*
½ *tsp salt*

Cook rice in the conventional way (see page 71).

Cut *shiso* leaves into short shreds. One quick way to do this is to stack the leaves and cut this stack in half lengthwise. Stack the halves, cutting the stack again in half lengthwise and then in half crosswise. Place cut leaves in a single pile and cut into shreds about ⅛ inch (½ cm) long.

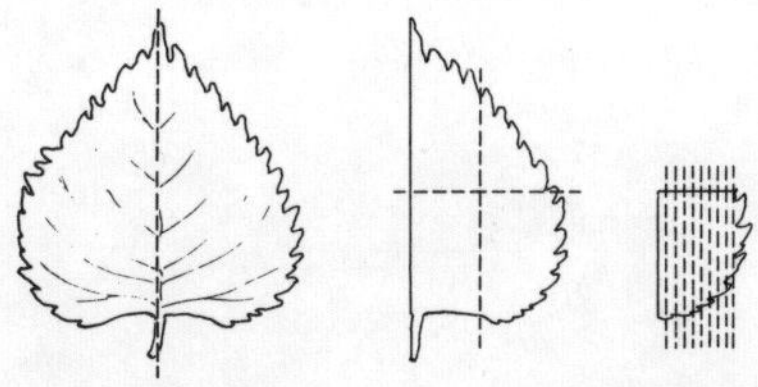

Place shredded *shiso* in a cloth napkin, rinse in water, then gently squeeze out moisture. Place *shiso* in a small bowl, add salt, and toss lightly, so that the *shiso* shreds separate and salt coats the shreds.

When the rice is cooked, add *shiso* and toss so that the shreds are well distributed in the rice. Serve hot!

August THICK-ROLLED SUSHI *(Futomaki Zushi)*

Sushi is a dish for special occasions in temples. This type of thick sushi roll, which originated in the Kyoto-Osaka area, can be a teatime snack, part of a large meal, or be a meal in itself completed by tea. In short, this sushi is the Japanese equivalent of a sandwich; and, like a sandwich, there are no rules or limits regarding what can be put into it.

same quantity of prepared sushi rice as in Pouch Sushi (page 189), but without yuzu *citron peel and with a little more salt added*
2 cakes dried-frozen tofu (Kōya-dōfu) *cut in fourths lengthwise*

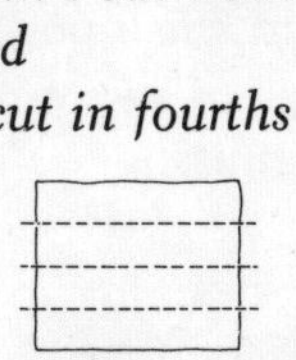

FOR FLAVORING KŌYA-DŌFU

1 1/4 cups water
1 Tbsp sugar
1/3 tsp salt
1 tsp soy sauce

3 sheets nori *seaweed*
3 1-inch (2 1/2-cm) pieces yuzu *citron (or lemon or lime) peel, cut in fine shreds (about 1/4 tsp per piece of peel)*
1/2 lb (225 gm) spinach, parboiled in lightly salted water, plunged into cold water to cool, and gently squeezed of moisture
soy sauce

Boil rice in the conventional way and make sushi rice by tossing rice while gradually adding vinegar-sugar-salt mixture (see page 189).

Reconstitute *Kōya-dōfu* by soaking in tepid water until soft, then pressing out milky liquid repeatedly in changes of water until no more is emitted. Simmer reconstituted *Kōya-dōfu* in its flavoring mixture over medium heat for 10 minutes.

Place *nori* sheet on clean kitchen towel or rolling mat (*maki-su*), shiny ("front") side down. Spread layer of sushi rice 1/2 inch (1 1/2 cm) thick on *nori*, with 3/8-inch (1-cm) margin in front and 1 1/4-inch (3-cm) margin on far side. Sprinkle 1/4 tsp finely shred-cut *yuzu* citron (or lemon or lime) peel over rice. Place *Kōya-dōfu* (2 1/2 sticks) across rice in a line 1 1/4 inches (3 cm) from front edge of rice.

Spread spinach on a plate. Dip fingertips in soy sauce and pat soy sauce across spinach a few times to add a small amount of flavor. Spread a line of spinach next to *Kōya-dōfu* on far side.

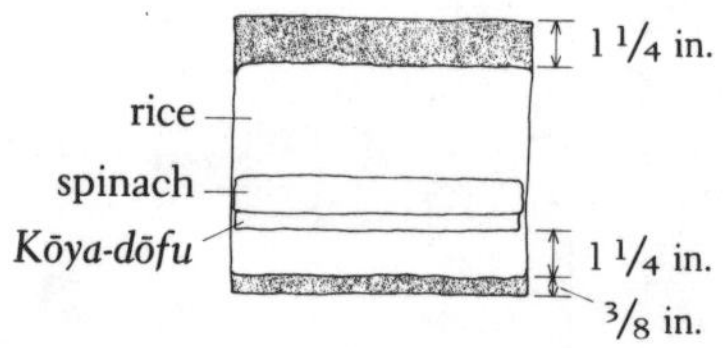

Roll sushi with towel (or rolling mat). Repeat for remaining two rolls. Cut 2 rolls into 9 pieces and 1 roll into 10 pieces. Each portion is 7 pieces; arrange 5 on bottom and 2 on top with cut side up. Place about 1/2 Tbsp Vinegared Ginger (see following recipe) in a neat mound next to sushi slices.

Vinegared Ginger (Sushōga or *Gari)*

Peel fresh ginger and slice as thin as possible. Place slices in bowl, pour boiling water on to cover and let rest about 2 minutes. Drain and cool. Mix ginger with sweet vinegar (3 parts vinegar; 1 part sugar; 1/6 part salt) and let rest at least 1 hour before using; best flavor is achieved after maturing 1 day.

September CHESTNUT RICE *(Kuri Gohan)* (4 very small servings)

This traditional autumn rice, eaten in small portions in both temples and homes, was one of the great treats before the age of sweet confections. The small amount of salt brings out the sweetness of the chestnuts.

1 cup short-grain rice
1 cup plus 2 Tbsps water

18 chestnuts, shells and skins removed and cut in half
1 ½ tsps salt
2 Tbsps saké

Combine all ingredients and cook in the conventional manner for rice (see page 71). Eat immediately.

October (1) GINKGO NUT RICE *(Ginnan Gohan)*

Ginkgo nuts are *ginnan* in Japanese and refer to the *gin* ("silver") in the list of precious materials mentioned in the introductory paragraph to Sweet Simmered Kumquats, page 167. In the Donke-in temple there is a marble slab that has been used only for cracking the shells of ginkgo nuts for about 300 years, and a hollow that just fits a ginkgo nut has been worn into the marble over the centuries.

40 ginkgo nuts, shelled and peeled (see page 148)
short-grain rice and water for 4 servings
1 tsp salt
2 tsps soy sauce
1 Tbsp saké

Combine all ingredients and cook rice in the conventional way (see page 71). Eat hot or at room temperature in the form of rice "balls" the same day as made.

October (2) SWEET POTATO RICE *(Satsuma Imo Gohan)*

During World War II, everyone in Japan stretched their rice with sweet potatoes—or whatever else was available. In Zen temples the food does not change with the economic weather—whatever is available is fully utilized as a matter of course. Here sweet potato is used with its skin, which is attractive, nourishing, and tasty.

½ medium sweet potato (about ⅓ lb/150 gm), washed, skin left intact
short-grain rice and water for 4 servings
1 tsp salt

Cut unpeeled sweet potato into ½-inch (1 ½-cm) cubes (there should be about 1 ¼ cups). Place in bowl and cover with water. Let stand 5 minutes in water, then drain and discard water.

Place all ingredients in a heavy saucepan or rice cooker and cook in the conventional way (see page 71).

Serve hot! Not good at room temperature.

November SHIMEJI MUSHROOM RICE *(Shimeji Gohan)*

This autumn rice is one of the seasonal rice dishes that is used for special occasions or for guests—both in the home and in temples. The mushrooms give off liquid when cooked, so the amounts of rice and water are the same (1 ⅔ cups each) for this recipe serving 4.

½ lb (225 gm) shimeji *mushrooms, dirty stem bases removed, clumps torn into pieces*
1 tsp salt
1 tsp soy sauce
1 Tbsp saké

Mix all ingredients and cook in the conventional manner (see page 71).

December (1) HOT SŌMEN NOODLES *(Onyūmen)* (serves 4)

Sōmen, the aristocrat of Japanese noodles, is the natural choice of a princess-abbess. Buckwheat noodles (*soba*) and the thick wheat noodles (*udon*) are far too coarse and plebeian. This simple yet satisfying dish was first eaten in nunnery-temples as an afternoon or teatime snack.

4 bundles thin ("hand stretched" or tenobe) sōmen *noodles*
BROTH
 2 *cups* konbu dashi (see page 81)
 8 *medium-sized fresh* shiitake *mushrooms, halved*
 2 *Tbsps soy sauce*
 ⅔ *tsp salt*
 1 *Tbsp saké*
4 sheets dried yuba, *deep-fried (see page 195)*
12 stalks trefoil (mitsuba), *cut into ½-inch (1 ½-cm) lengths (or about 4 generous Tbsps parboiled and roughly cut tender green vegetable)*
yuzu *citron (or lemon) peel as garnish*

Bring an ample amount of water to a boil in a large saucepan and add *sōmen* noodles. Boil until done, about 5–6 minutes. To test if noodles are done, throw a small piece against a wall; if it sticks, the *sōmen* is cooked. Rinse well in cold water.

Put the *konbu dashi* and *shiitake* mushrooms in a small saucepan and bring to a boil over medium heat. Add soy sauce, salt, and saké and simmer 2–3 minutes without cover.

Place one portion (¼ of total amount; about ⅚ cup) of noodles into broth, add 1 piece of deep-fried *yuba*, cover pan, and simmer about 20 seconds to warm noodles. Place each noodle portion and piece of *yuba* in a deep bowl, add trefoil (or 1 generous Tbsp of some other parboiled and chopped green) and ladle about ½ cup broth into each bowl.

Serve hot and eat with chopsticks, though forks and soup spoons will do. Garnish with a sliver of *yuzu* citron (or lemon) peel. Does not keep.

December (2) TEMPLE GRUEL *(Ojiya)* (serves 4–6)

In a Zen temple, the amount of rice to be used in preparing a meal is fixed for each day or time period. If an unexpectedly large number of people appears at a temple, the usual practice is to stretch the rice by adding more water. Another way of stretching rice and still staying within the limits of the rice commitment for the meal is to add flour dumplings. This dumpling gruel became a special recipe of the Donke-in temple. A good friend for frigid nights or for a delicate stomach.

3 ⅓ cups leftover cooked rice
3 ⅓ cups miso soup (miso shiru; *see page 86*), *leftover or freshly made*
7 Tbsps flour mixed with 5 Tbsps water
1 Tbsp saké

Bring rice and miso soup to a boil over medium heat then reduce heat to low and simmer for about 10 minutes, until rice begins to become "watery." Drop the flour batter into the simmering gruel, 1 tsp at a time to form small dumplings. Add 1 Tbsp saké at last minute. Serve piping hot. Does not keep.

All Season (1) AZUKI BEAN RICE *(Azuki Gohan)*

1/2 cup azuki beans, washed
short-grain rice and water for 4 servings
1/6 tsp salt

Place azuki beans in ample water, bring to a boil quickly, reduce heat to medium, and simmer with lid tilted. Add cold water three or four times during the simmering--this "surprises" the beans and hastens their softening. Simmer a total of about 40 minutes. The beans will still be somewhat hard but will soften when cooked with rice.

Mix with rice, add 3 Tbsps pot liquor of beans, and cook in conventional manner. Eat hot or in the form of rice "balls."

All Season (2) RICE "BALLS"—VARIATIONS *(Onigiri)*

There are four basic rice "ball" (*onigiri*) shapes—triangle, circle, sphere, and cylinder (rice bale). Playing with size creates various effects, and then coatings and flavor additions bring the variations possible to a very large number. The rice "balls" included here are some of the basic, classic ones found in temple cooking.

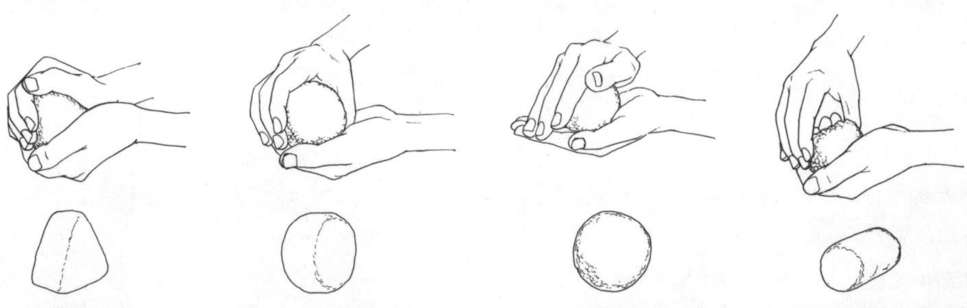

RICE BALES
Tororo Konbu no Onigiri

SERVES 4
1 cup white tororo *(shaved)* konbu *kelp*
3 1/2 cups cooked rice

Finely chop the *tororo konbu*. It comes finely shredded, so it needs only a little effort on the cutting board.

Make cylindrical rice "balls" (the shape of rice bales) using 1 ounce (30 gm)—about 2 Tbsps—of cooked rice for each. Roll each cylinder in finely chopped *tororo konbu*. One portion is five "bales."

GRILLED ONIGIRI
Grill both sides of a rice "ball" until unevenly browned and rice becomes crisp.

MISO
With your fingers, color the surface of a grilled or ungrilled rice "ball" with a small amount of salty or medium-salty miso. Do not overdo this—keep flavor delicate.
Soup: Place a small grilled and miso-coated rice "ball" in a deep soup bowl. Add about 1 Tbsp cut trefoil (or parboiled and chopped spinach) and enough hot *dashi* (page 81) to cover. Garnish with sliver of *yuzu* citron peel.

SOY SAUCE

Brush a bit of soy sauce on a grilled or ungrilled rice "ball."

SESAME

Toast and *roughly* grind white sesame seeds (and a few *sansho* seeds—optional). Roll each rice "ball" in the sesame. Do not use a grilled rice "ball" for this.

NORI

Pour some soy sauce onto a plate. Cut *nori* seaweed sheet into strips, dampen with soy sauce, and wrap around rice "ball" as you desire. An extravagant version is to dampen an entire sheet of *nori* in soy sauce and roughly wrap it around rice "ball."

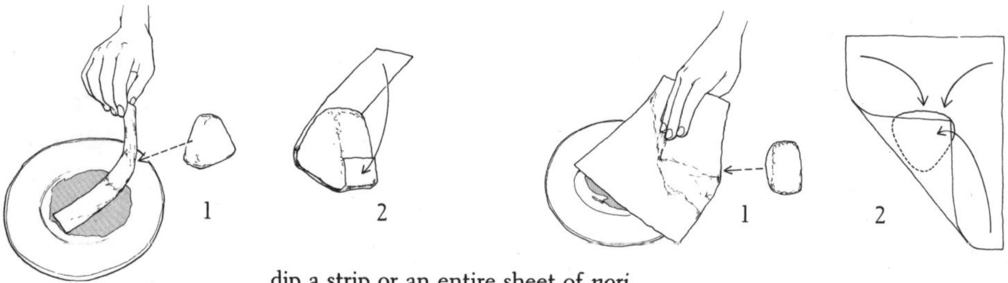

dip a strip or an entire sheet of *nori* into soy sauce before wrapping *onigiri*

All Season (3) TOFU RICE (*Otōfu Gohan*)

1 cake regular tofu
short-grain rice and water for 4 servings
1 1/2 tsps soy sauce
1 tsp salt
1 tsp saké

Place tofu in a large saucepan over medium heat and scramble it (4 chopsticks are convenient for this), stirring frequently until liquid evaporates and tofu resembles dry cottage cheese. This takes a little time—about 20 minutes—and you must stir constantly during the last 7 minutes or so.

Combine all ingredients and cook rice in the conventional manner (page 71).

SOUPS

Basic Stock (Dashi)

Konbu* kelp *Dashi (serves 4–5).

Use good-quality *konbu* with a flat, wide, thick leaf (about 10 in/25 cm wide). Avoid thin, wrinkled *konbu* unless there is no choice.

5 cups water
14-inch (35-cm) piece good-quality dashi konbu, *cut in thirds crosswise and wiped with a damp cloth*

Place water in large saucepan and add *konbu.* Cover and bring to a boil over high heat. Reduce heat to medium-low, place lid ajar, and simmer until water reduces 25 percent—until volume is about 3 1/3 cups. Add 1 2/3 cups cold water (enough to bring volume back to original 5 cups).

Simmer for another 20 minutes with lid ajar and again add enough cold water to bring liquid back to original volume.

Simmer for another 10 minutes with lid ajar. The stock will be a clear greenish amber. Remove *konbu.* The volume of stock will be 4 1/6 cups (1000 mL)—4 or 5 servings. Keeps 3–4 days refrigerated.

If the *konbu* expands greatly and develops soft blisters as it simmers, it is of good quality and the *dashi* will be good.

With larger amounts of *konbu* and water, the cooking times are longer: for an amount 4 times the one used here, the cooking time is a total of 3 hours.

ALTERNATE METHOD: Start with 8 1/3 cups (2000 mL) of water, add *konbu,* and simmer until the volume is halved, without adding water during the process.

Other Stocks

Shiitake* Mushroom *Dashi (serves 4)

8 medium dried shiitake *mushrooms*
4 cups boiling water
salt
soy sauce
saké

Add dried *shiitake* mushrooms to boiling water in a saucepan and simmer, with lid ajar, for 5–8 minutes. Remove *shiitake* and flavor to taste with salt, soy sauce, and saké

The simmering timing depends on the size and thickness of the *shiitake*: the larger and thicker, the longer the simmering time—8 minutes is about maximum. A good stock should be a thin amber color and it should have the fragrance of mushroom. Putting the *shiitake* in boiling water, rather than cold water, gives a stock with more punch.

Use the cooked *shiitake* mushrooms in other recipes. Mushrooms are little sponges and soak up flavor voraciously. For instance, stir-fry in a little oil and flavor with soy sauce and saké or soy sauce, sugar, and saké; cut in julienne strips or chop and mix with sushi rice; squeeze free of water and submerge in a sweet miso for 1 hour or more (wipe off miso, but do not wash before eating). Keeps 2 days refrigerated.

Daikon Radish *Dashi*

The skin of the daikon, which is removed for most dishes, can be simmered for at least 1 hour, uncovered, over very low heat. The amount of water will vary. Simmer it down to taste or dilute if too strong. (Or use entire daikon, with leaves, if you like. Simmering time is long.) Especially good with miso soup. Season with salt, saké, and soy sauce to taste. Does not keep. Use same day as made.

Vegetable *Dashi*

Use any and all parings, leftover, and pieces of vegetable. Place in pot with ample water and simmer, uncovered, over very low heat for a long time. The surface of the water should be barely roiling. Discard vegetables. Season with salt, soy sauce, and saké to taste. Replace water if level gets too low.

Sweet Potato (or Yam) *Dashi*

Peeled sweet potatoes (or yams) may be cut, placed in water to cover, and simmered over medium heat for about 1 hour—until potato disintegrates. Replace water if level gets too low. Excellent as a miso soup base; or season with salt and saké and eat as is, or with appropriate additions of deep-fried morsels and a small touch of some green vegetable.

Soy Bean *Dashi* (serves 4)

1/2 cup dried soy beans
1 1/2 cups cold water

Place dried beans in water and soak overnight then simmer over medium-low heat in soaking water for 3 hours, adding water to maintain the original level. Season with salt, saké, and soy sauce for clear soup; miso and saké will make miso soup. Add whatever vegetables and extra ingredients you like.

Clear Soups (Osumashi)

Clear soup is made by seasoning basic broth (*dashi*) with soy sauce (which gives it an amber tint) and salt. Too much soy sauce makes a dark and strong-flavored soup, which is good at appropriate times, such as after strenuous exertion. Generally, however, the flavor is delicate. *Dashi* flavored only with salt and saké (no soy sauce) results in a colorless, clear soup.

Since clear soups tend to be elegant, the things that are added, as a rule, should give an elegant impression. Ballet is not danced in hobnails; so, too, small sizes and quantities and a certain degree of delicacy should be maintained in the things added to clear soups. Yet, Buddhist temples use whatever is at hand. Therefore there is no rule or principle of adding things to soups as there is in fancy Japanese restaurant cooking. Add whatever you like to your soups; and in lean times, make the soups go a long way with lots of water.

The clear soups for the twelve months included here should be used as hints for your own creative cooking. Feel free to experiment as you like with the seasonal vegetables of your choice.

Basic Clear Soup (serves 4)

3 3/4 cups (900 mL) konbu dashi *(see page 81)*
1 tsp plus 1 pinch salt
1 1/2 tsps soy sauce
2 tsps saké
2 small dried shiitake *mushrooms (optional)*

Place all ingredients in a medium-sized saucepan and bring to a boil over high heat. Reduce heat to medium and simmer, uncovered, 5 minutes. (If mushrooms are included, remove them and reserve for some other use.)

In each soup bowl place appropriately small quantities of whatever solid ingredients you choose. Ladle the flavored *dashi* into the bowls and serve hot! Garnish each bowl with a sliver of *yuzu* citron (or lemon) peel or a young *sansho* sprig (*kinome*).

A number of different forms of wheat gluten, both dried and fresh (see page 66), are used decoratively in clear soups. *Hana fu* (clear soup for March) is dried wheat gluten in the form of small flowers; *komaru fu* (clear soup for May) is dried wheat gluten in the shape of small balls; *ita fu* (miso soup for October) is in sheet form; ***kuruma fu,*** seen in the clear soup of the tray serving for Spring (color, page 18) comes in ring form. Dry wheat gluten expands considerably in soup. The sizes of these forms vary: the flower form is small enough to have 3 or 5 pieces in a bowl of soup; the ball form only allows 2 pieces; and the wheel, only 1 piece. Wheat gluten in sheet form is cut into appropriate widths.

Clear Soups (Osumashi) ***for Twelve Months***

The amounts given are for 1 serving and are placed in each individual bowl unless otherwise stated. All clear soups should be served as hot as possible. Soup for 1 serving is between 5/6 cup (200 mL) and 1 cup (240 mL).

January (1) CHINESE CABBAGE AND USUAGE IN THICK BROTH (serves 1)

3 3/4×2-inch (2×5-cm) pieces Chinese cabbage
1 Tbsp thin deep-fried tofu (usuage) *cut into julienne strips*
1 Tbsp potato starch (katakuriko) *dissolved in 1 Tbsp water for each cup of* dashi
finely grated ginger as garnish

Separately parboil Chinese cabbage and *usuage* in either *dashi* or basic clear soup (page 81). Add potato starch to simmering *dashi* and stir until thickened. Place solid ingredients in a deep soup bowl; ladle on thickened *dashi* and garnish with a dab of finely grated ginger.

January (2) ICICLE RADISH (serves 1)

The use of entire small white radishes with leaves and root marks this as a dish for festive occasions. Whole radishes may also be used in *miso shiru,* in a thick translucent sauce (*ankake*), or at room temperature with a chunky nut dressing. Red salad radishes may also be used, though the red fades with parboiling.

1 small (2-in/5-cm) icicle or white radish, leaves and long root left intact
about 5/6 cup (200 mL) shiitake *mushroom* dashi *(page 81), seasoned with small amounts of salt, soy sauce, and saké*
1 slice cooked carrot (cut into leaf shape—optional)

Make 1-inch (2 1/2-cm) lengthwise slits at 3 points around circumference of each radish; this reduces cooking time. In a small pan of boiling water, boil radishes only, holding leaves out of boiling water (with chopsticks), until radishes are barely cooked (about 3 minutes), then place leaves in water and cook for 2 minutes more. Plunge radishes into cold water and drain.

February DEEP-FRIED MOCHI (serves 1)

1-inch (2 1/2-cm) square mochi, *deep-fried*
1 small fresh shiitake *mushroom, stem removed, simmered in* dashi *briefly, then cut into julienne strips*
1–2 stalks trefoil (mitsuba) *(or 1 Tbsp any parboiled green vegetable), cut into 3/4-inch (2-cm) lengths*

March GINGER (serves 1)

3 or 5 pieces hana fu *(dried wheat gluten in flower form)*

generous pinch finest shred-cut ginger
about $^1/_2$ *Tbsp parboiled green vegetable (green bean, spinach, asparagus), cut into* $^3/_4$*-inch (2-cm) lengths*

April (1) BAMBOO AND SEA GREENS (serves 1)

2–3 thin rounds or half-moons of cooked bamboo shoot
$^1/_2$ *Tbsp sea greens* (wakame), *reconstituted and cut into* $^3/_4$*-inch (2-cm) lengths*
1 young sansho *sprig* (kinome)

April (2) CHRYSANTHEMUM LEAVES (serves 1)

1 Tbsp parboiled chrysanthemum leaves
1 Tbsp cooked sōmen *noodles (see page* 78)
1 sliver yuzu *citron (or lemon) peel or 1 young* sansho *sprig* (kinome)

May SNOW PEAS (serves 1)

2 pieces komaru fu *(dried wheat gluten in ball form)*
3 parboiled snow peas

June JUNSAI (serves 1)

1 Tbsp junsai *(see page 124), washed once in water*

July SŌMEN NOODLES (room temperature or chilled) (serves 1)

$^1/_4$ *bundle cooked* sōmen *noodles (see page* 78)
2 small, fresh shiitake *mushrooms, stems removed and simmered briefly in* dashi
5 $^3/_4$*-inch (2-cm) lengths trefoil* (mitsuba) *or 1 Tbsp parboiled green vegetable*

August CUCUMBER IN CHILLED THICK CLEAR SOUP (recipe on page 129)

Substitute 3 small rings of cucumber for zucchini in each serving. Make cucumber rings by peeling cucumber, cutting 3-inch (8-cm) lengths, and removing seeds with a chopstick poked and rotated through the middle of each cucumber length. Cut into $^1/_2$-inch (1 $^1/_2$-cm) rings.

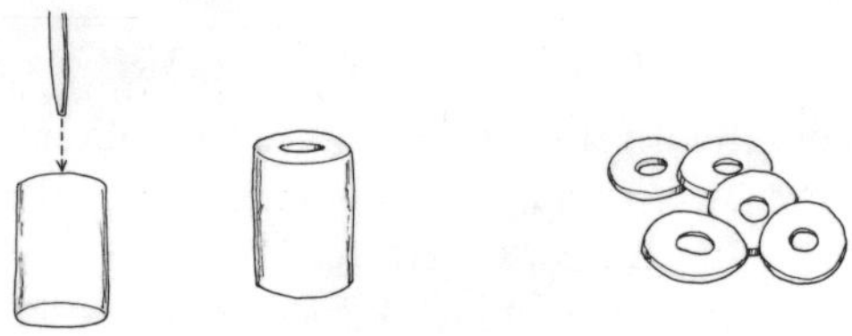

Chill thick clear soup in refrigerator before using.

September SESAME "TOFU" IN BROTH (recipe on page 198)

Rather than *yuzu* citron (or lemon) peel, garnish with a dab of finely grated ginger.

October MOUNTAIN YAM NUGGETS (serves 1)

2 Mountain Yam Nuggets (recipe on page 140)
1 Tbsp parboiled green beans cut on diagonal into julienne strips

November SHIMEJI MUSHROOMS (serves 1)

1–2 sprigs shimeji *mushrooms, dirty stem bases removed, and parboiled*

1 sliver yuzu *citron (or lemon) peel as garnish*

December **KENCHIN JIRU** (Vegetable Stew) (serves 4)

2 tsps vegetable oil
4-inch (10-cm) length burdock root, quartered lengthwise then thinly sliced lengthwise
3 ounces daikon radish, quartered lengthwise then thinly sliced
1 sheet thin deep-fried tofu (usuage), *cut in half lengthwise then cut into julienne strips*
2-inch (5-cm) length carrot, quartered lengthwise then thinly sliced lengthwise
4 medium fresh shiitake *mushrooms, stems removed and cut into julienne strips*
5 cups konbu dashi *(see page 81)*
salt
soy sauce } *to taste*
saké
1/2 cake regular tofu, cut into 3/4-inch (2-cm) cubes
4 green beans, parboiled and cut into julienne strips as garnish

Heat vegetable oil in a large saucepan and stir-fry burdock, daikon, *usuage,* carrot, and *shiitake* mushrooms briefly. Add *konbu dashi* and simmer over medium heat until cooked. Season to taste with salt, soy sauce, and saké. Add 1/4 of tofu cubes to each bowl and pour on vegetable broth, being sure all ingredients are present equally in each bowl. Garnish with cut green beans. Serve hot.

All Season **CHRYSANTHEMUM TOFU** (serves 1)

1/8 cake "silk" tofu, cut in same manner as Turnip Chrysanthemums (page 160)
1 Tbsp parboiled green vegetable of any kind cut into 3/4-inch (2-cm) lengths

Place cut tofu carefully in bottom of soup bowl and gently ladle on soup. If the "silk" tofu is thick, it might make things easier to cut the cake in half horizontally.

MISO SOUPS

These "thick" soups are made simply by dissolving miso paste into a small amount of hot *dashi,* then pouring this dissolved miso into the proper amount of simmering *dashi* and removing from heat as soon as it starts to simmer again. Do not let the miso soup boil, or it will loose its aroma and flavor.

Sweet miso is added to *dashi* in larger quantities than the saltier varieties. Personal taste plays the greatest role in making miso soup, and different kinds of miso soup use different quantities of miso, but, in general, for 4 servings, use

3 1/3 cups (800 mL) *dashi*
and
6 Tbsps sweet white miso
or
4 Tbsps medium-salty miso
or
4 Tbsps saltiest miso

There are no rules regarding the solid ingredients in miso soups, except, of course, to avoid adding so much to the soup that the miso flavor is obscured. Anything goes, as long as additions complement the miso flavor. The miso soups for the twelve months that follow should provide a good guide to what kinds of ingredients go well in such soups. Generally, such ingredients are parboiled or cooked in the *dashi* into which the dissolved miso is added.

Since the miso soup recipes mainly specify the solid ingredients added to the soups, recipes for single portions are given in most cases in the hope that this system makes it easy to figure out how to prepare soup for any number of diners. *The amount of miso soup for 1 serving is between 5/6 cup (200 mL) and 1 cup (240 mL).* Some of each ingredient should be present in each soup bowl. Add garnish to soup bowl last.

January (1) WHITE MISO OZŌNI (serves 1)

This New Year's soup uses more miso than the conventional formula given above—1/2 cup (120 mL) sweet white miso for 3 1/3 cups (800 mL) of *dashi* to serve 4.

1 generous Tbsp parboiled spinach cut in 1 1/2-inch (4-cm) lengths
1 piece grilled mochi
sliver yuzu *citron (or lemon) peel as garnish*

January (2) ZEN TEMPLE OZŌNI (serves 1)

miso type: sweet white
3/4-inch (2-cm) cube daikon radish
3 2-inch (5-cm) pieces gourd ribbon (kampyō), *reconstituted then knotted (see page 152)*
3 3/4-inch (2-cm) cubes grilled tofu (yakidōfu)
1/6 tsp basic Japanese mustard mix (see page 51)
3 boiled azuki beans

Simmer daikon cube and knotted gourd ribbon in *dashi* until tender—about 20 minutes. Add grilled tofu cubes and cook just until heated. Dissolve miso and add it to *dashi*, taking care not to break tofu.

Place mustard in soup bowl, then 3 azuki beans. Add solid ingredients and ladle in miso soup.

February TURNIP (serves 1)

miso type: medium salty
Prepare turnips and greens as in Turnips Above and Below (page 158), except slice turnips before simmering and then simmer in *dashi* until just tender. Parboil greens in *dashi* also.

3 slices cooked turnip
1 generous Tbsp parboiled turnip greens cut into 3/4-inch (2-cm) lengths

March MUSTARD GREENS OR RAPE BLOSSOMS (serves 1)

miso type: medium salty
2 generous Tbsps mustard greens or rape blossoms first parboiled in dashi *then cut into 3/4-inch (2-cm) lengths*

April BAMBOO SHOOT AND SEA GREENS (serves 1)

miso type: medium salty
3 thin rounds cooked bamboo shoot
1 generous Tbsp sea greens (wakame), *reconstituted (see page 102) and cut into 3/4-inch (2-cm) lengths*

young sansho *sprig* (kinome) *as garnish*

Heat bamboo and sea greens in *dashi,* add dissolved miso. Transfer to soup bowl and garnish with young *sansho* sprig.

May FIDDLEHEAD FERN (serves 1)

miso type: medium salty
2 generous Tbsps boiled fiddlehead ferns cut into 1 1/4-inch (3-cm) lengths

Heat fiddleheads in *dashi* then add dissolved miso.

June TOFU (serves 1)

miso type: medium salty
3 or 5 3/4-inch (2-cm) cubes regular tofu
1 generous Tbsp thin deep-fried tofu (usuage) *first rinsed under boiling water then cut into julienne strips*

Heat tofu and *usuage* in *dashi* then add dissolved miso.

July GREEN BEAN AND TOFU (serves 1)

miso type: sweet to medium salty
3 2 1/2-inch (6 1/2-cm) lengths green bean, stir-fried (or use raw green beans if very young and tender)
7 or 9 small (about 3/8-in/1-cm) cubes "silk" tofu

August EGGPLANT (serves 1)

miso type: saltiest (*hatchō*)
2 small (3-in/3-cm) whole Japanese eggplants, caps removed and simmered in dashi *until soft*

Dissolve miso and add to *dashi* after eggplants have been simmered.

September SWEET POTATO (serves 1)

miso type: sweet white
1 tsp saké
2 3/8-inch (1-cm) rounds sweet potato, skin intact

Add saké to *dashi* and simmer sweet potato rounds in *dashi* and saké over medium heat until just cooked. Dissolve miso and add to hot *dashi,* taking care not to break sweet potato slices.

October FLAT WHEAT GLUTEN (ITA FU) AND CHRYSANTHEMUM (serves 1)

miso type: medium salty
2 3/8-inch (1-cm) pieces flat wheat gluten (ita fu)
3 sprigs chrysanthemum leaves, parboiled in boiling water and cut into 1-inch (2 1/2-cm) lengths

Cut *ita fu* crosswise. Parboil chrysanthemum in water, not in *dashi.*

November SPINACH (serves 1)

miso type: medium salty
2 generous Tbsps spinach parboiled in dashi *and cut into 1-inch (2 1/2-cm) lengths*

December DAIKON RADISH AND USUAGE (1 portion)

miso type: medium salty
1 1/2-inch (4-cm) length daikon radish, peeled and cut into julienne strips
1/4 sheet thin deep-fried tofu (usuage), *rinsed under boiling water and cut into thick julienne strips*

Simmer daikon and *usuage* together in *dashi* until daikon is tender. Dissolve miso and add to *dashi.*

All Season SAKÉ LEES SOUP *(Saké Kasu Jiru)* (serves 4–6)

This is not a miso soup but is made of *saké kasu* (see page 53) and is more a vegetable stew than a soup. It is especially good on frigid, rainy days. This is eaten both in temples and homes, and in the cold and drafty temples it served the same function as central heating. Either soy sauce or miso may be used to season this.

3 1/3 cups water
1/4 lb (115 gm) saké lees (saké kasu)
4 tsps soy sauce
2/3 tsp salt
2 tsps vegetable oil
VEGETABLES
- *carrots*
- *burdock root*
- *thin deep-fried tofu* (usuage)
- *bamboo shoots*
- shiitake *mushrooms*
- *daikon radish*
- *field yams* (sato imo)
- *chestnuts*
- *waterchestnuts*
- *walnuts*
- etc.

This recipe is for the relatively thin broth to hold the vegetables. Water may be increased or decreased, as you like.

The various vegetables should be cleaned, sliced, and simmered until cooked before being added to the soup. There are no limits to the vegetables that can be used. The ones listed are traditional. Amounts are not given because there are too many variables. Use what you enjoy—either a single vegetable or twenty. Serve hot. Keeps about 3 days.

PICKLES

Light pickles are an integral part of every Japanese meal. Foreign visitors are sometimes surprised to know that the vegetables they are eating are pickles, for freshness and crispness are the results sought in pickling. Often a vegetable is pickled for only a few hours.

There are a number of pickling processes. The most common are pickling in miso, rice bran, saké lees (*saké kasu*), and with salt. Vinegar is also used, but not as much as in the West. Rice bran involves some complex preparation and a long waiting period for the pickling medium to mature. Miso, salt, and *saké kasu* may be used without lengthy preparation.

It is also very difficult to specify the number of servings. Japanese pickles can be eaten in quantity and often are as an accompaniment to saké. In the recipes that follow, where some indication of proportion of ingredients is necessary, an approximate number of servings is given. A little experience with these pickles and the appetites of your family and friends are the best criteria for judging how much to make. All these pickles are meant to keep more than one day, and quantities greater than for one meal can easily be prepared.

Pickling with Miso

Place a 1-inch (2 ½-cm) layer of medium-salty miso in the bottom of a nonmetallic, covered container—plastic is light and convenient; ceramic and enamel are good too. Add a layer of vegetable(s), then cover with miso. Either small or large amounts can be made, and a large crock or container is not necessary. This pickling method is particularly good for quick pickling. Also, a weight is not used in miso pickling.

Some water is given off by the vegetables in the miso. It is necessary occasionally to evaporate this water by cooking the miso in a saucepan. Salt and saké may be added to strengthen the flavor, or the "tired" miso may be used for miso soup.

Wash off miso from vegetables before slicing, if you desire.

January BURDOCK IN SWEET VINEGAR (serves about 6–8)

32-inch (80-cm) length burdock root, cut into 2-inch (5-cm) lengths then into julienne strips
4 cups boiling water
1 tsp vinegar
SWEET VINEGAR
6 Tbsps rice vinegar
2 Tbsps sugar
1 tsp salt
1 tsp soy sauce

Place burdock in water as soon as it is cut into julienne strips and let stand 1 hour. Drain. Place burdock in 4 cups boiling water and add 1 tsp vinegar. Mix sweet vinegar. Simmer burdock in boiling water 5 minutes over medium heat. Drain and put hot burdock in sweet vinegar immediately. Let stand 30 minutes at least. Keeps 3 days.

February DRIED DAIKON STRIPS IN SWEET VINEGAR (serves about 4)

¼ lb dried daikon radish strips (kiriboshi daikon), *reconstituted in water (10 minutes) then cut into 1-inch (2 ½-cm) lengths*
½ cup konbu dashi *(see page 81)*

SWEET VINEGAR

4 Tbsps rice vinegar
2 Tbsps sugar
½ tsp salt

Mix *dashi* with sweet vinegar. Add reconstituted dried daikon radish strips and place in bowl. Cover with plastic wrap or inverted plate and weight with 2 lbs (1 kg). Let stand at least 20 minutes. Keeps 2 days.

December–March WHOLE TURNIPS IN MISO

Turnip greens as well as bulbs may be used. Prepare bulbs as in Turnips Above and Below, page 158. Greens should be pickled whole. Cover turnips and greens with miso and let stand 2 days. Wash and slice bulbs and chop greens as in Turnips Above and Below.

March MUSTARD GREENS OR RAPE BLOSSOMS IN SALT

Dredge vegetable with salt, place in bowl, cover with plastic wrap or inverted plate, and weight with 2 lbs (1 kg) for 3 days.

April TOFU IN MISO

Wrap regular tofu in clean kitchen towel and drain for 1 hour on a tilted flat surface. Cut cake of tofu into quarters or use whole. Cover with sweet or medium-salty miso for at least ½ day. Cut the pickled tofu into pieces depending on how strong the flavor is; the stronger the flavor, the smaller the pieces and the servings.

May OKRA IN MISO

For every 20 okra pods, use ½ cup of any type of miso blended with 2 Tbsps saké. Dredge okra with salt and wash immediately. Drain and pat dry. Place okra in miso-saké mixture and let stand at least 2 hours in a covered container or bowl. Wash okra and slice if desired. Keeps 2 days.

June–September (1) CUCUMBERS IN MISO

Dredge washed and dried cucumbers with salt, knead briefly, submerge in miso in a covered container or bowl, and let stand 1 day. Wash and slice diagonally. Keeps 2 days.

June–September (2) EGGPLANTS IN MISO

Wash small Japanese eggplants and pat dry, leaving cap intact. Dredge with salt and knead briefly. Imbed in miso in a covered container or bowl and let stand 2 days. Wash, remove cap, and slice diagonally. Keeps 2 days.

June–September (3) TWO-HOUR EGGPLANT PICKLE (serves about 4)

4 Japanese eggplants, caps removed, cut in half lengthwise, then cut in thin slices either lengthwise or crosswise
1 Tbsp vegetable oil
1 Tbsp sweet white Kyoto (saikyō) *miso*
1 Tbsp saké

Stir-fry eggplant slices briefly in vegetable oil. Add miso to hot stir-fried eggplant and cool. When cool, add saké and mix well. Place in bowl, cover with plastic wrap, and let stand 2 hours. Wash before eating. Keeps 2 days.

June–September (4) THREE-MINUTE EGGPLANT PICKLE

Cut Japanese eggplants into thin slices crosswise, dredge with salt, and knead well. Let stand 3 minutes. Wash, and season with soy sauce to eat.

June–September (5) CELERY IN MISO

Cut celery stalks into appropriate lengths, submerge in miso in a covered container, and let stand 1 day. Wash and slice diagonally. Keeps 2 days.

September TWO-HOUR PUMPKIN PICKLE (serves about 4)

1/3 lb pumpkin or winter squash, peeled and cut into 1/8×1 1/2-inch (1/2×4-cm) slices
1/2 cup any kind of miso
2 Tbsps saké

Parboil pumpkin slices. Blend miso and saké and mix with pumpkin. Place in covered container and let stand 2 hours. Wash before eating. Keeps 2 days.

October SHIITAKE MUSHROOMS IN SWEET MISO (serves 2–4)

8 medium-sized fresh shiitake *mushrooms*
sweet white Kyoto (saikyō) *miso*
1 Tbsp saké

Grill *shiitake* mushrooms briefly on both sides. Blend miso and saké and mix with *shiitake*. Place in covered container or bowl and let stand 1 hour. Not necessary to wash before eating. Keeps 1 week.

November SHIMEJI MUSHROOMS IN SAKÉ LEES (serves 2–4)

1/4 lb shimeji *mushrooms, dirty stem bases removed*
1/4 cup saké lees (saké kasu; *see page 53)*
2–3 Tbsps saké
1/2 tsp salt

Parboil *shimeji* mushrooms in ample lightly salted water. Dissolve saké lees in saké. Add salt, then parboiled *shimeji*, and mix well. Place in covered container and let stand at least 1 hour. Not necessary to wash before eating. Keeps 2 days.

December (1) CABBAGE IN MISO

Tear cabbage leaves to fit size of container. Submerge in miso, cover container, and let stand 1 day. Wash before eating. Keeps 2 days.

December (2) DAIKON RADISH AND GREENS IN SALT (serves about 4)

1 3/4 lbs daikon radish, peeled and cut into julienne strips
1/2 lb daikon radish greens, chopped coarsely
1 Tbsp salt

Mix radish strips and chopped greens, sprinkle with salt, and knead well. Gently press out water. Place in bowl, cover with plastic wrap or an inverted plate, weight with 2 lbs (1 kg), and let stand 1 to 3 days. Wash before eating. Season with soy sauce if you like.

December (3) TURNIPS WITH CITRON (serves 2–4)

4 medium turnips, stalks cut off about 1/2 inch (1 1/2 cm) above bulb (see page 159)

1 tsp finely shred-cut yuzu *(or lemon) peel*
2 tsps salt

Cut turnips into thin (1/8-in/1/2-cm) slices lengthwise. Mix turnip slices and citron (or lemon) shreds. Add salt and mix. Place in bowl and cover with plastic wrap or an inverted plate and weight with 2 lbs (1 kg). Let stand overnight. Keeps 1 week.

All Season CARROTS IN SALT (serves about 4)

1/4 lb carrots, scraped and cut into julienne strips
1/2 tsp salt

Sprinkle carrot strips with salt, place in bowl, cover with plastic wrap or an inverted plate, and weight with 1 lb (450 gm). Let stand overnight. Keeps 2 days.

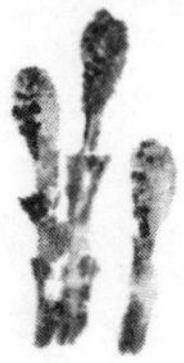

Spring

Rape Blossoms with Mustard-Miso Dressing

Na-no-Hana no Karashi-Miso Ae

菜の花の辛子あえ

Rape blossoms are a harbinger of spring. Although they are now available year-round in Japanese supermarkets, they were once a luxury food. Even now only small quantities are eaten because consuming the leaves and blooms of this plant is like eating spring itself.

SERVES 4

½ lb (225 gm) rape blossoms (na-no-hana), *washed and hard stem ends removed*

MUSTARD-MISO DRESSING

4 Tbsps sweet white Kyoto (saikyō) *miso*

1 tsp basic Japanese mustard mix (see page 51)

1 tsp saké

Parboil rape blossoms in lightly salted water about 2–3 minutes, depending on the tenderness of the greens. Rinse in cold water, drain, and gently but firmly squeeze out water. Cut into ½-inch (1 ½-cm) lengths.

Blend mustard-miso dressing ingredients in a bowl. Add rape blossoms and toss until well coated.

Serve on small individual dishes or family style in one bowl. Eat at room temperature. Keeps about 3–4 hours.

Flavor-Simmered Rape Blossoms

Na-no-Hana no Usudaki

菜の花の薄炒き

Quick simmering in a soy-flavored broth brings out the sweetness of this flowering green. If preparing this dish ahead of time, remove the vegetable from the pot liquor and let it drain in a colander.

SERVES 4

½ lb (225 gm) rape blossoms (na-no-hana), *washed and hard stem ends removed*

FOR SIMMERING

¾ cup plus 1 Tbsp konbu dashi *(see page 81)*
4 tsps soy *sauce*
4 tsps saké
2 pinches salt

Parboil rape blossoms in lightly salted water about 2–3 minutes, depending on the tenderness of the greens. Rinse in cold water, drain, and gently but firmly squeeze out water. Cut into 1-inch (2 ½-cm) lengths.

Place greens and simmering ingredients in a medium-sized saucepan over medium heat and simmer, stirring occasionally, for about 3 minutes, until flavor is absorbed by greens.

Serve hot or at room temperature. Keeps 1 day refrigerated.

Seven Herbs Rice Gruel

Nanakusa no Okayu

七草のおかゆ

The eating of this dish is a very ancient custom associated with Japan's protracted New Year celebrations. The original seven herbs are *seri* (water dropwort), *nazuna* (shepherd's purse), *gogyō (Gnaphalium multiceps), hakobera (Stellaria media), suzuna* (turnip greens), *suzushiro* (daikon greens), *hotokenoza (Lapsana apogonoides). Mochi* (glutinous rice) cakes are an integral part of Japanese New Year. This gruel of rice and herbs (including their roots) is said to act as a tonic for people who have overindulged in New Year's *mochi.* Since these herbs are even difficult to find in Japan (in urban areas), some interesting Western herbs have been substituted.

SERVES 4

1 cup short-grain rice, washed
7 cups water
½ tsp salt
1 tsp each parboiled and finely chopped
fennel leaves
watercress
curly chicory
chervil
turnip greens

Romaine lettuce
trefoil or sorrel (or appropriate slightly sour green)

Bring rice and water to a boil quickly, reduce heat to medium-low, and simmer about 40 minutes, until rice is very soft. Add salt and finely chopped greens, mix well, and remove from heat.

Eat immediately. Does not keep.

VARIATION: Use any of your favorite greens or herbs, but avoid any with strong flavors.

Herb Mochi

Kusamochi

草 餅

In Kyoto temples, where the old lunar calendar is still used to determine annual festivals and rituals, the Dolls' Festival occurs about one month later than its date in the solar (Western) calendar. By early April, spring herbs are plentiful. The traditional herb used in making this is *mochigusa* (or *yomogi; Artermisia princeps*). In Kyoto the tiny confections made of this herb *mochi* have a center of sweet azuki bean paste. Curly endive is used here simply because its flavor is good and not because it resembles the traditional Japanese herb.

SERVES 4

1 2/3 cups shiratamako *(glutinous rice flour)*
1 cup water
2 cups curly chicory, green parts of leaves only, parboiled 10–20 seconds in lightly salted water and plunged into cold water
cornstarch

Add water to *shiratamako* a little at a time, mixing and kneading with your hand to make a smooth mixture. The aim is a mixture that is firm, smooth, and soft—like your earlobe, as the Japanese say. Be careful when adding water—toward the end, a little goes a long way. A Tbsp or 2 more than 1 cup may be necessary.

Line steamer with a clean kitchen towel or 2 layers of cheesecloth, then place it on medium-high heat.

Break *shiratamako* mixture into 1 1/2-inch (4-cm) rough lumps and place lumps in hot steamer. Cover with ends of cloth and steam 10–15 minutes, until soft throughout. The steaming transforms the *shiratamako* mixture into a form of *mochi* (glutinous rice) cake.

While steaming, finely chop parboiled chicory and then grind in a *suribachi* grinding bowl or mortar (or use processor to cut it very finely, but *do not puree*).

Add steamed *mochi* to *suribachi* and mix with pestle until chopped green is evenly distributed in the tacky mass (or use a processor for this, working carefully).

Dredge a working surface (or baking pan) generously with cornstarch, place green *mochi* on cornstarch, and dredge entire *mochi* surface. Shape either into a single flat rectangle or small rounds, as you like.

Eat immediately with sweet azuki bean paste (*anko*), soy powder (*kinako*), *yuzu* citron and sweet miso, jam, marmalade, or whatever you like. This also can be toasted just like *mochi*.

Keeps 2–3 days.

Savory Dried Horsetails

Hoshi Tsukushi

干つくし

The common Japanese field horsetail (*Equisetum arvense*), gathered as soon as it appears in spring, becomes a marvelous snack with little effort. The same variety of horsetail grows in other countries, but I am not sure whether or not other varieties can be prepared in the same manner. Nonetheless, this little snack is a great luxury and is worth including here just because it exists. (A *note of caution*: horsetail contains a toxin—thiaminase—which is destroyed by heat. Do not eat horsetail raw.)

SNACK; SERVES 6–8

1 cup field horsetails (firm fresh young heads and 3/8 inch [1 cm] of stalk)
2 Tbsps soy sauce

Place horsetails and soy sauce in a small saucepan and bring to a boil quickly. Reduce heat to medium, then simmer, covered, for 3–5 minutes. Set pan lid ajar and continue simmering until heads are just soft. Drain.

Place horsetails in a shallow colander or basket supported between bricks and dry in the sun for 1 week. It obviously is important to have a week of continuous sunny weather to dry the horsetails.

Keeps indefinitely in a closed container, though the flavor changes with time. If horsetails get a little moist, just dry for 1/2 day or so.

Bamboo Sushi

Takenoko no Sugata-Zushi

竹の子の姿ずし

This is the dish for which the Donke-in temple is known—its specialty, as it were. There is a nun's diary of the late seventeenth century recording the experience of eating this sushi at the Donke-in. There are also dishes extant today at the temple that date from about the same time as the diary (or perhaps earlier) and that are known to have been used to serve this bamboo sushi. It is likely that the dish itself originated at a much earlier time.

SERVES 4

4 small (2 1/2 in/6 1/2 cm) whole (or 8 half) bamboo shoots, hard bases cut off

FOR FLAVORING BAMBOO SHOOTS

1 cup water
1 tsp soy sauce
1 Tbsp saké
1/2 tsp salt

2 2/3 cups prepared sushi rice (see page 189)

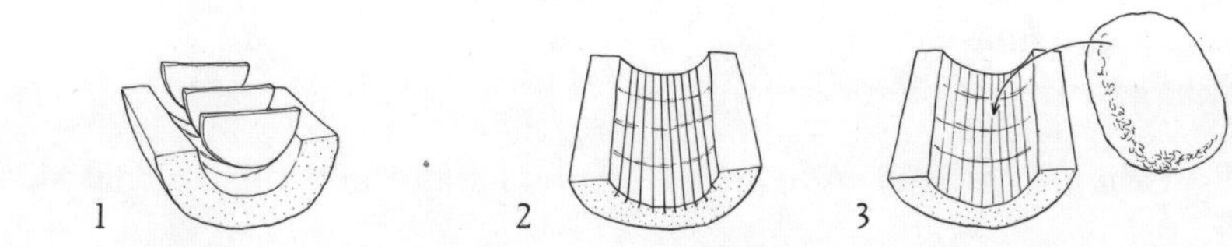

remove membranes from bamboo shoot score inside and insert sushi rice

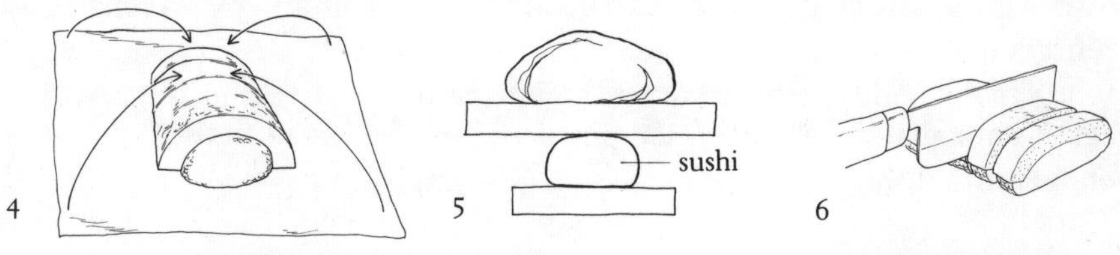

wrap well and weight overnight slice before serving

Cut bamboo shoots in half lengthwise, then remove membranes from inside, leaving a cavity. With the tip of a knife, score the inside of each cavity 8–10 times lengthwise to allow the sushi rice flavor to penetrate the bamboo shoot.

Simmer bamboo and flavoring ingredients over low heat in small saucepan with lid ajar for 30 minutes. Cool in pot liquor.

For small bamboo shoots, use about 1/3 cup sushi rice; for larger shoots, use more. Firmly press rice into the inverted bamboo shoot and form into a neat shape.

Wrap each bamboo sushi very firmly with foil or plastic wrap. (Originally bamboo sheath was used to wrap the sushi.)

Place wrapped sushi on a flat surface. Place a chopping board on top of the sushi and weight with a 2-lb (1-kg) weight overnight.

Cut crosswise into 1-inch (2 1/2-cm) slices and serve pressed sushi at room temperature. Dips are unnecessary. Keeps 3 days. Do not refrigerate.

Bamboo Shoots with Vinegar-Miso Dressing

Takenoko no Sumiso Ae

竹の子の酢味噌あえ

This dish is used both as everyday and as guest food in Kyoto temples. The texture and earthiness of bamboo shoots are as much a part of their appeal as the flavor.

SERVES 4

VINEGAR-MISO DRESSING

2 Tbsps sweet white Kyoto (saikyō) *miso*

2 tsps saké

2 tsps rice vinegar

1 small (3 1/2 oz/100 gm) boiled or canned bamboo shoot, cut in half lengthwise, washed, and sliced thinly crosswise into half-moons

finely grated yuzu *citron (or lemon) zest*

Blend dressing in a bowl. Add sliced bamboo shoot and toss to coat slices evenly.

Serve at room temperature or chilled, in small dishes or in one bowl. Garnish with a dab of finely grated *yuzu* citron (or lemon) zest. Keeps 1/2 day refrigerated.

VARIATIONS: Add 1 tsp powdered green tea to the dressing; this should be eaten immediately. About 1/4 tsp powdered *sansho* added to the dressing will enliven the dish.

Bamboo Shoots with Sansho Dressing

Takenoko no Kinome Ae

竹の子の木の芽あえ

This is both household and temple food and is representative of bamboo shoot cookery. The best time to use the young *sansho* sprigs is the brief period in spring before the sprigs reach a length of about 2 1/2 inches (4 cm).

SERVES 4

4 Tbsps young sansho *sprigs* (kinome)
4 Tbsps sweet white Kyoto (saikyō) *miso*
1 Tbsp saké
1 cup sliced bamboo shoot (canned is fine)

Place young *sansho* sprigs in a bowl, pour on boiling water, then drain after about 10 seconds. Place in mortar or *suribachi* grinding bowl and grind well. Add miso and blend, then add saké and blend again. Add sliced bamboo shoot and toss to coat well.

Eat at room temperature, served in small individual dishes or in one bowl. Keeps no more than 3 hours.

Konbu Kelp and Bamboo Shoots

Konbu to Takenoko no Nimono
昆布と竹の子の煮物

This is actually two dishes in one. It can be eaten hot or left overnight. In the latter case, something in the bamboo acts to dissolve the *konbu* into a jamlike consistency and transforms the same ingredients into something quite different yet equally delicious. This second dish should be eaten at room temperature.

SERVES 4

1-foot (30-cm) length dried konbu *kelp, cut into 2 pieces*
2/3 lb (300 gm) canned or boiled sliced bamboo shoots, washed (take care to remove white material inside shoot)
4 cups water
SIMMERING I
1 Tbsp saké
2 tsps soy sauce
1/2 tsp salt
SIMMERING II
1/3 tsp salt
1 tsp sugar
young sansho *sprigs* (kinome) (*optional*)

Place *konbu* on the bottom of a medium-sized saucepan. Add bamboo shoots and water. Bring to a boil over medium heat, reduce heat to low, and simmer, with pot lid ajar, until *konbu* becomes soft—about 50 minutes.

Remove *konbu* and cut into 1 1/4-inch (3-cm) squares. Reserve.

Add simmering I ingredients to pot liquor and bamboo shoots and simmer 10 minutes over medium heat, with pot lid ajar.

Add *konbu* squares and simmering II ingredients, then simmer over medium heat again with pot lid ajar for 30 minutes.

Arrange portions of both ingredients in individual bowls, with *konbu* and bamboo shoot side by side (do not mix), and pour about 1 Tbsp pot liquor over each serving. Garnish with young *sansho* sprigs (*kinome*) if you desire. Eat hot. Keeps 5 days if ingredients are refrigerated in separate containers. Can be reheated in the pot liquor.

Or, combine ingredients and allow the bamboo to transform the *konbu* overnight, as described above. Eat at room temperature.

Bamboo Shoot Tempura

Takenoko no Tempura

竹の子の天ぷら

The bamboo is first given flavor by simmering then is tempura-fried. It is thought that bamboo cookery at the Donke-in temple may well date from some time near its founding (1349). Further, the name Take-no-Gosho ("Bamboo Palace") was given to this temple by an emperor some time in the eighteenth century. It seems likely that both the name and the cookery are results of the fact that there is an extensive and ancient bamboo grove in the temple precincts, but there is no direct evidence to support this view.

SERVES 4

1 medium (2 1/2-in/6 1/2-cm diameter) canned or boiled bamboo shoot, white material washed away, cut into 16–20 3/8-inch (1-cm) thick half-moon slices (4–5 slices per serving)

FOR FLAVORING BAMBOO SHOOT

1 cup water
1 Tbsp soy sauce
1 Tbsp saké
2 tsps sugar
1/6 tsp salt

BATTER

1/2 cup flour
1/2 cup water
1/2 tsp salt

vegetable oil for deep-frying

Place sliced bamboo shoot and flavoring ingredients in a small saucepan, place pot lid ajar, and bring to a boil over medium heat. Reduce heat to medium-low and simmer 5 minutes.

Mix batter until there are no lumps of flour.

Heat oil to medium temperature (340°F/170°C). Dip bamboo slices in batter to coat, and deep-fry about 1 minute. The color should not be brown, but a light tan.

Eat hot! Serve in small dishes with a decorative garnish of green. Does not keep.

Bamboo Shoot and Green Pea Sushi

Takenoko to Endo no Sushi

竹の子とえんどうのすし

This unusual recipe is both colorful and elegant. It is a Donke-in original and is usually made with shoots of the *madake* bamboo variety, which appear at the same time that garden peas ripen.

SERVES 4

1 cup thinly sliced bamboo shoot cut into 3/4 × 1/8-inch (2 × 1/2-cm) rectangles

FOR FLAVORING BAMBOO SHOOT

- *1 cup water*
- *1 Tbsp saké*
- *1/2 tsp sugar*
- *1/6 tsp salt*

1/2 cup green peas (frozen are fine), parboiled in lightly salted water (add a bit of sugar if you like)

2 cups prepared sushi rice (see page 189)

Simmer bamboo shoot in flavoring ingredients over medium heat for 5 minutes. Drain and cool.

Toss bamboo shoot with remaining ingredients.

Eat at room temperature. Keeps 1/2 day. Do not refrigerate.

Fiddlehead Ferns

Warabi no Ohitashi

わらびのおひたし

This is the simplest way of preparing fiddlehead fern sprouts and is a part of Japanese home cooking.

SERVES 4

$1/2$ lb (225 gm) water-packed fiddlehead ferns (warabi), *cut into 1 $1/2$-inch (4-cm) lengths*
4 tsps soy sauce
sesame seeds or crushed nuts (optional)

Parboil fiddleheads in ample water for 3 minutes. Drain and cool.

Divide into 4 portions in small dishes and pour 1 tsp soy sauce on each portion. Garnish with sesame seeds or crushed nuts if you like. Serve at room temperature. Keeps 2–3 days refrigerated.

Vinegared Sea Greens

Wakame no Sunomono

わかめの酢のもの

Most households in Japan make this dish with sea greens (*wakame*) only or combine sea greens and cucumber. However, any crisp vegetables may be combined with this basic recipe, for example, fennel, small raw zucchini, and chayote. Avocado is delicious.

SERVES 4

$1/2$ cup (30 gm) salt-preserved sea greens (wakame), *washed well in cold water, then reconstituted for 10–15 minutes in fresh cold water, changing water once or twice*

SWEET VINEGAR
3 Tbsps rice vinegar
1 Tbsp sugar
$1/6$ tsp salt
1 tsp saké
1 tsp water

Spread out reconstituted sea greens and trim away hard membrane. (Reserve this for some other use if you desire. It may be added to vegetables in vinegar dressings, to simmered vegetables, etc.) Cut sea greens into bite-sized pieces.

Bring water to a boil in a small saucepan. Add sea greens and wait until water comes to a boil again. Drain immediately and let cool naturally. This process improves the color and tenderness.

Prepare the sweet vinegar and add to sea greens. Eat at room temperature or chilled. Keeps 1 day refrigerated.

Vinegared Sea Greens and Turnip

Wakame to Kabura no Sunomono

わかめとかぶらの酢のもの

This is guest food at Kyoto temples. Sea greens are often used in Kyoto temple food because that city is not far from Wakasa Bay on the Japan Sea, which is noted for the quality of its ocean harvest.

SERVES 4

1/3 cup (20 gm) salt-preserved sea greens (wakame), *washed well in cold water then reconstituted in fresh cold water for 10–15 minutes, changing water once or twice*

1 large (1/4 lb/115 gm) turnip

1/6 tsp salt

SWEET VINEGAR

2 Tbsps rice vinegar

1 Tbsp sugar

1/6 tsp salt

4 drops soy sauce

Cut away any hard parts of reconstituted sea greens. (Save these for some other use, if you like.)

Cut turnip in half from top to bottom, then cut each half into thin slices. Place slices in a bowl and add 1/6 tsp salt; toss well to coat slices with salt. Let stand 5 minutes. Rinse well to remove salt. Drain.

Cut sea greens into 3/4-inch (2-cm) squares (or 3/4-inch lengths if ribbons are narrow). Place sea greens and turnip slices together in a small bowl and toss.

Mix sweet vinegar, taking care that sugar is dissolved. Pour sweet vinegar over turnip-sea greens mixture and toss to coat.

Serve at room temperature or chilled in small dishes. Keeps 2 days refrigerated.

Fava Beans with Sea Greens

Soramame no Wakame-Ni

空豆のわかめ煮

The Donke-in temple in Kyoto received large quantities of fava beans from its parishioners, so when dishes using these beans appeared, portions were always plentiful. Sea greens (*wakame*) harmonize with the color, texture, and flavor of fava beans—a delicious combination of the harvests of land and sea.

SERVES 4

½ cup boiled and shelled small fava beans
⅔ cup (40 gm) salt-preserved sea greens (wakame), *reconstituted (see previous recipes) and cut into ¾-inch (2-cm) lengths*
1⅔ cups water
2 Tbsps saké
⅔ tsp salt
1 tsp sugar
squirt soy sauce

Combine all ingredients in a medium-sized saucepan and simmer over medium heat until flavors are well blended—about 8 minutes. Drain. Reserve pot liquor for another use.

Serve hot or at room temperature, in individual dishes or in one bowl. Keeps 2 days refrigerated.

Konbu Kelp Sushi Rolls

Konbu no Makizushi

昆布の巻きずし

Various Kyoto temples housing imperial prince-abbots or princess-abbesses became famous for special dishes. The Hōkyō-ji temple is known for its marvelous doll collection and also for its *konbu* kelp cookery. This recipe comes from that temple and is the special dish associated with its name, as Bamboo Sushi is associated with the Donke-in. This makes an unusual hors d'oeuvre.

SERVES 4

4 8-inch (20-cm) lengths of the widest (5-in/13-cm) and best-quality konbu *kelp remaining after* dashi *has been made, trimmed so that corners are right angles*
3 cups prepared sushi rice (see page 189)

Place *konbu* with long side toward you on a clean kitchen towel or rolling mat (*maki-su*). Spread ¾ cup sushi rice on *konbu* in the same manner as for a *nori* roll (see page 64)—with a ⅜-inch (1-cm) margin near you and a 1¼-inch (3-cm) margin on the far side. Roll as firmly as possible, using more pressure than for a *nori* roll, then firmly wrap roll in plastic wrap. Repeat process for remaining 3 rolls.

Place plastic-wrapped rolls in a baking pan or on a cookie sheet. Place a chopping board or another baking pan on top of the sushi rolls and weight with 1½–2 pounds (675 gm–1 kg)—a thick iron saucepan or bowl filled with water will do. Let rest under pressure 6 hours. The result will be flat oval rolls.

Cut into ½-inch (1 ½-cm) lengths. One portion is one roll. Serve on individual dishes or on a decorative plate. Keeps 3 days. Do not refrigerate.

Chrysanthemum Leaf Roll

Shungiku no Nori-Maki

春菊の海苔巻き

The *nori* seaweed roll (*nori-maki*) idea is often used in the Donke-in temple cookery. Here aromatic chrysanthemum leaves are used. This dish should be eaten as soon after making as possible, because the *nori* quickly becomes soggy and loses its shape.

SERVES 4

½ lb (250 gm) chrysanthemum leaves (shungiku), *washed and hard stems removed*

1 sheet nori *seaweed*

CITRON-SOY SAUCE

1 ½ Tbsps soy sauce

2 tsps yuzu *citron (or lemon) juice*

Bring an ample amount of lightly salted water to a rolling boil. Because the leaf stems are thick, they need a bit longer to cook. Therefore, to parboil this vegetable, first put any thick stems into the boiling water, holding the leaves above the boiling water for 30 seconds or so, then drop in the entire stalk and cook for 1 minute more. The length of parboiling time of course depends on the size and tenderness of the vegetable. Rinse in cold water, drain, then roll in a bamboo rolling mat or kitchen towel and squeeze out water gently but firmly.

Place a sheet of *nori* seaweed on a rolling mat or *dry*, clean kitchen towel with the long (8-in/20-cm) side toward you. Place the chrysanthemum across the *nori* sheet with a ⅜-inch (1-cm) margin on the side near you and a 1 ¼-inch (3-cm) margin on the far side. Alternate thick stems and leaves to make an even layer.

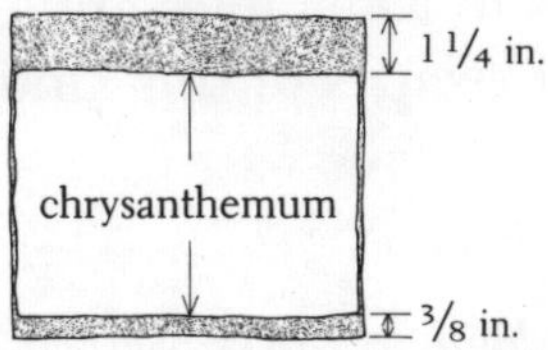

Using the rolling mat or towel, roll the *nori* around the vegetable. Press firmly to form an even, attractive roll. With a *sharp* knife, cut roll in half and each half into fourths.

Place 2 pieces, cut side up, in each small dish. Pour about 1 tsp citron-soy sauce over both pieces. Eat immediately! Does not keep.

Chrysanthemum Leaves

Shungiku no Ohitashi

春菊のおひたし

This vegetable has two names because there are two crops per year—in spring it is known as *shungiku*; in autumn, as *kikuna*. This simple dish is everyday food throughout Japan.

SERVES 4

¼ lb (115 gm) chrysanthemum leaves, washed and hard stem ends removed

CITRON-SOY SAUCE

4 parts soy sauce

1 part yuzu *citron (or lemon) juice*

⅛ sheet nori *seaweed, cut into fine shreds with scissors*

To parboil chrysanthemum leaves, bring an ample amount of lightly salted water to a boil, hold chrysanthemum by leafy tops and plunge any thick stems into boiling water to cook for about 30 seconds, depending on thickness. Drop entire sprigs into water and parboil for 1 minute or so more. Rinse in cold water, drain, and gently squeeze out moisture.

Cut chrysanthemum into 1¼-inch (3-cm) lengths. Serve at room temperature in mounds in 4 small dishes. Top each mound with 1 tsp citron-soy sauce and garnish with a pinch of *nori* seaweed shreds. Keeps no more than 3 hours.

Chrysanthemum Leaves with Sesame Dressing

Shungiku no Goma Ae

春菊のごまあえ

Vegetables with sesame dressing are a standard part of temple cooking. In addition to being delicious, sesame masks any harsh flavors or bitterness in vegetables and is a rich source of nourishment. A number of recipes of this kind are scattered throughout the book.

SERVES 4

¼ lb (115 gm) chrysanthemum leaves, washed and hard stem ends removed

SESAME DRESSING

1 ounce (30 gm) white sesame seeds, toasted and ground (see page 65)

2 tsps soy sauce

1 Tbsp saké
1 tsp sugar
1/6 tsp salt

Bring an ample amount of lightly salted water to a rolling boil. Because the leaf stems are thick, they need time to cook. To parboil, first put stems in the boiling water, holding leafy tops above the pot, for about 30 seconds or so, then drop in entire vegetable and parboil for about 1 minute longer. Rinse in cold water, drain, and gently squeeze out moisture. Cut greens into 1 1/4-inch (3-cm) lengths.

Blend ground sesame, soy sauce, saké, sugar, and salt. Add chrysanthemum and toss to coat.

Serve at room temperature in small portions or family style in one bowl. Keeps 1 day.

VARIATIONS: See Green Beans with Sesame Dressing, page 113.

Quick Oden

Haya-Oden

早おでん

This is served in May, when young *sansho* sprigs (*kinome*) appear. The dish was developed at the Donke-in temple as a fresh, delicious food that can be quickly prepared when unexpected guests appear. Now, of course, young *sansho* leaves are available almost year round. When preparing this in summer, chill the tofu in cold water; in winter, warm it in hot water.

SERVES 4

1 cake "silk" or regular tofu

MISO TOPPING

- *1 generous Tbsp young* sansho *sprigs* (kinome)
- *2 scant Tbsps sweet white Kyoto* (saikyō) *miso (or the sweetest miso available)*
- *2 tsps saké*
- *1/2 tsp sugar (optional; increase this amount if a saltier miso type is used)*

Cut tofu into four pieces crosswise (one portion should measure about 1 1/3×1 1/4×2 1/4 in/3 1/2×3×6 cm).

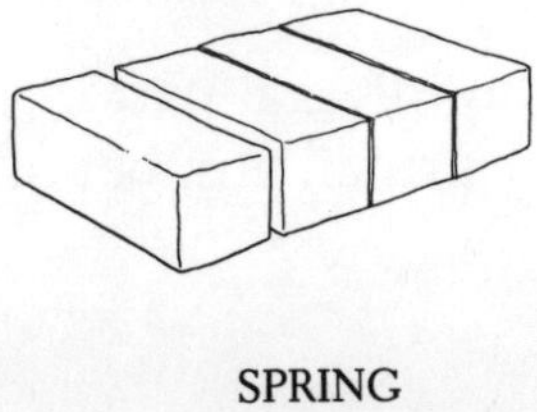

In a *suribachi* grinding bowl or mortar, pound young *sansho* sprigs to a paste. Blend in miso, saké, and sugar (optional).

Place each piece of tofu in a small, deep bowl and spread with about 1 ½ tsps or so of topping. Eat immediately.

VARIATION: Substitute 1 tsp powdered green tea (*matcha*) for the young *sansho* sprigs in the topping. Green tea darkens in time, so this topping may appear a little light when first made.

Note: To heat tofu, bring ample water to a boil in a saucepan, remove from heat, and add tofu immediately; cover pan and let stand 5 minutes.

Sansho Pods and Konbu Kelp Relish

Sansho no Mi to Konbu no Tsukudani

山椒の実と昆布つくだ煮

This simple "relish" is one of a great family of strongly flavored saké-and-soy-simmered foods (*tsukudani*) that go well with plain rice. If you do not have a *sansho* bush nearby as a source of the fresh young pods (they look like small green berries), then the bottled, pickled *sansho* pods can be used.

MAKES ABOUT 1 CUP

½ cup of 1-inch (2 ½-cm) squares dried konbu *kelp (cut with scissors)*
¼ cup green (young) sansho *pods, without stems (or bottled, pickled* sansho *pods)*
1 cup saké
1 cup water
2 Tbsps soy sauce

Combine all ingredients in a small saucepan, cover, and bring to a boil over medium heat. Place pot lid ajar, reduce heat to low, and simmer until pot liquor is almost gone. There should be just enough liquid to keep the *konbu* kelp moist.

Serve in tiny quantities at room temperature as a relish or with rice. Keeps indefinitely refrigerated.

Simmered Hijiki

Hijiki no Takimono

ひじきの炊きもの

This type of seaweed is an integral part of Japanese home cooking, but it appears only in a small number of dishes, of which this is the most common.

SERVES 4

1-ounce (about 35-gm) pack dried hijiki *seaweed*
1 cake thin deep-fried tofu (usuage)
1/3 ounce (10 gm) dried gourd shavings (kampyō), *scrubbed, reconstituted in water, and cut into 3/4-inch (2-cm) lengths.*
1-inch (2 1/2-cm) length carrot, cut in julienne strips and parboiled (optional—carrot is mainly for color)

FOR SIMMERING

3 1/2 Tbsps soy sauce
2 Tbsps sugar
2 Tbsps saké
1 2/3 cups water
1 tsp vegetable oil
1/3 tsp salt
1/2-inch nubbin fresh ginger, peeled and sliced

Wash *hijiki* well, then let stand in tepid water until soft, about 30 minutes.

Pour boiling water over *usuage* to remove oil. Cut into 1 1/2-inch (4-cm) widths then into thick julienne strips.

Place *hijiki, usuage,* reconstituted gourd shavings (and carrot) in a medium-sized saucepan. Add simmering ingredients and simmer over medium heat until *hijiki* swells and its aroma is strong, about 15 minutes. Cool in pot liquor.

Serve at room temperature in individual dishes or in one bowl. Keeps 1 week refrigerated. Goes well with rice.

Saké-Braised Snow Peas

Kinu Saya no Mushi-Ni

絹さやのむし煮

This Kyoto temple dish is versatile as guest or everyday food. If the broad type of snow pea (called *Horanda saya* in Japan) is available, use it; that is the type of pea originally used for this recipe.

SERVES 4

40 snow peas

FOR BRAISING

2 Tbsps saké
2 pinches salt
1/2 tsp vegetable oil
dash soy sauce

Place all ingredients in saucepan over medium heat. Cover pan and braise 3 minutes over medium heat.

Eat hot (10 peas per portion).

Snow Peas and Rōbai Stir-Fry

Kinu Saya to Rōbai no Itamemono

絹さやとろうばいの炒めもの

Any favorite vegetable can be used in this tasty combination of a green with vegetable protein (wheat gluten). This is an original recipe for this book.

SERVES 4

1 tsp vegetable oil

1 round of deep-fried Rōbai *(see page 192), cut into bite-sized pieces*

1/4 lb (115 gm) snow peas, washed and strings removed

salt

pepper

red pepper

Heat large frypan or wok over medium-high heat, add oil, then *rōbai,* and stir-fry for about 2 minutes. Add snow peas, season to taste with salt, pepper, and a dash of red pepper, and stir-fry until done, about 2 minutes more.

Serve hot in individual dishes or family style in one dish. Does not keep.

Summer

Simmered Plums

Ni-Ume

煮　梅

Here is what might be called a Japanese "jam." The flavor is complex, and the dish is eaten during the rainy season in June, when the hard green *ume* appear on the market. Good as a dessert, a snack, or as a relish with a meal.

SERVES 4

12 hard green ume *or green apricots*
4 Tbsps sugar
4 tsps soy sauce

Place fruit and ample water in an enameled saucepan. (Do not use a metal pan—it will affect the flavor.) Bring to a boil over high heat, reduce heat to very low, and simmer 10 minutes. Drain.

Place plums in ample cold water and let water run (slowly, to be sure) over *ume* overnight to remove harshness (2–3 hours in running water should suffice for green apricots). Drain.

To serve, place 3 fruit on each small dish, sprinkle with 1 Tbsp sugar, then top with 1 tsp soy sauce. Keeps 3 days.

Sweet Green Plums

Ao-Ume no Satō-Zuke

青梅の砂糖づけ

Unripe Japanese plums (*ume*) are usually used to make a kind of sweet cordial, but here they are sweetened and kept crisp. This dish is originally from the mountains of the Shinshū region, west of Tokyo, and was adopted by the Sankō-in. In fact, the *ume* is not a plum at all, but a type of apricot. Hard green apricots may be used.

SERVES 4

8 hard green ume *or green apricots*
1 tsp salt
1–2 Tbsps "white liquor" (shōchū) *or vodka*
2 Tbsps sugar

Prick each fruit 3–4 times with a needle or toothpick. Cover with water and let stand 24 hours. Drain. Sprinkle with 1 tsp salt while still wet and toss well to coat fruit. Let salted fruit stand 72 hours in a colander or bowl. Wash well to remove salt. The seeds should be easily removed at this point either by squeezing fruit or by cutting each fruit open.

Again place fruit in water and let soak 12 hours to get rid of all salt. Drain. Sprinkle with 1–2 Tbsps "white liquor" (*shōchū*) or vodka. Sprinkle with 2 Tbsps sugar. Place in airtight jar and keep in cool dark place for at least 2 months before using.

Fruit may be served whole, cut in half, or with each half cut in arc-shaped slices. Serve 2 fruit per person with 1–2 tsps of the sweet liquid. Keeps indefinitely.

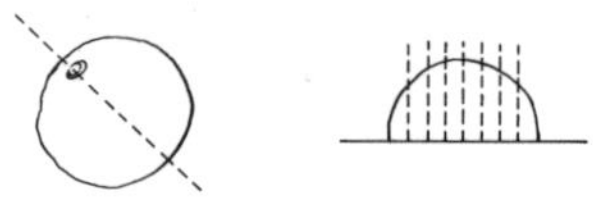

Gingered Green Beans

Ingen no Ohitashi

いんげんのおひたし

This is another example of daily temple food—a simple dish that can easily be made in large quantities.

SERVES 4

$\frac{1}{4}$ lb (115 gm) green beans, ends snapped off
2 tsps finely grated fresh ginger
2 tsps soy sauce

Put ample lightly salted water in a medium-sized saucepan and bring to a boil over high heat. Reduce heat to medium-high and add beans. Boil, uncovered, for about 4 minutes (time depends on size of beans), until just barely tender-crisp and still bright green. Plunge into cold water to cool and arrest cooking. Cut beans into 2-inch (5-cm) lengths.

About 20 pieces of bean are 1 portion. Arrange each portion into a pyramid on a small dish. Place about $\frac{1}{2}$ tsp of finely grated fresh ginger on each mound of beans and pour on $\frac{1}{2}$ tsp soy sauce. Serve at room temperature or chilled. Does not keep.

Green Beans with Sesame Dressing

Ingen no Goma Ae

いんげんのごまあえ

SERVES 4

$^1/_4$ lb (115 gm) green beans, ends snapped off

SESAME DRESSING

1 ounce (30 gm) white sesame seeds, toasted and ground (see page 65)
1 Tbsp soy sauce
1 Tbsp saké
1 tsp sugar

Parboil green beans in lightly salted water until just barely cooked and still crisp—about 4 minutes (time depends on size of beans). Plunge into cold water to cool and arrest cooking. Drain and cut into 2-inch (5-cm) lengths.

Blend ground sesame, soy sauce, saké, and sugar. Add green beans and toss until well coated with dressing.

Serve at room temperature in small portions in individual dishes or family style in one bowl.

VARIATIONS: Many green vegetables may be parboiled in lightly salted water (soaked to remove harsh flavor, if necessary), cooled, chopped, and mixed with sesame dressing. Some Japanese vegetables are *seri, mitsuba* (trefoil), spinach, chrysanthemum leaves (see page 106); Western vegetables are water-cress, chard, beet tops, fennel, asparagus, kale, and broccoli. See also Spinach Crowns with Sesame Dressing, page 177.

Any nuts roughly ground in a mortar may be used instead of sesame seeds.

Green Beans with Miso Dressing

Ingen no Miso Ae

いんげんの味噌あえ

Green beans (*ingen*) are an important part of daily menus of Zen temples. When the Chinese monk Yinyuan (Japanese: Ingen) brought the Huangbo (Japanese: Ōbaku) sect of Zen to Japan in the seventeenth century, he apparently also brought green beans; thus this vegetable carries his name in Japanese.

SERVES 4

$^1/_2$ lb (225 gm) green beans, ends snapped off

MISO DRESSING

3 Tbsps sweet white Kyoto (saikyō) *miso*
3 Tbsps saké

1/3 tsp basic Japanese mustard mix (see page 51)
pinch grated lemon zest

Parboil green beans in ample lightly salted water until just cooked but still crisp. Plunge into cold water to cool and arrest cooking. Drain and cut into 1 1/2-inch (4-cm) lengths.

Blend miso dressing ingredients. Add beans and toss until coated.

Serve at room temperature in individual dishes or in one bowl. Color of beans will change quickly, but flavor does not change. Keeps 1 day.

Simmered Green Beans

Ingen no Nimono

いんげんの煮もの

This representative *shōjin* dish has a deep flavor yet can be eaten in quantity. It goes well with hot rice.

SERVES 4

1/4 lb (115 gm) green beans, ends snapped off

FOR SIMMERING

1 2/3 cups water (or dashi)
2 1/2 Tbsps soy sauce
2 Tbsps saké

Snap or cut beans into 2-inch (5-cm) lengths.

Put simmering ingredients and beans in a medium-sized saucepan over medium heat, cover pan, and bring to a boil. Reduce heat to low and simmer, covered, until tender-crisp.

Serve 20 pieces of bean in small individual saucers or serve family style in one bowl. May be eaten hot, at room temperature, or chilled. Keeps 2–3 days refrigerated.

Green Beans in Thick Sauce

Ingen no Kuzutoji

いんげんの葛とじ

The Sankō-in had its own fields at one time and reaped great harvests of green beans. This is one easy way to prepare them—chilled, it is a summer dish; at room temperature it can be eaten at any time; hot, it warms the body.

SERVES 4

1/2 lb (225 gm) young green beans, ends snapped off

THICK SAUCE

5/6 cup (3/4 cup plus 1 Tbsp) dashi *(see page 81)*
2 Tbsps sugar
1 Tbsp saké
1/6 tsp salt
2 Tbsps potato starch (katakuriko) *dissolved in 2 Tbsps water*

4 tsps fresh ginger juice
lemon juice

Parboil green beans in ample lightly salted water over high heat until just cooked but still crisp. The time will vary with age and tenderness of beans. Plunge immediately into cold water to cool and arrest cooking. Drain, pat dry, and cut into 1 1/4-inch (3-cm) lengths.

Bring *dashi*, soy sauce, saké, and salt to a boil over medium heat. Add dissolved potato starch and stir until thickened.

Place one-fourth of the beans in each dish and pour on 2 Tbsps thick sauce. Add 1 tsp ginger juice and a squirt of lemon juice to each portion just before serving. Serve hot, at room temperature, or chilled. Keeps 2 days.

Cucumbers with Sesame-Mustard Dressing

Kyūri no Goma-Zu-Karashi Ae
きゅうりのごま酢辛子あえ

This is guest, and not daily fare. It is part of the cuisine developed in Kyoto temples housing offspring of the imperial family.

SERVES 4

2 Japanese cucumbers, ends trimmed and thinly sliced
1 tsp salt
2 Tbsps white sesame seeds, toasted and ground (see page 65)
1 Tbsp rice vinegar
1 tsp soy sauce
1 1/2 tsps sugar
1/4 tsp basic Japanese mustard mix (see page 51)

Place sliced cucumber in one bowl, add 1 tsp salt, and toss with fingers until slices are salt coated. Let rest 10 minutes, then rinse well in water and gently squeeze out moisture. Slices should be slightly limp but still crisp.

Blend the remaining ingredients, increasing the sugar if you like a sweeter dressing—this is not sweet. Add cucumber slices and toss until all slices are coated with dressing.

Serve at room temperature or chilled in small mounds in small deep bowls or family style in a bowl. This should be eaten immediately. Does not keep.

Vinegared Cucumbers

Kyūri no Sunomono

きゅうりの酢のもの

This is a basic vinegared "salad" that is popular in homes throughout Japan as well as in temples. It has many variations.

SERVES 4

1/2 sheet thin deep-fried tofu (usuage)

FOR FLAVORING USUAGE

- *2 Tbsps water*
- *1 tsp soy sauce*
- *1 scant tsp sugar*

2 small (or 1 large) shiitake *mushrooms, stems removed*

FOR FLAVORING SHIITAKE

- *1 tsp vegetable oil*
- *1/2 tsp soy sauce*
- *1/2 tsp saké*
- *1/2 tsp sugar*

1/2 ounce (15 gm) cellophane noodles (harusame)

VINEGAR DRESSING

- *3 Tbsps rice vinegar*
- *1 1/2 Tbsps sugar*
- *pinch salt*

1 1/2 Japanese cucumbers, ends trimmed and thinly sliced

Pour boiling water over the *usuage* to remove excess oil. Cut in half and then, placing one half atop the other, cut into thick julienne strips. Place strips in a small saucepan with the *usuage* flavoring ingredients and cook over medium heat until liquid disappears, stirring frequently. Spread on plate to cool.

Cut *shiitake* mushrooms into thin slices. Place in small saucepan over medium heat, add 1 tsp oil, and stir-fry about 30 seconds. Remove from heat and add remaining ingredients for flavoring *shiitake*. Return to heat and cook about 30 seconds, stirring constantly. Spread on plate to cool.

Place cellophane noodles in ample boiling water and boil until soft—about 2–3 minutes. Drain, place in a mound on a cutting board, and make 2 parallel cuts through the mound. Spread on plate to cool.

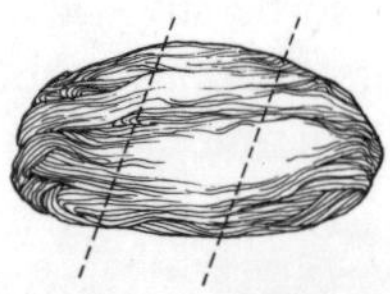

Mix vinegar dressing in a medium-sized bowl until sugar dissolves. Add all solid ingredients to vinegar dressing and toss well.

Serve chilled in small mounds in small deep bowls. Keeps 1 day.

VARIATION: Add 1 perilla (*shiso*) leaf cut into thin julienne strips.

Pressed and Vinegared Cucumbers

Oshi-Kyūri no Sunomono

押しきゅうりの酢のもの

This equivalent of a summer salad is Kyoto temple food. The complementary flavors of *konbu* kelp and cucumber are brought together by a sweet vinegar.

SERVES 4

3 Japanese cucumbers (or 1 1/2 Western cucumbers, seeded)
1/2 tsp salt
1 1/2×2 1/4-inch (4×6 cm) piece of good quality dashi konbu *kelp, wiped with a moist cloth*

SWEET VINEGAR
3 Tbsps rice vinegar
1 Tbsp sugar
2–3 drops soy sauce
pinch salt

With a peeler or knife, peel 1/8-inch (1/2-cm) strips of cucumber skin at 3/8-inch (1-cm) intervals. With Japanese cucumbers, do this only along the 2 1/2 inches (6 1/2 cm) or so where the skin is a darker green. Western cucumbers should be entirely strip-peeled in this manner, because their skin is much more bitter than that of the Japanese variety.

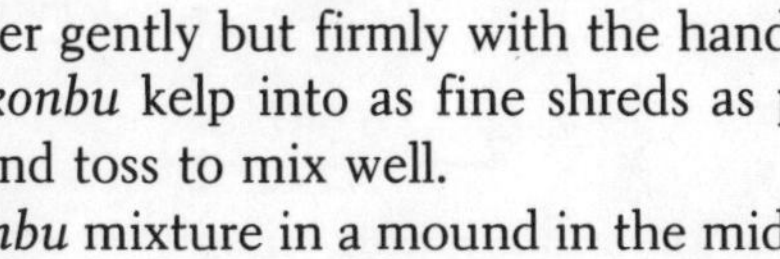

Cut cucumbers into 1/8-inch (1/2-cm) slices on the diagonal. Place slices in a bowl and sprinkle with 1/2 tsp salt. Shake bowl to toss and coat cucumber evenly with salt, then let rest 5 minutes. Rinse cucumber well to remove salt, then squeeze out water gently but firmly with the hands.

With scissors, cut *konbu* kelp into as fine shreds as possible. Add *konbu* shreds to cucumber and toss to mix well.

Place cucumber-*konbu* mixture in a mound in the middle of a dinner plate or very shallow bowl.

Mix the sweet vinegar ingredients until sugar is dissolved. Spoon the vinegar mixture over the cucumber and *konbu*. Invert a plate or place a wooden drop-lid on the cucumber-*konbu,* add a 2-pound (1-kg) weight (a water-filled bowl or pot is convenient; a stone is best), and let rest in a cool, dark place for 3 hours.

Place cucumber-*konbu* mixture in a bowl with the liquid given off during the pressing and toss well.

Serve at room temperature or chilled in small dishes with a portion of the liquid. Keeps only 2–3 hours.

VARIATION: Cut cucumber into thick slices (lengthwise or crosswise). Make alternate layers of sheets of *konbu* and cucumber, sprinkle each layer with some of the sweet vinegar mixture, and press under a weight for ½ day. Serve and eat as described above.

Cucumber Rolls

Kyūri no Nori-Maki

きゅうりの海苔巻き

This is a midsummer dish. The aroma of *nori* and its crispness combined with that of freshly cut cucumber makes this one of the most refreshing of summer foods.

4 PIECES—SERVES 1 OR 2

1 Japanese cucumber, ends trimmed
1 sheet nori *seaweed, cut in half crosswise (across long side)*

WASABI-SOY SAUCE
basic wasabi *horseradish mix (see page 57)*
soy sauce

Cut cucumber in half, then cut each half into medium julienne strips. Keep these half-cucumber portions separate.

Place ½ *nori* sheet with narrow side toward you on bamboo rolling mat (*maki-su*) or clean kitchen towel folded in half. Place julienne strips of ½ cucumber in an even mound across the *nori,* about 2 inches (5 cm) from the near edge. The mound will seem rather large.

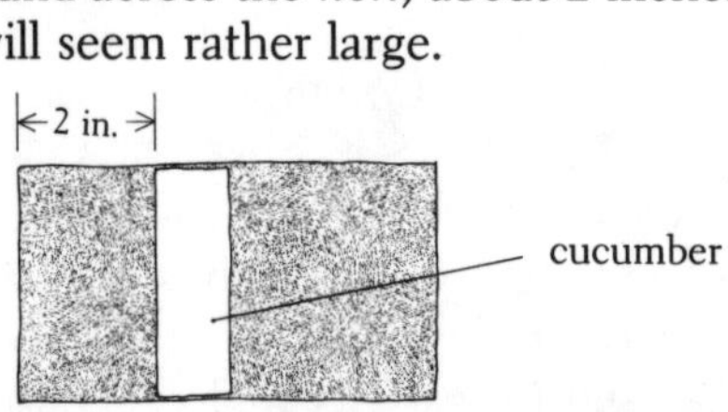

Roll *nori* around the cucumber, using the mat or cloth. The roll should be fairly loose. Repeat process for remaining half cucumber.

Cut each roll in half, making a total of 4 pieces.

Place a dab of basic *wasabi* horseradish mix on the side of a small dish or saucer, put a small amount of soy sauce in the saucer and mix in *wasabi* to taste. Dip cucumber rolls in this mixture.

Must be eaten immediately! This is a very light food that can be eaten in quantity.

Whole Simmered Eggplants

Nasu no Maru-Ni

なすの丸煮

In Kyoto temples, this dish appears at the time of the Japanese All Souls' (Obon) observances in mid August, when eggplants are at their best. The appearance of plump eggplants cooked whole is itself considered a feast for the eyes. It is worth finding (or growing) the 4-inch (10-cm) eggplants for this dish.

SERVES 4

8 4-inch (10-cm) eggplants, caps left intact

FOR SIMMERING

- *1 2/3 cups water*
- *5 Tbsps soy sauce*
- *4 Tbsps saké*
- *1 generous Tbsp sugar*

With the point of a knife, score each eggplant 3 times. Each cut should begin just below the cap and extend almost to the bottom and should be deeper in the middle than at the beginning and end. The cuts should be equidistant around the vegetable.

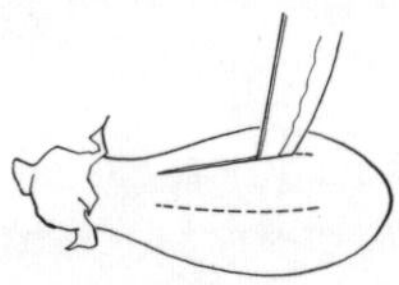

Mix simmering ingredients in a medium-large saucepan, making sure sugar is dissolved. Add scored eggplants, cover with a drop-lid, and bring to a boil over high heat. Reduce heat to medium, and simmer for 15 minutes, turning the eggplants every 5 minutes or so. Drain.

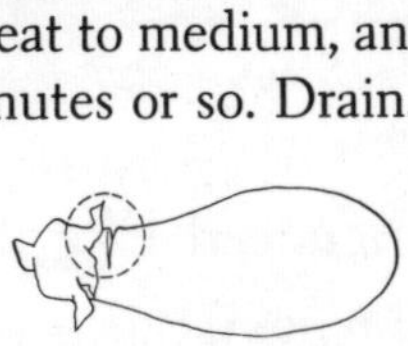

Cut almost through the neck of each cooked vegetable just below the cap. This makes the eggplant easier to eat, especially with chopsticks. Serve 2 whole eggplants in each individual medium-sized dish. May be eaten hot, at room temperature, or chilled. Does not keep.

Simmered Eggplant with Ginger Sauce

Nasu no Ohitashi

なすのおひたし

Eggplant blends well with the flavor of ginger, which brings out the sweetness of the vegetable. The common preliminary step of soaking in water or lightly salting eggplant is not done in any of the eggplant recipes here.

SERVES 4

4 4-inch (10-cm) eggplants, caps removed, and cut in half lengthwise

GINGER-SOY SAUCE

1/3 ounce (10 gm; 1-inch cube) fresh ginger, peeled and finely grated
1 Tbsp soy sauce

Bring about 4 cups water to a boil in a medium-sized saucepan over high heat. Add eggplant halves, cut side up, and reduce heat to medium. Simmer, uncovered, until just cooked (about 5 minutes), turning eggplant after about 3 minutes. Test by pricking with toothpick or skewer. Flesh should be soft but not mushy.

Drain with skin side up. Press gently with your hand to squeeze out water without crushing. Cool.

When cool, cut each half lengthwise into 1/8-inch (1/2-cm) slices. The vegetable can be cut when hot, but the result is messy.

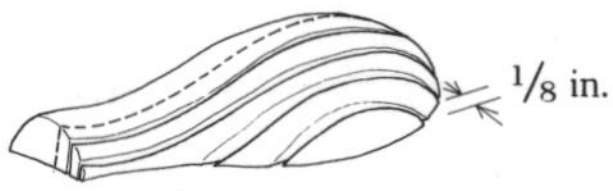

Mix ginger-soy sauce.

On small dishes or saucers, make a quick, casual arrangement of 8 slices for each serving. Top with 1 Tbsp ginger-soy sauce, mixing lightly before eating. Best eaten hot, but may be eaten at room temperature or chilled. Does not keep well.

Note: If large eggplants are used, cut into slices about 1/8 inch thick × 3 inches long × 1 inch wide (1/2 × 8 × 2 1/2 cm). Prepare as above.

Light Vinegared Eggplant

Nasu no Achara

なすのあちゃら

This eggplant dish appears among the foods served at Japanese All Souls' (Obon) in August and also may be part of the offering on household Buddhist altars at that time. It is a light, typical summer dish.

SERVES 4

4 4-inch (10-cm) eggplants, caps removed

SWEET VINEGAR

3 Tbsps rice vinegar
1 1/2 Tbsps sugar
pinch salt

Cut eggplants into fourths lengthwise. Cut each fourth crosswise into 1/8-inch (1/2-cm) slices.

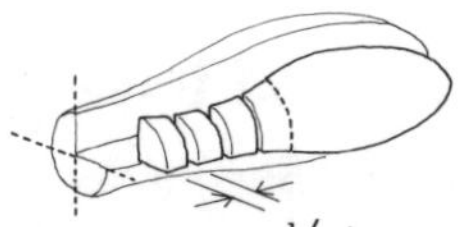

In a medium saucepan, bring eggplant slices and ample water to a boil over high heat, reduce heat to medium, and simmer until cooked. The cooking time varies greatly, depending on the season and eggplant.

Drain eggplant and cool to room temperature. Place cooled slices in a bowl and add sweet vinegar dressing. Toss until well coated.

May be served at room temperature or chilled, in separate small dishes or in one dish family style. Does not keep.

Eggplant with Sesame Dressing

Nasu no Goma Ae
なすのごまあえ

This dish, which brings together the flavors and aromas of eggplant and sesame, is also summer fare. In Japan, rich foods—such as broiled eel—are thought to counteract summer's debilitating, sultry weather.

SERVES 4

vegetable oil for deep-frying
4 4-inch (10-cm) eggplants, caps removed, and cut in half lengthwise

SESAME DRESSING

4 Tbsps white sesame seeds, toasted and ground (see page 65)
3 Tbsps soy sauce
1 Tbsp saké

Heat vegetable oil to medium temperature (340°F/170°C) over medium heat. Slide eggplant halves into oil, skin side down. Turn after about 3 minutes and deep-fry about 1 minute more—until eggplant flesh is just soft. Test by pricking with toothpick or skewer.

Drain with cut side down on rack or absorbent paper. Cut diagonally into ³/₈-inch (1 cm) slices.

Combine ground sesame seed, soy sauce, and saké. Add cooked eggplant slices and toss to coat eggplant evenly with dressing.

Serve at room temperature. Does not keep.

Eggplant and Fava Beans

Nasu no Soramame Ae

なすの空豆あえ

This early summer dish is a marriage of fresh colors and flavors. Its luxury lies in the effort involved in peeling the fava beans. Small portions go a long way.

SERVES 4

vegetable oil for deep-frying
4 *4-inch (10-cm) eggplants, caps removed, and cut in half lengthwise*
28 *large (or 36 small) fava beans*
4 *tsps sugar*
1/6 tsp salt

Heat vegetable oil to medium temperature (340°F/170°C) over medium heat. Slide eggplant halves into oil skin side down. Turn after about 3 minutes and deep-fry about 1 minute more—until just soft. Test by pricking with toothpick or skewer.

Drain with cut side down on rack or absorbent paper. Cut diagonally into ³/₈-inch (1-cm) slices.

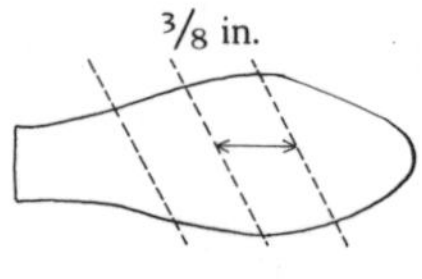

Bring an ample amount of lightly salted water to a boil, add beans, and boil over medium-high heat until tender. Cooking time depends on the size of the beans. Drain and remove bean skins.

Place beans in a bowl or mortar and crush with pestle or potato masher. The crushed beans should be lumpy, containing pieces of partially crushed bean. Mix in sugar and salt. Add eggplant slices and mix.

Serve at room temperature in individual dishes or in a bowl family style. Does not keep.

Eggplant with Miso Sauce

Nasu no Oden

なすのおでん

This happy marriage of eggplant and sweet miso is often known by the name of eggplant *dengaku.*

SERVES 4

vegetable oil for deep-frying
4 4-inch (10-cm) eggplants, caps removed, and cut in half lengthwise

MISO TOPPING

- *4 level Tbsps sweet white Kyoto* (saikyō) *miso*
- *1 1/2 Tbsps saké*
- *1 tsp sugar*

1 tsp or so grated yuzu *citron zest (optional)*

Bring vegetable oil to medium temperature (340°F/170°C) over medium heat. Slide eggplant halves into oil skin side down. The number of eggplant halves you can cook at one time depends on the quantity of deep-frying oil and the area of its surface. Turn eggplant after about 3 minutes and cook about 1 minute more—until just soft. Test by pricking with toothpick or skewer.

Drain on rack or absorbent paper with cut side down.

Combine all miso topping ingredients in a small saucepan. Cook over medium heat, blending until smooth and shiny, about 1 minute or so.

Hold hot eggplant halves with a napkin or paper towel and spread cut side with miso topping.

Place 2 eggplant halves in each small dish, garnishing the middle of each half with a dab of grated *yuzu* zest, and decorating each dish with a small green leaf or two from the garden. If *yuzu* citron is not available, omit the zest.

Serve hot. Does not keep.

Eggplant Purple

Nasu Murasaki no Itamemono

なす紫の炒めもの

Some recipes call for peeled eggplant. But why throw away the delicious skin? This original dish from the Sankō-in uses eggplant skin only and takes advantage of its slight bitterness and beautiful color, which becomes more intense with stir-frying.

SERVES 4

4 4-inch (10-cm) eggplants, caps removed
2 tsps vegetable oil
pinch salt
pinch pepper

Peel each eggplant in thick (1/8 in/1/2 cm) and wide slices. Four-inch (10-cm) eggplants should yield 4 wide slices. Do not use narrow strips or bits of skin. (Place the peeled eggplants in water and reserve for other uses. Or, make this dish when preparing recipes calling for peeled eggplant, such as Eggplant and *Shimeji* Mushrooms, page 143.)

Heat 2 tsps vegetable oil in frypan over medium heat. Add eggplant skin and stir-fry until just tender, about 1 minute. Season to taste with salt and pepper.

Fold skin slices in half and serve 4 slices in each small dish. Serve hot or at room temperature. Keeps 1 day.

Junsai

じゅん菜

Junsai are plant sprouts found only on the bottoms of old ponds. There are (or were) many such ponds in Kyoto, so this is considered Kyoto food, though there are some regional variations, particularly where daimyo lived. Clear soup with *junsai,* eaten either hot or chilled, is considered an aristocrat of summer temple cooking. This soup is made simply by putting 2 *junsai* buds, in *dashi* (made from *konbu* kelp plus a little *shiitake* mushroom *dashi*) and adding a touch of ginger juice.

This dish, in fact, is not cooking at all, since *junsai* come bottled. They are still quite expensive and one of Japan's true luxury foods.

SERVES 4

1/2 cup junsai
1/6 tsp salt
4 pinches pepper

Mix all ingredients. Serve in small deep bowls at room temperature. Opened bottle keeps 3–4 days refrigerated.

Cold Sōmen Noodles in Dipping Sauce

Ozoro to Tsuke-Jiru

おぞうとつけ汁

Cold noodles appear in summer, especially in temples as part of the All Souls' (Obon) observances during the heat of August. Many kinds of food are served between rituals, which continue for three days—Cold Sōmen Noodles and Light Vinegared Eggplant (page 120) are but two. In fact, one school of thought believes *shōjin* cooking might have developed out of the food that appears at the Obon observances.

SERVES 4

4 bundles thin ("hand stretched" or tenobe) *sōmen noodles*

DIPPING SAUCE

- 1 ⅔ *cups* konbu dashi *(see page 81)*
- *7 Tbsps saké*
- *4 Tbsps soy sauce*
- *½ tsp salt*
- *½ tsp sugar*

1 sheet nori *seaweed, toasted and cut into fourths*

basic wasabi *horseradish mix (see page 57)*

Bring an ample amount of water to a boil in a large saucepan and add *sōmen* noodles. Boil until done, about 5–6 minutes. To test if noodles are done, throw a small piece against a wall; if it sticks, the *sōmen* is cooked. Rinse well in cold water.

To arrange cooked cold noodles attractively, insert a chopstick into the noodles and pick up an amount that covers about a 4-inch (10-cm) length of chopstick. Swish back and forth once or twice in cold water, then gently lay in a medium-sized dish or bowl as if folding cloth. The final result should have all noodles neatly aligned and folded across the diameter of the dish.

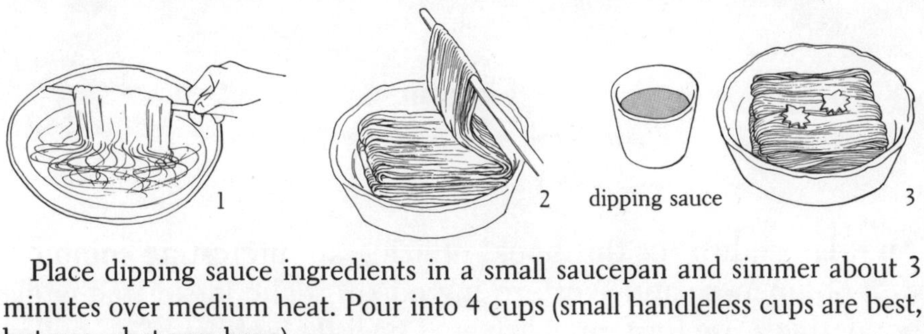

Place dipping sauce ingredients in a small saucepan and simmer about 3 minutes over medium heat. Pour into 4 cups (small handleless cups are best, but use what you have).

Crumble a piece of *nori* seaweed into each cup of broth, add a dab of *wasabi* horseradish, and mix well.

Eat immediately, picking up noodles with chopsticks (best) or fork and dipping into sauce.

Fennel Stir-Fry

Amauikyō Itame

あまういきょういため

Fennel is an excellent vegetable that lends itself to *shōjin* cooking. Other Western vegetables might do as well, but fennel has an interesting flavor, and both leaves and bulb can be used separately to get different textures and effects.

SERVES 4

1 Tbsp vegetable oil
1 fennel bulb, cut into 1-inch (2 1/2-cm) widths then into julienne strips
2 sheets thin deep-fried tofu (usuage), *or 1/4 round* Rōbai *(see page 192), or 6 sheets reconstituted dried* yuba, *cut into small pieces*
1/2-inch (1 1/2-cm) piece fresh horseradish, peeled and finely shred-cut
salt
soy sauce

Heat oil in deep frypan or wok over medium-high heat. Add fennel and *usuage* (or *Rōbai* or *yuba*) and stir-fry until done, about 1–2 minutes.

Remove to bowl and sprinkle with horseradish shreds and season to taste with salt and soy sauce. Toss to mix.

Eat hot! Does not keep.

Flotsam

Amauikyō no Kampyō Musubi

あまういきょうのかんぴょう結び

An original dish for this book, utilizing an interesting combination of Japanese and Western ingredients. The idea came while pondering a use for fennel leaves. The little bundles of parboiled fennel looked a bit more bedraggled than expected, thus the English name. One way of serving this would be to spread the sand-colored miso dip over a plate and place the "flotsam" bundles on this "shore." An attractive and delicious hors d'oeuvre.

SERVES 4

12 3-inch (8-cm) lengths fennel leaves and small stems (use 2 thin or 1 thick stem with leaves), keeping volume of lengths roughly equal

SWEET VINEGAR

1/2 cup rice vinegar
1 Tbsp sugar
1/6 tsp salt

1/3 ounce (10 gm) dried gourd ribbons (kampyō), *scrubbed in water then reconstituted in tepid water for 5 minutes*

MISO DIP

4 Tbsps sweet white Kyoto (saikyō) *miso*
4 Tbsps rice vinegar
1 Tbsp vegetable oil
1 Tbsp sugar

Make small bundles of fennel leaves by bending lengths in half. Parboil for about 30 seconds in lightly salted water, holding each bundle with chopsticks (chopsticks make it easier, but you can let the leaves float around loose if you like). Drain.

Mix sweet vinegar, add reconstituted gourd ribbons, and let stand 5 minutes or more. Cut gourd ribbons into 4 1/2-inch (12-cm) lengths and tie 1 length around each fennel bundle so that the ends of the gourd ribbon are not too long.

Blend miso dip.

Dip each fennel bundle into miso dip before eating. Finger food. Does not keep.

Cellophane Noodle, Fennel, and Nori Explosion

Harusame to Amauikyō to Momi-Nori Age

春雨とあまういきょうともみ海苔揚げ

This original dish for this book is fun food—fun to make and fun to eat. The basic idea can be expanded and explored in many ways. Serve with paper napkins.

SERVES 2–6

vegetable oil for deep-frying
1 cup fennel leaves, cut into 1-inch (2 ½-cm) lengths and thick stalks removed
1 cup cellophane noodles (harusame), *cut or broken into 1-inch (2 ½-cm) lengths*
1 sheet nori *seaweed, toasted until crisp then crumbled into medium-sized pieces*
salt

Heat oil to medium temperature (340°F/170°C).

Mix fennel, cellophane noodles, and *nori.* Drop a small handful at a time into the hot oil. The cellophane noodles will expand spectacularly. Turn over immediately. Work quickly—total frying time is not more than 10 seconds.

Drain on absorbent paper and salt lightly. Eat as a snack or saké (or beer) accompaniment. Small paper napkins are a help, because this is a little oily. Gets soggy in a few hours.

VARIATION: *Konbu* kelp cut into fine shreds or filaments and *thoroughly dried* in the sun or oven can be combined with cellophane noodles and deep-fried.

Flowery Peppers Stir-Fry

Hanayaka Piiman Itame

花やかピーマン炒め

This recipe is included here to show how a sweet miso sauce can be used with Western vegetables. The same sauce can be used in many other ways. Sweet peppers are relatively late arrivals in Japan and thus are not part of the classical *shōjin* cooking.

SERVES 4

2 Tbsps sweet white Kyoto (saikyō) *miso*
2 Tbsps saké
½ Tbsp vegetable oil
1 small green sweet pepper, cut into ¼-inch strips
1 small red sweet pepper, cut into ¼-inch strips
1 small yellow sweet pepper, cut into ¼-inch strips
dash cayenne pepper

Blend miso and saké.

Heat oil in frypan or wok, add peppers, and stir-fry until heated but still crisp—about 2 minutes (timing depends on thickness of peppers). Remove from heat, add miso-saké mixture and dash of cayenne, and toss to coat well.

Serve hot! Does not keep. Goes well with saké or beer.

Zucchini with Sesame-Miso Sauce

Zukini no Goma Ankake

ズッキーニ炒めごまあんかけ

A bit of oil and zucchini (also eggplant) combine well. This is a rich dish.

SERVES 4

SESAME-MISO SAUCE

- *2 Tbsps white sesame seeds, toasted and ground (see page 65)*
- *2 Tbsps sweet white Kyoto* (saikyō) *miso*
- *2 Tbsps saké*

1 Tbsp vegetable oil

2 young zucchini, cut in half lengthwise then cut into 2-inch (5-cm) slices

Blend sesame-miso sauce ingredients.

Heat oil in a frypan or wok over medium-high heat. Add zucchini slices and stir-fry until barely cooked. The zucchini should not become translucent.

Place slices amounting to 1/2 zucchini in each small dish. Top each mound with 1/4 of the sesame-miso sauce. Serve hot. Mix well before eating. Does not keep.

VARIATIONS: Slice raw very young zucchini in half lengthwise and spread sesame-miso sauce on cut surface. Other summer squash—pattypan and yellow squash—can also be used in this recipe.

Zucchini in Thick Clear Soup

Zukini no Kuzutoji no Otsuyu

ズッキーニの葛とじのおつゆ

Zucchini was introduced to Japan in the 1970s; if it had been known in earlier times, it would certainly have been a part of Japanese cooking. It is a marvelous vegetable with a myriad uses. Here its slight bitterness is deliciously used to make an unusual and brightly flavored soup. The recipe itself is an old one; zucchini takes the place of Japanese cucumber.

SERVES 4

4 small young zucchini, ends removed, cut into 3/8-inch (1-cm) lengths

2 cups konbu dashi *(see page 81)*

1 Tbsp soy sauce
1 Tbsp saké
1/6 tsp salt
1 Tbsp potato starch (katakuriko) *dissolved in 1 Tbsp water*
1 tsp finely grated fresh ginger

Parboil zucchini about 1 minute if very young, a little longer if older. Drain.

Combine *dashi,* soy sauce, saké, and salt and bring to a boil over medium heat. Add dissolved potato starch and stir until liquid thickens.

Place zucchini slices amounting to 1 whole zucchini in each deep soup bowl, ladle on the thickened broth, and garnish with 1/4 tsp finely grated fresh ginger. Stir before eating.

Eat hot, at room temperature, or chilled, but add ginger just before serving. Keeps 1 day.

Steamed Zucchini with Three-Color Miso

Mushi Zukini no Sanshoku Miso

むしズッキーニの三色味噌

A third zucchini recipe, this one a bit of a fantasy using three original miso mixtures.

SERVES 4

2 young zucchini
1/2 small tomato, peeled and seeds removed
3 Tbsps sweet white Kyoto (saikyō) *miso*
1/2 tsp vegetable oil
1 sheet nori *seaweed*
2 tsps saké
1/6 tsp basic wasabi *horseradish mix (see page 57)*

Place zucchini in hot steamer and steam until *almost* soft (time depends on size of zucchini). Plunge into water to cool. Trim off stem when cooled.

Red miso: puree tomato—a mortar or *suribachi* grinding bowl and pestle make quick work of it. Blend 1 Tbsp miso with 2 Tbsps pureed fresh tomato and 1/2 tsp vegetable oil. The flavor of fresh tomato is desired here, but if you like, use 2 Tbsps canned tomato sauce.

Black miso: Toast *nori* seaweed well on both sides by waving it over a gas flame until it is crisp—30 seconds or so. Crumble the crisp *nori* over a dry cloth napkin. Hold the edges of the napkin to make a pouch containing the crumbled *nori* so that no *nori* escapes. Crush and knead the pouch so the *nori* is finely crumbled. Blend 1 tsp saké with 1 Tbsp miso. Add 1 Tbsp finely crushed *nori* and blend.

Green miso: Blend 1 Tbsp miso, 1 tsp saké, and 1/6 tsp basic *wasabi* horseradish mix.

Cut zucchini in half lengthwise. Place a healthy dollop of each kind of miso at even intervals on the cut face of the zucchini so that a bit runs down onto the dish in an attractive way. Eat at room temperature. Keeps only about 2 hours before zucchini flavor begins to change.

Simmered Japanese Pumpkin

Kabocha no Nimono

かぼちゃの煮もの

This is a typical temple dish, using seasonal vegetables and the simplest cooking techniques. Japanese pumpkins are in season in August and September. Pumpkins with a small bottom spot (where the blossom was) are said to have better flavor than ones with a large bottom spot.

SERVES 4

1 lb (450 gm) Japanese pumpkin (kabocha) *or any winter squash*

FOR SIMMERING

2 1/2 cups water
5 Tbsps sugar
1 tsp salt

If the skin of the Japanese pumpkin or winter squash is tender, leave it intact; otherwise cut it off. In the latter case, do not peel it clean, but allow a few bits and stripes of rind to remain. Cut pumpkin into 12 1×1 1/2-inch (2 1/2×4-cm) wedges.

Mix simmering ingredients in a medium-sized saucepan until sugar dissolves. Add the pumpkin wedges and bring to a boil over medium heat.

Boil, covered, for 5 minutes. Reduce heat to low and simmer until soft—about 20 minutes. Test occasionally by pricking with skewer or toothpick.

Carefully place wedges on a plate to cool, skin side up. This allows the wedges to keep their shape. Pour a bit of the pot liquor over the wedges; this lets the pumpkin absorb flavor while cooling. Cool to room temperature.

Serve three slices on each small plate (one attractive arrangement is 2 slices skin side up and 1 slice on its side resting on top of the other two), and pour about 1 Tbsp of pot liquor over each serving. This is usually eaten at room temperature, but may also be eaten chilled. Keeps 1–2 days.

Pumpkin with Sesame Sauce

Kabocha no Goma Ankake

かぼちゃのごまあんかけ

This rich dish from the Donke-in temple is best eaten in small portions. Any pumpkin or yellow-fleshed winter squash may be substituted for Japanese pumpkin. A little oil—in this case the oil in the ground sesame—brings out the flavor and richness of all these vegetables.

SERVES 4

20 1 1/2-inch (4-cm) triangles pumpkin or winter squash, skin left intact, edges on skin side beveled about 1/8 inch (1/2 cm)

1/8 in. bevel

FOR SIMMERING PUMPKIN

1 2/3 cups water
4 Tbsps sugar
1 Tbsp saké
1/2 tsp salt

SESAME SAUCE

4 Tbsps black (or white) sesame seeds, toasted and ground (see page 65)
6 Tbsps pot liquor from simmering pumpkin
pinch salt

finely grated yuzu *citron (or lemon) zest*

Cook pumpkin (or squash) in simmering liquid in medium-sized saucepan over medium heat until just cooked—about 5–10 minutes, depending on thickness of pumpkin. Remove from heat and transfer pumpkin to a plate to cool, skin side up. Take care not to break up pumpkin.

Blend ground sesame seed, pot liquor, and salt.

Place 5 pumpkin triangles decoratively on each dish and pour on 1/4 of the sesame mixture. Garnish with a dab of finely ground *yuzu* citron (or lemon) zest.

Delicious hot or at room temperature. Keeps for 2 days if pumpkin and sauce are kept separate until just before serving. Does not keep once they are combined.

VARIATION: The sauce can be enriched further with additions of sweet white Kyoto (*saikyō*) miso and saké to taste.

Pumpkin Tempura

Kabocha no Tempura

かぼちゃの天ぷら

This is a simple and common way of cooking pumpkin (or any other winter squash) that brings out its sweetness. In Japan, the pumpkins begin to appear at the end of summer and thus are considered a summer vegetable; because they keep well, they are eaten mainly in autumn and winter. This dish and Ginger Tempura (page 143) are excellent served together.

SERVES 4

1/2 lb (225 gm) pumpkin or winter squash, peeled
BATTER
2 Tbsps flour
2 Tbsps water
pinch salt
vegetable oil for deep-frying

Cut pumpkin (or squash) into 1/8×2-inch (1/2×5-cm) slices.

Mix batter well. Place pumpkin slices in batter and coat well.

Heat oil to low temperature (320°F/160°C). Deep-fry pumpkin until just cooked—about 1 minute.

Serve 3 slices per portion (together with Ginger Tempura and a tempura-fried green such as parsley or watercress dipped partially in batter, if you like).

Eat hot! Does not keep.

Sweet Bean Balls

Ohagi

おはぎ

This is perhaps the most representative of Japan's sweet confections. Originally it was served at both equinoxes and at the All

Souls' (Obon) observances in August. Sweet azuki bean paste (*anko*) is available canned, but the fresh homemade kind always tastes better than commercial preparations.

SERVES 4

1 cup cooked short-grain rice
salt
1 cup chunky sweet azuki bean paste (anko; *see page 44*).

If using leftover rice, steam it. Place hot freshly cooked or steamed leftover rice in a bowl or large mortar and mash with pestle until some of the rice is well mashed—about 30 seconds to 1 minute of pestle work.

Moisten hands well, touch salt with fingertips of one hand, then rub this bit of salt over both hands.

Form ball of rice about the size of a large walnut by pressing the rice hard between the fingers of both hands until it forms a coherent mass, then forming this into a ball. This is a bit tricky at first but a little practice will bring results. Wash and resalt hands between each ball (oval shapes are also traditional).

Wet a clean cloth napkin and wring it out thoroughly. Place napkin over one palm (hands should be totally dry) and spread 2 Tbsps sweet bean paste over napkin on hand. Place rice ball in center of bean paste, then wrap napkin around rice, gently pushing and teasing the bean paste until it covers the rice completely in as even a layer as possible.

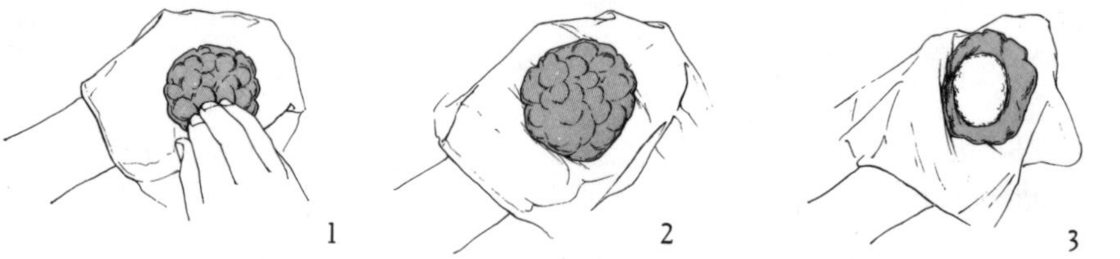

1, 2. spread sweet bean paste on damp cloth

3. place rice on sweet bean paste

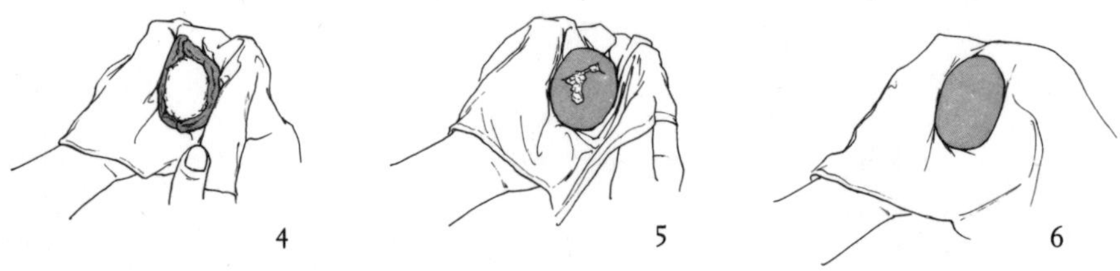

4–6. gently push bean paste around rice

Rinse the napkin thoroughly and wring it out between each use. Repeat process for each rice ball.

Serve 2 balls per portion. Keeps 1–2 days.

VARIATION: Glutinous rice is commonly used for this confection. Because it involves more fuss and skill than regular rice, which is just as good according to many people, glutinous rice is mentioned as a variation.

Autumn

Carrot Greens with Sesame Dressing

Ninjin no Ha no Goma Ae

人参の菜のごまあえ

This is really pretty basic everyday fare, but today carrot greens have become so rare (carrots are sold without greens in Tokyo) and are so little appreciated as a food that this simple dish has been elevated to guest food at the Sankō-in. The harsh flavor of the greens is eliminated by soaking, and the greens must be well chopped. A few flat slivers of boiled carrot make this very attractive.

SERVES 4

1/3 lb (150 gm) carrot greens, washed and long stems removed

SESAME DRESSING

- *3 Tbsps white sesame seeds, toasted and ground (see page 65)*
- *2 tsps soy sauce*
- *1 Tbsp saké*
- *1/6 tsp sugar*

a few boiled carrot slivers

Place carrot greens in ample lightly salted boiling water and parboil 2 minutes. Plunge into cold water, drain, and gently squeeze out moisture.

Place parboiled greens in ample water in a bowl and let stand 8 hours or overnight, changing water 2–3 times to eliminate bitter and harsh flavor. Gently squeeze moisture from greens, place on cutting board and cut into 1/2-inch (1 1/2-cm) lengths, then turn 90° and cut again.

Combine the ground sesame, soy sauce, saké, and sugar. Add chopped carrot greens and toss until well coated with dressing.

Serve at room temperature in small portions in individual dishes or family style in one bowl. Garnish with carrot slivers. Best eaten immediately, but keeps 1 week refrigerated.

Potatoes and Sea Greens

Jagaimo to Wakame no Nitsuke

じゃがいもとわかめの煮つけ

Potatoes are not part of traditional *shōjin* cooking because they were introduced into Japan only in the middle part of the last century. Here is one potato dish, which, as might be expected, is good everyday food, not guest cuisine.

SERVES 4

5 medium potatoes, peeled and cut into ½-inch (1 ½-cm) pieces

FOR SIMMERING

1 ⅔ cups water
2 Tbsps soy sauce
2 Tbsps sugar
2 tsps vegetable oil

1 ⅓ ounces (40 gm) salt-preserved sea greens (wakame), *washed in water, then reconstituted in cold water, changing water 1–2 times*

Place potato pieces and water in a saucepan, cover pan, and bring to a boil quickly. Reduce heat to medium, remove pot lid, and simmer 10 minutes. Add soy sauce, sugar, and oil, and simmer another 5 minutes.

Meanwhile, cut reconstituted sea greens into 4-inch (10-cm) lengths and tie a knot in the middle of each length. There should be 12 knotted pieces.

Add sea greens to potatoes and simmer 5 minutes.

Serve on individual dishes or in one bowl, family style. Eat hot or at room temperature. Keeps 3 days.

Jade Nuggets

Kizami Nattō no Ao-Jiso Age

刻み納豆の青じそ揚げ

Nattō has been described as "bean cheese," and indeed this popular food made by subjecting soy beans to the action of special bacteria resembles cheese in flavor. The texture of *nattō*, however, is its own. Here the flavor of *nattō* is complemented by the minty fragrance of fresh perilla (*shiso*) leaves. The dish is a Sankō-in original.

SERVES 4
3 Tbsps (50 gm) nattō, *finely chopped*
pinch salt
½ tsp basic Japanese mustard mix (optional; page 51)
BATTER
1 tsp cake flour
1 Tbsp water
pinch salt
8 green perilla (shiso) *leaves, washed and patted dry*
vegetable oil for deep-frying

Place the *nattō* in small bowl, add a pinch salt and mix well. The *nattō* should be quite sticky (mix in Japanese mustard, if you desire).

Mix tempura batter well.

Place a perilla leaf on the palm of your hand, with the "front" (greener) side down and the stem facing you. Place about 1 ½ tsps chopped *nattō* in the middle of the leaf (amount depends on size of leaf). Fold leaf so that the stem comes just below the point of the leaf and pinch sides; the stickiness of the *nattō* filling will seal the leaf. Too much filling results in a mess.

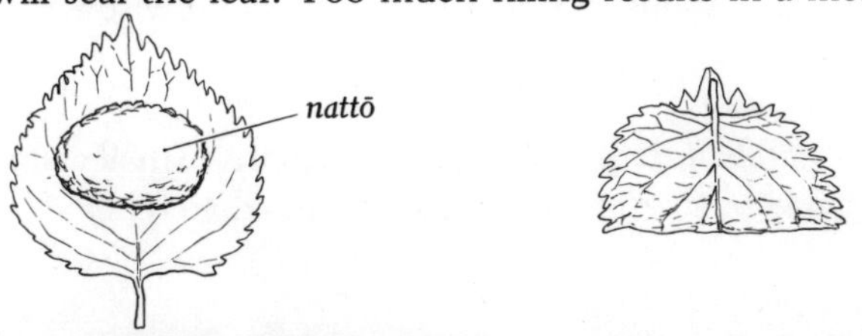

Heat oil to medium-hot (340°F/170°C).

Holding leaf by the point and stem, dip fold into batter about halfway up the leaf. Place in hot oil and deep-fry for only 10–20 seconds. The batter

coating should be creamy in color, not gold or brown. With a little practice, you can fry 2–3 pieces at once.

Serve hot! Two leaves in a small dish are one portion. Does not keep.

Grilled Matsutake Mushrooms

Yaki Matsutake

焼き松茸

This dish, so closely associated with autumn, is considered the height of luxury in the temple and, for that matter, throughout

Japan. *Matsutake* mushrooms defy cultivation and must be sought on pine-clad hillsides. Thus they always fetch premium prices. The Donke-in temple once owned its own mountain, which produced great quantities of *matsutake*. Today, for various reasons, the temple can no longer rely on this source of *matsutake*, but the memory of eating generous quantities of this mushroom is still alive, and this food is part of the temple tradition.

SERVES 4

1 large matsutake *mushroom*

CITRON-SOY SAUCE

2 tsps soy sauce
2 tsps yuzu *citron (or lemon) juice*

Cut *matsutake* in half lengthwise. (If there is evidence of worms in the stem, place in medium-strength brine for 10 minutes.) Place *matsutake* halves, cut side down, on a grill and broil over charcoal (best) or gas for about 5 minutes, turning occasionally. While hot, tear each half lengthwise with fingers into 8 pieces.

Mix citron-soy sauce.

Serve 4 pieces *matsutake* per portion in decorative small dishes. Spoon a bit of citron-soy sauce over each serving. Eat immediately! Does not keep.

Mountain Yam with Plum Dressing

Yamato Imo no Bainiku Ae

大和芋の梅肉あえ

In this dish, diced and cooked mountain yam (the type known as *Yamato imo* is best) takes the place of lily root, the traditional vehicle for plum dressing. Pickled plums are ubiquitous in Japan and are considered to be very good for the health.

SERVES 4

1/3 lb (160 gm) mountain yam (Yamato imo, *if available; any other mountain yam variety can be used), peeled and coarsely diced*
1/2 ounce (15 gm) pickled plum flesh (bainiku), *or about 1 ounce (25–30 gm) pickled plums* (umeboshi), *seeds removed*
1/3 tsp salt
2 tsps sugar
1 tsp saké

Place diced mountain yam in lightly salted water in medium-sized saucepan over medium heat and simmer until just cooked—about 3 minutes. Rinse in cold water to cool. Drain.

Place the pickled plum flesh in a *suribachi* or mortar and mash coarsely, leaving small bits of pickled plum skin. Add the salt, sugar, and saké and mix well.

Add cooked mountain yam and toss gently until all pieces are coated with dressing. Adjust seasonings to taste by adding a bit more salt, sugar, or saké. The plum dressing flavor should be smooth and deep with a gentle "bite." Divide into 4 portions and serve in small, deep bowls. Keeps 1 day refrigerated.

Mountain Yam Rolls

Yamato Imo no Nori-Maki

大和芋の海苔巻き

This dish is both delicious and decorative and will keep even experienced cooks guessing what it is made of. In fact, this is a variation of a dish made in Kyoto temples adapted to foods available around Tokyo.

SERVES 4

7 ounces (200 gm) mountain yam (the Yamato imo *type of yam is dryest and easiest to use)*
1/4 tsp basic wasabi *horseradish mix (page 57)*
2 Tbsps sugar
1/2 tsp salt
1 sheet nori *seaweed*

Peel the mountain yam and remove any black spots. If your hands itch a little after peeling the yam, just rub them together with a small amount of vinegar.

Cut the yam into 1-inch (2 1/2-cm) lengths. Place in a small saucepan with water to cover, and boil over medium heat until cooked—about 15 minutes. Test with a skewer or toothpick. The cooked yam has almost the same consistency as cooked potato. Discard water, then return saucepan to medium heat and shake until the liquid in the yam evaporates. Be careful not to scorch.

Remove from heat or keep on lowest heat (especially with the moister varieties of yam), and while yam is still hot, mash it in the saucepan with a pestle or potato masher. Mash until smooth if you like, but a slightly lumpy texture is more interesting and tasty. Cool.

Add the sugar and salt to the cooled and mashed yam, and then mix and knead yam with the hand. Using the hand is important. Mash any large lumps with the fingers, and mix until the surface is powdery.

On a clean dry kitchen towel or a bamboo rolling mat (*maki-su*), place sheet of *nori* with shiny side down and long side facing you.

Form yam into a ball and spread on *nori* as illustrated. The yam should be about 1/8–1/4 inch (1/2–3/4 cm) thick and should extend to about 1/8 inch (1/2 cm) from the *nori* edge near you and to about 1 1/4 inches (3 cm) from the far edge, and right up to the sides. Smooth the yam layer to a uniform thickness.

Spread a line of *wasabi* horseradish across yam as shown in sketch.

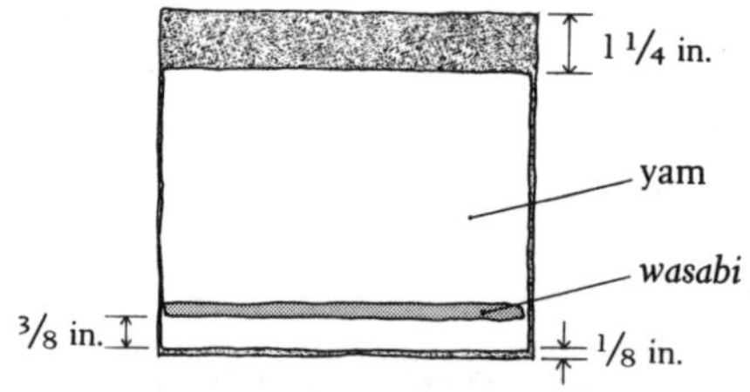

Roll *nori* from the near edge, using the towel or the bamboo mat on which it has been placed. At first, your *nori* rolls might be a bit saggy, but as you quickly acquire the knack, they will become firm and tight. (Actually, with a little practice, you can roll the *nori* without a supporting towel or mat.) Firm up the shape by rolling it back and forth a few times with the palms of the hands.

Cut roll in half with a *sharp*, dry knife, cut each half into halves, and then each quarter into thirds. If the knife is not very sharp, the roll will not cut cleanly, and all your work will be in vain. Use a slicing motion toward you, wiping the knife between cuts.

Place 3 slices on each small dish, either on edge or in a neat pile with cut side facing up. Keeps about 1/2 day.

Deep-Fried Mountain Yam Nuggets

Yamato Imo no Iso-Age

大和芋の磯揚げ

This is luxury food. The nuggets may also be served in clear broth (see page 83).

SERVES 4

6 ounces (180 gm) mountain yam (the Yamato imo *type is best, but use whatever variety is available)*
1 1/2 sheets nori *seaweed*
vegetable oil for deep-frying

GINGER-SOY SAUCE

1 tsp fresh ginger juice (made by pressing juice from finely grated fresh ginger)

2 tsps soy sauce

Peel the mountain yam, removing any black spots, and finely grate the yam. If your hands itch a little, rub them with some vinegar.

Cut whole sheet of *nori* into eighths and half-sheet into fourths.

Heat vegetable oil to medium temperature (340°F/170°C) over medium heat.

Mix ginger-soy sauce.

Place a cut piece of *nori* flat on the work surface (or on a clean kitchen towel), put a portion (1/12 of total amount) of grated yam about 3/8 inch (1 cm) from near edge, and roll. Slide nugget immediately into hot oil and deep-fry until yam is a very light gold—about 1 minute. As each nugget is cooked, roll once in ginger-soy sauce to coat. It is best to work quickly, without interruption.

Serve hot, with three nuggets on each small dish. Eat immediately. Does not keep.

VARIATION: Instead of coating nuggets with ginger-soy sauce, mix together finely grated daikon radish and finely grated fresh ginger in the proportion of 5 parts daikon to 1 part ginger and serve as a garnish on top of the nuggets.

Mountain Yam and Mushroom Croquettes

Yamato Imo no Nichirin Age

大和芋の日輪揚げ

This dish was invented at the Sankō-in temple one day when a certain guest requested more and more food. There was not much left in the kitchen, and hasty improvisation was necessary. This dish was one result, and the response was enthusiastic. The guest in question turned out to be one of Japan's most famous food writers.

SERVES 4

1/2 lb (225 gm) mountain yam (Yamato imo *or any available variety), peeled and cut into 2-inch (5-cm) lengths*

1 *Tbsp sugar*
⅓ *tsp salt*
1 *large (or 2 small) dried* shiitake *mushrooms, reconstituted in tepid water, stems removed, and finely chopped*

FOR FLAVORING SHIITAKE

- 1 *tsp vegetable oil*
- 2 *Tbsps water* or dashi *(see page 81)*
- 1 *tsp sugar*
- 1 *tsp soy sauce*
- 1 *tsp saké*

1 *Tbsp flour*
2 *Tbsps water*
1 *cake freeze-dried tofu* (Kōya-dōfu), *finely grated* (**do not** *reconstitute)*
vegetable oil for deep-frying

Boil mountain yam until done and mash while hot in the same manner as in Mountain Yam Rolls, page 139. Add 1 Tbsp sugar and ⅓ tsp salt and mix well.

Place chopped *shiitake* mushroom in a small saucepan, add flavoring ingredients, and simmer over medium heat until liquid is reduced and flavor is absorbed, about 5 minutes.

Add *shiitake* mushroom to mashed mountain yam and mix well. Form into 4 oblong shapes about 2 inches (5 cm) long and 1 ¼ inches (3 cm) thick at the middle.

Place 1 Tbsp flour in a small bowl. Roll croquettes in the flour and set them aside. Then mix 2 Tbsps water with the flour. Roll croquettes in this flour-water mixture to coat, then roll them in the powdery, finely grated freeze-dried tofu to coat evenly. (There will be some freeze-dried tofu powder left over. It will keep indefinitely in the freezer and can be added to other batters and coatings of fried foods.) It is important to coat the mountain yam with the flour and flour-water batter before dipping in freeze-dried tofu powder. This forms a firm layer that contains the yam and keeps the croquettes from slowly disintegrating in the hot oil.

Heat oil to hot temperature (360°F/180°C) and fry croquettes until light gold—about 3 minutes apiece.

Serve hot, one croquette per person. Does not keep.

VARIATION—Deep-Fried "Sandwiches": If you have some of the freeze-dried tofu powder and fresh mountain yam left over, peel and finely grate the raw yam to form a sticky paste and mix a bit of this with freeze-dried tofu powder and a bit of water to form an elastic dough. Pat this dough out thinly and use it to sandwich some ingredient such as *nattō, konbu* kelp relish (*tsukudani*), walnuts, etc. Make small "sandwiches." Deep-fry them in medium-low temperature (330°F/165°C) oil until light gold. Serve 1 or 2 "sandwiches" per portion. Eat hot.

Ginger Tempura

Shōga no Tempura

生姜の天ぷら

This Sankō-in original is starkly simple and startlingly delicious. Fresh ginger acts as an appetizer, freshens the palate, and also warms the body. Good as an hors d'oeuvre or between courses of a heavy meal, or served with, say, Pumpkin Tempura (page 133).

SERVES 4

3 ounces (90 gm; 3 2 ½-in/6 ½-cm pieces) fresh ginger, peeled

BATTER

3 Tbsps flour
⅙ tsp salt
3 Tbsps water

vegetable oil for deep-frying
salt

Cut ginger into medium-thin rounds across the fiber grain, then cut rounds into fine julienne strips.

Mix batter well. Place ginger in batter and toss to coat well.

Heat oil to medium temperature (340°F/170°C) and deep-fry ginger in 4 portions. Drain and sprinkle with salt.

Serve hot! Does not keep.

Eggplant and Shimeji Mushrooms

Nasu to Shimeji no Takimono

なすとしめじの炊きもの

A dish of early autumn, when the eggplant and mushroom seasons overlap. This Sankō-in original is yet another startlingly simple yet delicious dish—one that should be eaten hot as soon as possible to savor the freshness of the vegetables, as compared to dishes heavily seasoned by condiments (such as soy sauce), which may have to mature a bit for the flavor to be at its peak.

SERVES 4

2 *4-inch (10-cm) eggplants, peeled, cut into quarters, then cut into ⅛-inch (½-cm) thick slices lengthwise (this is roughly ½ lb; use the equivalent weight of a large eggplant)*

$^1/_4$ lb (115 gm) shimeji *(or other) mushrooms, washed and dirty stem bases removed*
1 tsp vegetable oil
2 Tbsps saké
1 tsp soy sauce
$^1/_6$ tsp salt

Place eggplant and *shimeji* mushrooms in a medium-sized saucepan and add remaining ingredients. Place on medium-high heat, cover pan, and bring to a boil. Reduce heat to medium, mix ingredients well, and simmer, covered, 3 minutes. Do not overcook.

Best served hot (in individual dishes or family style in one bowl), though it may be eaten at room temperature as well. Keeps 3 days refrigerated.

Saké-Braised Enokidake Mushrooms

Enokidake no Saké-Iri
えのき茸の酒入り

This simple dish is a Sankō-in original and is a delicious accompaniment to saké.

SERVES 4

2 bunches enokidake *mushrooms (sometimes packaged as* enok *in the U.S.), spongy bottoms removed and cut in half crosswise*
2 Tbsps saké
2 pinches salt
$^1/_2$ tsp soy sauce
$^1/_2$ tsp vegetable oil

Place all ingredients in a medium-sized saucepan over medium heat. Cook, stirring constantly, until done, about 2–3 minutes.

Eat hot. Does not keep.

Braised Shiitake Mushrooms

Hoshi-Shiitake no Iri-Ni
干し椎茸の炒り煮

This Donke-in dish is a good companion to other foods and is also delicious eaten alone as an hors d'oeuvre. It is guest food and part of Buddhist altar offerings. Here the recipe calls for whole mushrooms, but it can also be made with sliced *shiitake.* Excellent with rice.

SERVES 4

1 tsp vegetable oil
12 medium-sized dried shiitake *mushrooms, reconstituted in tepid water and stems cut off*
1 Tbsp saké
1 Tbsp soy sauce

Place oil in a small frypan or saucepan over medium heat. Add mushrooms and sauté on both sides for a total of 3 minutes. Add saké and soy sauce and stir-fry 30 seconds (15 seconds on each side).

Serve hot or at room temperature. Keeps 1 week.

Autumn Leaves

Fukiyose

ふき寄せ

Chisen Nikō (fourteenth century), the grandmother of Shogun Ashikaga Yoshimichi, founded the Donke-in temple in about 1349. The anniversary of her death on November 24 is a special occasion at the nunnery, and this dish is one of the special foods that appear at this time. It represents a garden in late autumn. Each ingredient is independently flavored, which involves a small amount of fuss, but the result is worth it.

SERVES 4

1/3 lb (150 gm) burdock root (gobō), *scrubbed with a stiff brush*

FOR FLAVORING BURDOCK

- *2 cups water or* dashi *(see page 81)*
- *2 Tbsps saké*
- *2/3 tsp salt*
- *1 1/2 Tbsps sugar*
- *1 Tbsp soy sauce*

8 chestnuts, shelled and peeled

FOR FLAVORING CHESTNUTS

- *1 1/2 cups water*
- *1 Tbsp sugar*

1/2 tsp salt
2 Tbsps whiskey or saké
12 ginkgo nuts, shelled and peeled (see page 148)
FOR FLAVORING GINKGO NUTS
3 Tbsps water
2 tsps sugar
pinch salt
1 1/2-inch (4-cm) length small carrot, scraped well
FOR FLAVORING CARROT
3 Tbsps water
2 tsps sugar
pinch salt
12 1/8-inch (1/2-cm) slices millet gluten (awa-fu) *(optional)*
FOR FLAVORING MILLET GLUTEN
3 Tbsps water
2 tsps sugar
pinch salt
1 medium turnip, peeled (traditionally aotsuto-fu*—a green-colored gluten preparation—is used)*
FOR FLAVORING TURNIP
3 Tbsps water
2 tsps sugar
pinch salt
1–2 drops green food coloring

Cut burdock in 2-inch (5-cm) lengths, then cut each piece lengthwise into julienne strips. Place in water immediately upon cutting to avoid discoloration. Drain. Simmer burdock with water to cover over medium heat until soft, about 20 minutes. Drain and discard cooking water.

Simmer cooked burdock in its flavoring liquid, with pot lid ajar, over medium heat until flavor strengthens, about 25 minutes. Let cool in pot liquor so flavor is absorbed.

Place chestnuts in saucepan with water to cover and simmer over medium heat until nuts just *start* to get soft. Do not cook fully. The time varies with size of chestnuts. Drain. Discard cooking water.

Simmer partially cooked chestnuts in their flavoring liquid over medium-low heat until completely cooked. Test with toothpick to see if nuts are cooked through. Let cool in pot liquor so flavor is absorbed.

Simmer ginkgo nuts 3 minutes in their flavoring liquid, then cool in pot liquor so flavor is absorbed.

Notch the length of carrot to form a leaf shape when sliced, then cut into 1/8-inch (1/2-cm) slices. (There are small metal cutters in Japan that are used to cut maple and other leaf shapes from vegetable slices.) Any leaf shape will do, but this is an autumn dish, so the maple leaf is most fitting. There should be 12 small carrot "leaves."

Cut each millet gluten (*awa-fu*) slice into a leaf shape (or sculpt a length of millet gluten first, then slice).

Cut turnip in the same manner as carrot (using a different leaf shape), then cut into 12 ⅛-inch (½-cm) leaf-shaped slices. A second turnip may be required. (The *aotsuto-fu* comes already formed—the slices will be leaf-shaped.)

The three leaf shapes—carrot, millet gluten, and turnip (or *aotsuto-fu*, if available, which it probably is not)—must be flavor-simmered independently, although the content of the flavoring liquid is the same for each—3 Tbsps water, 1 tsp sugar, and a pinch of salt. Fresh flavoring liquid should be made for each ingredient.

Simmer carrot for 3 minutes and let cool in its pot liquor. The millet gluten needs only 2 minutes of simmering before being allowed to cool. The turnip leaf shapes should be simmered about 3 minutes, then cool and add a drop or two of green food coloring to dye the leaves. This touch of green is an integral part of the visual effect of this festive dish.

Place 1 chestnut at either side of each individual dish. Fill space between chestnuts with burdock, add a few "leaves" in three colors, then add more burdock. Place remaining "leaves" on the burdock then add 3 ginkgo nuts to balance the composition. Each serving should contain 2 chestnuts; 3 carrot, 3 millet gluten, 3 green-dyed turnip "leaves"; 3 ginkgo nuts; and burdock (which represents dried pine needles).

Keeps 3 days refrigerated.

Ginkgo Nuts

Iri Ginnan

炒りぎんなん

There is a saying that if you eat more than seven ginkgo nuts, you will become a little funny in the head. This recipe is the simplest and most delicious way of preparing these beautifully colored fresh nuts and it will tempt you to challenge the validity of the bit of folklore just cited.

SERVES 4

1 tsp vegetable oil
28 fresh ginkgo nuts, shelled, but inner skin left intact
2 generous pinches salt

Place oil in medium-sized frypan over medium heat. Add nuts and stir-fry for about 4 minutes. The skins will split and come off some of the nuts, and the nuts will turn a vivid, soft green color. Remove from heat, then remove all skins with chopsticks or your fingers (the nuts are hot!). This should be easy, but is fussy. Sprinkle 2 pinches salt over nuts.

Serve 7 nuts per portion in tiny dishes. Eat hot!

Ginkgo Nuts in Thick Sauce

Ginnan no Kuzutoji
ぎんなんの葛とじ

A light-catching translucent sauce embraces the gentle green of the ginkgo nuts.

SERVES 4

28 fresh ginkgo nuts, shelled, but inner skin left intact

SAUCE

- *1/3 cup water*
- *3 pinches salt*
- *2 tsps sugar*
- *1 1/2 Tbsps potato starch* (katakuriko) *dissolved in 2 Tbsps water (2 1/4 Tbsps cornstarch may be substituted, but the effect and flavor are not as good)*

Place ginkgo nuts in water to cover in a small saucepan. Bring quickly to a boil, reduce heat to medium or medium-low, then press and stir nuts with the back of a slotted spoon or wire-mesh skimmer. The inner skins will loosen and come off, and the nuts will turn a delicate jade green, somewhat cloudier than when they are stir-fried in oil as in the preceding recipe. Cooking time is about 5 minutes. Remove skins with chopsticks, fingers, or by rubbing nuts in a clean kitchen towel. If the skin is very stubborn, discard the nut—it is probably bad.

Place sauce ingredients in a small saucepan over medium heat and stir until thick. Drops formed when chopsticks are lifted from sauce should hang and not fall immediately. Add nuts.

Serve hot, with 7 nuts per portion and some sauce in small dishes. Does not keep.

Deep-Fried Ginkgo Nut Rolls

Ginnan no Yuba-Maki Age
ぎんなんの湯葉巻き揚げ

This simple dish combines the protein of *yuba* and the delicate flavor of ginkgo nuts. An excellent hors d'oeuvre.

SERVES 4

4 sheets dried yuba
32 ginkgo nuts, shelled and skins removed (see preceding recipe)
vegetable oil for deep-frying
salt

Reconstitute *yuba* by quickly submerging each sheet in cold water then letting drain and soften on a clean kitchen towel.

Place a *yuba* sheet with long side toward you. Arrange about 8 ginkgo nuts in a row about 3/8 inch (1 cm) from near edge of *yuba*. Roll once, then add a bamboo skewer to stabilize the roll. Do not skewer the roll, just put in a skewer and roll once more, then remove skewer from one end of roll. Tuck in ends of roll so nuts do not fall out, then finish rolling. Repeat, making 3 more rolls.

Heat oil to medium temperature (340°F/170°C) and deep-fry each roll until color deepens—about 20 seconds at most. Sprinkle with salt.

Serve hot; can be enjoyed at room temperature, but flavor is best when hot.

Chestnut, Persimmon, and Ginkgo Nut Tempura

Kuri to Kaki to Ginnan no Tempura

栗と柿とぎんなんの天ぷら

This autumn feast is an original Sankō-in recipe, combining bright flavors and colors.

SERVES 4

BATTER

5 Tbsps flour
4 Tbsps water
1/3 tsp salt

vegetable oil for deep-frying
8 chestnuts, boiled, then shelled and skins cut off
12 1-inch (2 1/2-cm) slices firm ripe Japanese persimmon, peeled and cut into wedges
24 fresh ginkgo nuts, shelled and skins removed (see page 148); 3 nuts skewered on 1 toothpick

Mix batter well, but do not beat it.

Heat oil to medium temperature (340°F/170°C).

Delicate things should be deep-fried last, so the order of frying is chestnuts, persimmon, then ginkgo nuts. Drain on a rack or absorbent paper.

Coat chestnuts with batter and deep-fry one at a time until a light gold—about 1 minute.

Batter-coat each persimmon slice and deep-fry one at a time for 1 minute.

Coat skewered ginkgo nuts with batter and deep-fry for 10 seconds.

Attractively arrange individual servings of 2 chestnuts, 3 persimmon slices, and 2 skewers of ginkgo nuts on each small plate or dish with a sprig of green leaves from your garden. Serve hot! Does not keep.

Persimmons in Saké Sauce

Kaki no Saké Kuzutoji

柿の酒葛とじ

This simple preparation of a chilled fruit and a warm sauce is one of the recipes created while this book was being written. It is a proper *shōjin* dish and shows interesting contrasts between texture, flavor, and temperature. The same concept could be adapted to other fruits and liquors.

SERVES 4

SAUCE

1 cup saké
1 Tbsp potato starch (katakuriko) *dissolved in 1 Tbsp water (cornstarch does not substitute well)*

2 firm ripe Japanese persimmons, peeled and well chilled in refrigerator, each cut into eighths

Simmer saké until all alcohol has been given off. Add potato starch mixture (make sure there are no lumps) and stir constantly until thickened. It should be relatively runny.

Place 4 slices (1/2 persimmon) attractively on each individual small dish and top with sauce. Eat immediately!

Pine Cones

Matsukasa

まつかさ

Before the commuter train station was completed about 10 minutes' walk from the Sankō-in, the temple area was as quiet and isolated as Tibet. At that time, in autumn one could hear odd popping sounds coming from some parts of the temple grounds. The little cones of the red pines had dried and were opening up percussively. In this event was born the idea for this dish. The ingredients are just tofu and *shiitake* mushrooms, and the result is amazingly delicious. The commuter train made the area a convenient place to live, so houses and apartments surround the temple today. The quiet that allows one to hear pine cones popping open is part of the past.

SERVES 4

1 cake regular tofu

3 large dried shiitake *mushrooms, reconstituted in tepid water, stems cut off, and finely chopped*

FOR FLAVORING SHIITAKE

1 tsp vegetable oil

2 tsps soy sauce

1/2 tsp sugar

vegetable oil for deep-frying

GINGER-SOY SAUCE

1 part fresh ginger juice

2 parts soy sauce

Place tofu in a medium-sized saucepan with water to cover. Bring to a boil over medium heat and simmer 1 minute. Drain. Wrap tofu in a clean kitchen towel, place on cutting board, and weight with about 1 pound (450 gm) for 45 minutes.

Pour 1 tsp vegetable oil in small pan. Add chopped *shiitake* mushrooms and stir-fry about 30 seconds. Add the soy sauce and sugar and stir-fry until liquid is absorbed—about 1 minute.

Place pressed tofu in a bowl and mash with your hand, leaving some small lumps. Add flavored *shiitake* mushroom and mix gently by hand.

Heat oil to medium temperature (340°F/170°C) over medium heat.

Form tofu-*shiitake* mixture into 12 small pine-cone shapes about 1 1/2–2 inches (4–5 cm) long and weighing about 1 ounce (30 gm) each. Deep-fry until golden brown. Drain on rack or absorbent paper.

Mix ginger-soy sauce. Eat hot! Dip one side into ginger-soy sauce before serving, or serve it as a dip accompanying the pine cones. Serve in individual dishes or family style on one plate. Decorate serving with pine needles.

Vinegared Gourd Ribbons

Kampyō no Sunomono

干ぴょうの酢のもの

Gourd (*kampyō*) shaved into ribbons is a dried food that keeps a long time. It was developed by mountain farmers who lacked fresh vegetables in winter. The Enshō-ji temple, a nunnery founded in the seventeenth century by a daughter of Emperor Gomizuno-o, is located in the mountains of Nara Prefecture and specializes in dishes featuring gourd ribbons. This is one such dish from that temple.

SERVES 6

1-ounce (about 35-gm) package dried gourd ribbons (kampyō)

SWEET VINEGAR

4 Tbsps rice vinegar

4 tsps sugar

1 tsp salt

1/3 tsp soy sauce

Scrub the dried gourd ribbons well in cold water (the way you would scrub socks or a spot out of a shirt) for about 1 minute. Rinse well, then let them stand in tepid or cold water until fully reconstituted—about 5 minutes or so. Drain in colander for about 30 minutes, then cut into 4 1/2-inch (12-cm) lengths and tie a knot in the middle of each.

Mix sweet vinegar, add knotted gourd ribbons, and let stand 30 minutes. Eat at room temperature or chilled. Keeps 1 week refrigerated.

Note: Reconstituted gourd ribbons (not vinegared) may be cut into 1 1/2-inch (4-cm) pieces and mixed with sesame dressing (*goma ae*; page 113), walnut dressing (*kurumi ae*; page 176), or sesame-miso (*goma*-miso; page 129) as well as used in salads. They are also very convenient for tying rolls of various kinds because they are relatively strong and can be eaten.

Lightly Pickled Gourd Ribbons

Kampyō to Konbu no Sunomono

干ぴょうと昆布の酢のもの

The sweetness of *konbu* kelp is transmitted to gourd ribbons in this decorative and light saladlike pickle. This is a food for special occasions, to be served to close friends and people who really enjoy food.

special equipment: 2 shallow wooden, plastic, or stainless steel pans; a convenient size is 8×6 1/2×1 1/4 inches (20×16×3 cm)

1-ounce (about 35-gm) package dried gourd ribbons (kampyō)

dried konbu *kelp*

rice vinegar

Gourd ribbons come in various widths, and the amount of *konbu* kelp and rice vinegar required depends on the width of the gourd ribbon and the size of the container you use. Therefore, only the simple principles of this pickle will be given here, and you can make any amount you like.

Scrub the dried gourd ribbons well in cold water (the way you would scrub socks or a spot out of a shirt) for about 1 minute. Rinse well, then let them rest in tepid water until fully expanded—about 5 minutes. Drain in colander for about 30 minutes. Stretch ribbons on cutting board and cut in lengths just slightly shorter than the width of your container.

Cut dried *konbu* kelp with scissors to fit the width or the length of the container, covering the entire bottom of the container with it.

Cover the *konbu* completely with lengths of gourd ribbon, taking care not to overlap ribbons.

Dip your fingers into vinegar and sprinkle about 1/2 tsp over the gourd ribbon. This seems a very small amount, but is correct—do not use too much vinegar.

Repeat this process for as many *konbu* kelp-gourd ribbon-and-vinegar layers as you like. The top layer should be *konbu.*

Place another container on the last layer (over plastic wrap, if container is metal) and add a 2-lb (1-kg) weight—a thick pot or bowl filled with water is convenient. Let rest in a cool, dark place 3 days.

Only gourd ribbon is eaten. (Reserve *konbu* for another use, such as the miso pickles described below.)

Serve in an attractive manner (see sketch for example). Eat pickled gourd ribbon at room temperature, either as is or with lemon-soy sauce (4 parts soy sauce; 1 part lemon juice).

MISO-PICKLED VINEGARED KONBU KELP

Place the *konbu* kelp used in this recipe in miso of your preference (sweet or salty) and let stand 3 days. Remove miso (use for soup or whatever), wash *konbu,* and cut into julienne strips. Sprinkle with a touch of red pepper (or black pepper) and serve as desired.

Sweet Potato, Pumpkin, and Mountain Yam Balls

Satsuma Imo, Kabocha, to Yamato Imo no Chakin Shibori

さつま芋，かぼちゃと大和芋の茶巾しぼり

This charming sweet potato confection is known to every Japanese household. Here pumpkin and mountain yam are prepared in the same manner to provide color and flavor contrasts. This is usually considered to be a sweet, but the sugar can be omitted and the plump little balls may accompany an entree or be a course by themselves.

MAKES 4 BALLS OF EACH TYPE

½ lb (225 gm) sweet potato, cut into ½-inch (1 ½-cm) rounds, skin left intact
1 ½ tsps sugar
⅙ tsp salt
½ lb (225 gm) pumpkin or winter squash, cut into 1-inch (2 ½-cm) pieces, skin left intact
1 ½ tsps sugar
⅙ tsp salt
1 Tbsp saké
½ lb (225 gm) mountain yam (the type known as Yamato imo *is best), peeled and cut into 1-inch (2 ½-cm) pieces*
2 Tbsps sugar
½ tsp salt

Simmer sweet potato in ample water over medium heat, with pot lid ajar, about 10 minutes. Drain, cool, and peel.

Mash cooked sweet potato in a bowl (or put through ricer or use food processor). Blend in 1 ½ tsps sugar and ⅙ tsp salt.

Simmer pumpkin or squash in enough water to cover over medium heat, with pot lid ajar until just cooked. The timing depends on tenderness and thickness of pumpkin or squash. Do not allow the vegetable to get mushy. Drain, cook, and peel.

Mash the pumpkin with sugar, salt, and saké in the same manner as the sweet potato.

Simmer the pieces of mountain yam in ample water over medium heat until cooked, about 15 minutes. Test with a skewer or toothpick. Cooked mountain yam and cooked potato have about the same consistency. Discard water and return saucepan to medium heat, shaking it until the water in the yam evaporates. Be careful not to scorch. Remove from heat and mash while hot. (Mountain yam types other than *Yamato imo* contain more moisture. If you are using such a yam, it may be necessary to keep the pot on lowest heat while yam is being mashed with sugar and salt.) A food processor is quick, but results in too smooth a puree. Cool.

Divide mashed sweet potato, pumpkin, and mountain yam each into 4 parts and form each part into a rough ball.

Wet and wring out a cloth napkin or handkerchief. Place a ball of sweet potato, etc. in the damp cloth, pinch cloth just above ball and shake ball gently like a bell (this settles the ball), then and twist until it is firmly squeezed. Unwrap and place finished shapes on a small plate. Rinse and squeeze out the napkin between balls.

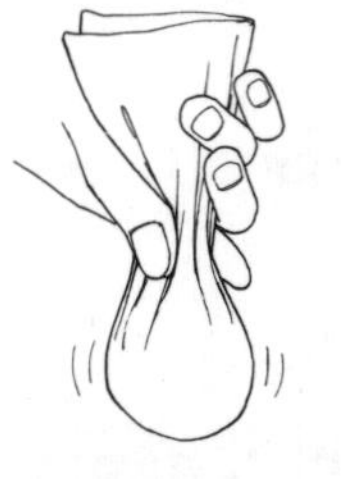

shake ball gently in cloth

twist cloth around ball

This process of squeezing a plump, chestnutlike ball from mashed sweet potato and the like is basically very simple, but it is a bit tricky at first to get attractive shapes, like the ones in the photograph on page 25. A little experimentation and practice is necessary.

Serve cold. Garnish serving plate or individual dishes with a touch of green from your garden. Eat with fingers, chopsticks, or dessert forks. Keeps 2–3 hours.

VARIATIONS: Mix about 1 1/2 tsps mashed sweet potato or mountain yam with 1/3 tsp powdered green tea (*matcha*). Place a dab of this green mixture near (not on) the top of a roughly formed ball, before squeezing in the napkin, then

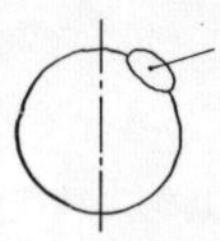

squeeze as described above. (If the balls are not sweet, *wasabi* horseradish powder can be used.) Powdered tea darkens in time, so the initial mixture will appear a little light. Sweet azuki bean paste (*anko*) may also be used in this manner to provide a touch of contrasting color.

The mountain yam is white and takes coloring well. A touch of red food coloring will produce a delicate pink.

The plump balls in the photograph on page 25 are two mountain yam that have been tinted pink and one pumpkin, showing color touches of green tea and azuki bean paste. There are many decorative ways to vary color and flavor of these confections. A touch of brandy or liquor added when the potato is mashed is delicious. Feel free to experiment.

Winter

Burdock with Spicy Sesame Dressing

Tataki Gobō

たたきごぼう

The Japanese name for this dish, which means "pounded burdock," is derived from pounding the burdock root to allow flavors to penetrate and to tenderize it. In this variation, however, it is just cut and boiled. *Sanshō* or black pepper brightens the sesame dressing in this Donke-in temple version of a dish known to all Japanese.

SERVES 4

1 burdock root (about 1 ½ ft/45 cm long), scrubbed well with a stiff brush
½ tsp whole dried sanshō *pods (or black peppercorns)*
4 Tbsps white sesame seeds, toasted (see page 65)
4 tsps soy sauce
1 tsp saké

Cut burdock in quarters lengthwise, then cut into 2-inch (5-cm) lengths. Immediately place in medium-sized saucepan with ample water to avoid discoloration. Bring to a boil quickly, reduce heat to medium, and simmer until tender—about 30 minutes. Drain and cool.

Parch *sanshō* pods (or peppercorns) in a dry frypan for about 2 minutes over medium heat. Place in *suribachi* grinding bowl or mortar with toasted sesame seeds and grind together to form a flaky paste.

Add soy sauce and saké to ground seed and mix well, adjusting flavor to taste. Add burdock and toss until well coated.

Flavor matures in 2–3 hours, but can be served immediately if necessary. Pile 7–10 pieces of burdock in a pyramid in each dish. Keeps 2 days refrigerated.

Arrow Feathers

Yabane

やばね

This simmered burdock dish is made in homes and temples alike. The cut pieces of burdock are arranged to resemble arrow feathers, which in Buddhist symbolism represent the arrow used to rout evil. This dish, considered to be one of the more "difficult" of the simmered foods in *shōjin* cooking, should be made slowly and carefully.

SERVES 4

8-inch (20-cm) length of burdock root, scrubbed well with a stiff brush
2 cups dashi *(see page 81)*
1 Tbsp sugar
2 tsps soy sauce
2 Tbsps saké
½ tsp salt

Cut burdock diagonally into 12 ½-inch (1 ½-cm) slices (excluding ends). Place in water immediately when cut to avoid discoloration. Discard water.

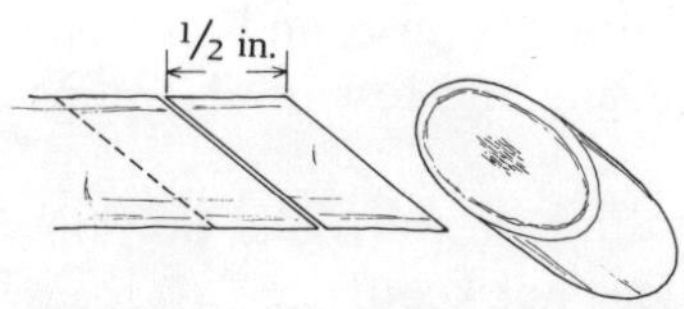

Place burdock in ample water, bring to a boil quickly, reduce heat to medium, and simmer until tender—about 20 minutes. Drain.

Place cooked burdock and remaining ingredients in a medium-sized saucepan and simmer over medium heat for 20 minutes. Remove burdock and reserve pot liquor.

Cut each slice of burdock through the center, then place on a plate, taking care to keep the two halves of each slice together. Pour pot liquor over burdock, and cool to room temperature. Flavor will be absorbed from the pot liquor as the vegetable cools. Reserve pot liquor for some other use.

When cool, turn each half of a slice 90° and place together to form a chevron shape. Three such chevrons are one portion. Keeps 1 week refrigerated.

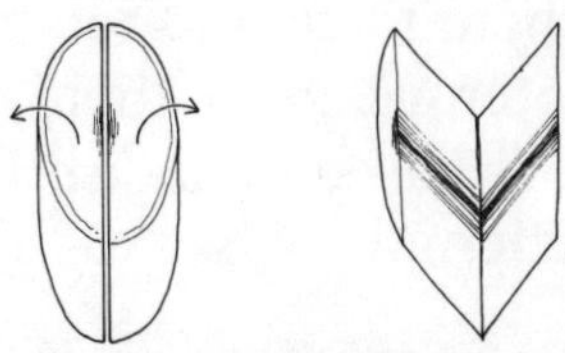

Crisp Turnip with Sesame-Miso Dressing

Kabura no Sankō-in Miso-Ae

かぶらの三光院味噌あえ

The delicate flavor of turnips harmonizes well with this dressing, which is a Sankō-in original. The dressing keeps well refrigerated.

SERVES 4

3 medium turnips (2 oz/60 gm each), trimmed and peeled
1 tsp salt

SESAME-MISO DRESSING

3 Tbsps white sesame seeds, toasted and ground (see page 65)
1 1/2 Tbsps sweet white Kyoto (saikyō) *miso*
1 Tbsp saké
1/2 tsp basic Japanese mustard mix (see page 51)

Cut turnips into julienne strips by first cutting crosswise into thin (1/8-inch/1/2-cm) rounds, then stacking rounds and cutting into strips. Add 1 tsp salt and toss to coat thoroughly. Let stand for about 20 minutes.

Rinse salt from turnips and gently but firmly squeeze out water. Turnip slivers should be slightly limp.

Mix the freshly ground sesame, miso, and saké. Add Japanese mustard and blend. Add turnips to dressing and toss until turnips are evenly coated with dressing.

Serve at room temperature in individual portions or family style in one bowl. Eat immediately; does not keep.

VARIATIONS: Just before serving, add a dab of finely chopped or grated *yuzu* citron, lemon, or lime zest to the top of each serving. Mix before eating. Or, mix in a little lemon or lime juice before serving.

Turnips Above and Below

Kabura no Ohitashi

かぶらのおひたし

That turnips are delicious is proven by this simple recipe that utilizes both greens and bulbs. The natural flavor of turnips is preserved by allowing them to cool to room temperature slowly. Force-cooling in cold water will make them watery in flavor. This original Sankō-in recipe is based on a dish from Toyama Prefecture (there is an affiliate temple of Sankō-in in Takaoka, Toyama Prefecture).

SERVES 4

4 medium turnips (2 oz/60 gm each), with roots trimmed but greens left intact
soy sauce

Cut off greens about 1 inch (2 ½ cm) above bulb—either straight or at an angle—and reserve. Leave stem stubs attached to bulb. Trim skin from around base of stems and also any smashed or messy stubs. Take care to remove dirt and grit from between stem stubs, using a toothpick if necessary. This step is slightly fussy, but the nutritive value of the entire turnip is being retained, and the result is very attractive.

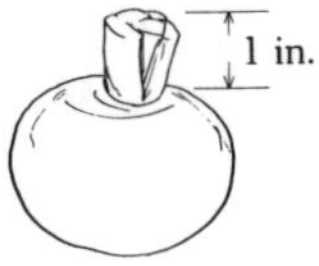

Place turnips in boiling water to cover and boil, uncovered, over medium-high heat until just barely cooked—about 15 minutes. Take care not to overcook, or the turnip will be mushy. Test with toothpick or skewer.

Remove turnips from water and allow to cool to room temperature naturally—about 1 hour. Do not force-cool in cold water.

Wash turnip greens well. Place an ample amount of the water from boiling the bulbs or fresh lightly salted water in a large pot and bring to a boil over medium-high heat. Add greens and parboil for 3–4 minutes, depending on tenderness of leaves. Remove from boiling water, spread in a colander or basket, and let cool naturally; do not plunge into cold water or flavor will be lost.

Cut each turnip lengthwise into ⅛-inch (½-cm) thick slices. Cut 3 boiled leaves (and stems) into ¾-inch (2-cm) lengths. (Reserve remainder of boiled leaves for some other use.)

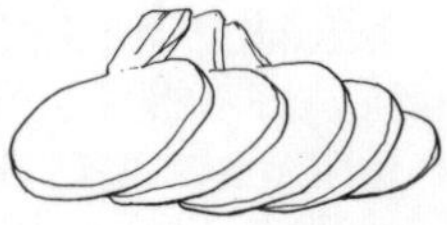

Arrange 1 sliced turnip and a small mound of chopped leaves attractively on each small individual dish. Pour on about 1 tsp soy sauce. Serve at room temperature or chilled. Eat within 3 hours.

Turnip Chrysanthemums

Kikka Kabura no Sunomono

菊花かぶらの酢のもの

This delightful way of cutting and serving turnips is not limited to temple cooking, but is a part of Japanese cuisine in general. Good also with a touch of soy sauce.

SERVES 4

2 medium (2 oz/60 gm) turnips or 4 tiny turnips, tops removed, peeled
1 tsp salt
SWEET VINEGAR
3 Tbsps rice vinegar
1 Tbsp sugar
1/6 tsp salt
red pepper

Cut about 1/8 inch (1/2 cm) from tops of turnips so that they are stable on the cutting board. Place a disposable wooden chopstick on either side of a turnip to prevent the knife from cutting all the way through. Slice turnip as finely as

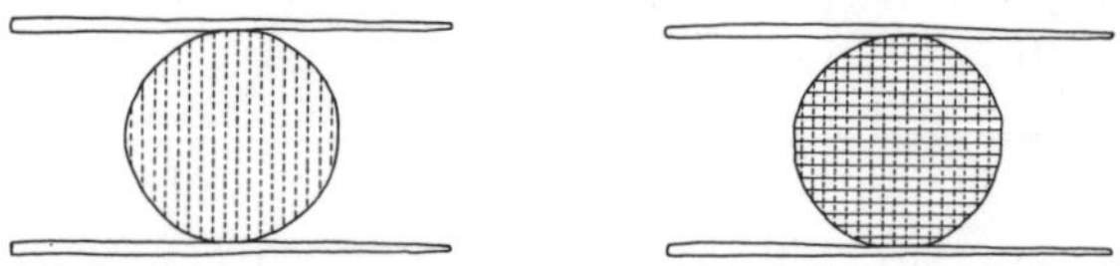

possible, then rotate turnip 90° and again slice as finely as you can. A very sharp knife is important—a dull knife may spread butter well, but will not make chrysanthemums out of turnips. Repeat process for each turnip.

Place prepared turnips in a medium-sized bowl and sprinkle with 1 tsp salt. Bounce and jiggle the bowl vigorously to coat turnips with salt (turnips can bounce around a bit without breaking up) and let stand 10 minutes. Rinse thoroughly to remove salt and drain well. Return to bowl.

Mix sweet vinegar and stir until sugar dissolves. Pour vinegar over turnips. Invert each turnip and press gently in the liquid to allow the vinegar to come in contact with all surfaces. Let turnips stand in vinegar 5 minutes.

If using medium-sized turnips, place each one on a cutting board and break in half carefully with the fingers. Disarrange the turnip "petals" a bit to resemble a chrysanthemum.

Place each turnip chrysanthemum in a small dish and decorate with fresh green leaves from the garden (flowering chrysanthemum leaves are excellent). Sprinkle a touch of coarse red pepper into the center of each. Serve at room temperature or chilled. Keeps 2–3 days refrigerated.

Steamed Savory Cup

Kabura no Chawan Mushi

かぶらの茶碗むし

This hearty, warming dish, which emphasizes the brightness and sweetness of turnips, is one of the "greats" of *shōjin* cooking and one of the stars of this book. Unless you have an immense steamer, this dish is best made for intimate dinners.

SERVES 4

special equipment: 4 large handleless Japanese teacups (*yunomi*) or the special lidded cups made for *chawan-mushi*; the capacity should be about 5/6 cup (200 mL)

4 generous Tbsps freshly cooked or leftover short-grain rice

4 small (1 1/2 oz/50 gm) unpeeled turnips, finely grated and drained (not squeezed) of excess liquid; a total of 8 Tbsps grated turnip is needed

4 medium-sized fresh shiitake *mushrooms, cut into thirds*

12 small snow peas, parboiled

12 carrot slices, cut into maple leaves or any simple shape, parboiled (cut slices in half if you like)

12 ginkgo nuts, shelled and skins removed (see page 148)

2 chestnuts, shelled, skins removed, and cut in half

1 tsp vegetable oil (or 4 small pieces Deep-Fried Dried Yuba *(page 195)*

THICK SAUCE

1 2/3 cups konbu dashi *(see page 81)*

1/2 tsp salt

1 tsp soy sauce

1 Tbsp saké

2 Tbsps potato starch (katakuriko) *dissolved in 2 Tbsps water (cornstarch is not a substitute)*

basic wasabi *horseradish mix (see page 57)*

Place rice on chopping board and chop until grains are roughly cut into thirds. Mix with grated turnip. The ratio of turnip to rice here is 2:1, but you may vary this to taste. Some people like equal amounts of turnip and rice.

In each cup, place 3 pieces *shiitake* mushroom; 3 parboiled snow peas; 3 slices carrot (or 6 half-slices); 3 ginkgo nuts; 1 piece chestnut; and 1/4 tsp vegetable oil (or a piece of Deep-Fried Dried *Yuba*, page 195). A small amount of oil is important—a bit of deep-fried *Rōbai* I (page 192) or a deep-fried

Piquant Waterchestnut Ball (page 166) may also be used in place of oil or deep-fried *yuba.*

Spoon 2 ½ Tbsps turnip-rice mixture over these ingredients in each cup. Press down the turnip-rice mixture evenly and firmly with the fingertips to fill the bottom of the cup. Do this thoroughly, taking about 1 minute per cup.

Heat steamer. Place cups in hot steamer, covering them with a clean kitchen towel so that water does not drip in during steaming. Cover steamer, and steam 10 minutes.

While the steaming proceeds, place all the thick sauce ingredients except the potato starch in a small saucepan. Bring to a boil over medium heat, then dribble in the starch-water mixture and cook, stirring until thick and a clear, light amber in color. If you think the mixture is thickening too quickly, reduce the heat to medium-low.

Spoon or ladle ¼ of the thick sauce into each cup in the steamer, cover cups again with towel, replace steamer lid, and steam another 5 minutes.

Remove cups from steamer, place a dab of prepared *wasabi* horseradish in the middle of each, and serve hot. If a little time must elapse before eating, place lids on the cups. Improvise if you like. If the cups are rustic, small rounds of wood make attractive lids. Plastic or lacquered lids for porcelain cups should be available in Japanese gift shops.

Eat hot (!) with spoons or chopsticks. Mix ingredients well before eating.

Grilled Saké Lees

Saké Kasu no Tsuke-Yaki

酒粕のつけ焼き

Saké is brewed in winter, and this is the season when fresh *saké kasu*—the lees of saké brewing—is available. *Saké kasu* freezes well and keeps indefinitely. This minute yet hearty snack for winter afternoons is a Donke-in temple dish and is considered gourmet food, if really fine *saké kasu* is available.

SERVES 4

FLAVOR DIP

1 Tbsp saké
⅓ tsp soy sauce
pinch salt
pinch sugar

12 *½×2-inch (1 ½×5-cm) rectangles saké lees* (saké kasu; *this is usually packaged in pressed sheets about ⅛-inch [½ cm] thick)*

Mix flavor dip.

Grill *saké kasu* rectangles over a gas flame or under the broiler, keeping pieces as close to flame as possible, until nicely spotted on both sides.

Dip quickly into flavor dip and serve immediately, 3 pieces per portion. Keeps well, but flavor is best when hot.

Sweet Saké (nonalcoholic)

Saké Kasu no Ama-Zaké
酒粕の甘酒

In December there is a rigorous Zen ritual and meditation. This drink warms and cheers on such winter nights, and it nourishes as well. The ginger gives it added zest and also acts to heat the body.

SERVES 4–6

1/4 lb (115 gm) saké lees (saké kasu)
2 1/2 cups water
4 Tbsps sugar
2 citrus leaves, crumbled (optional) or a bit of orange zest
4 tsps ginger juice

Soak the saké lees in the water for a few hours or overnight, then whirr in processor or blender until smooth. (Or, after soaking, mash the lees in the water with a spoon, squeezing away any lumps by hand.) The saké lees can be made into a drink without soaking, but there will be stubborn lumps that will resist dissolving.

Heat the mixture over low heat, stirring constantly. Add sugar and stir until dissolved. Add citrus leaves (if available), crumbling them to release the aroma, or use a bit of orange zest. Add ginger juice and serve immediately in tall cups. Drink hot.

This recipe is for a rather thick, hearty mixture. You can thin this as you wish by increasing the amount of water.

Keeps 1 week.

Carrots in Sweet Saké

Ninjin no Saké Kasu Ni
人参の酒粕煮

In this Sankō-in original the smell of carrots is reduced and the sweetness is enhanced—an everyday dish that should appeal even to those who do not like carrots.

SERVES 4

1 ounce (30 gm; about 1/6 cup) saké lees (saké kasu)
1/2 cup water
1/2 lb (225 gm) carrots, scraped and cut into 1/8-inch (1/2-cm) thick half-moons
5 Tbsps saké
2 Tbsps sweet white Kyoto (saikyō) *miso*
1 slice fresh ginger

Soak saké lees in 1/2 cup water for a few hours or overnight and puree (a food processor or blender makes this very easy) until there are no lumps.

Place carrot in ample water in a saucepan and bring to a boil quickly. Reduce heat to medium and simmer until carrot is just cooked. Do not overcook. Plunge carrot slices in cold water to cool, then drain.

Place carrot and 5 Tbsps saké in a saucepan over low heat. Add saké lees, miso, and ginger slice and stir well. Heat only until carrot is warm throughout.

Serve hot or at room temperature in individual dishes or family style in one bowl. The flavor improves with time. Keeps about 5 days refrigerated.

Vinegared Chinese Cabbage

Hakusai no Nihaizu

白菜の二杯酢

This dish resembles a light, bright sauerkraut. It is everyday fare, not guest food, at the Donke-in temple. For some reason Chinese cabbage is almost not present in Donke-in cooking, perhaps because this vegetable was not used much in Kyoto in times past. This dish is also good with a light sprinkling of small dried red chili pepper seeded and cut into rings.

SERVES 4

3 Chinese cabbage (hakusai) *leaves*

FLAVOR VINEGAR
- *2 Tbsps rice vinegar*
- *1/6 tsp salt*
- *4 drops soy sauce*
- *1/2 tsp sugar*

The Chinese cabbage leaves should be from just inside the outer covering and measure about 6×10 inches (15×25 cm). Use the equivalent amount from a small head, if heads this size are not available. (American markets tend to sell smaller heads of Chinese cabbage than those in Japan.)

Trim off ragged edges of leaves and cut each leaf in half crosswise.

Bring water to a boil in a large saucepan. Remove from heat, add Chinese cabbage leaves, and let stand for 2 minutes. Drain.

Stack leaf halves and cut into julienne strips.

Mix flavor vinegar in a bowl. Add Chinese cabbage shreds and toss well. Let flavor mature 30 minutes.

Serve chilled or at room temperature in small dishes or in one bowl. Keeps 1 day.

Waterchestnut Chips

Kuwai no Usu-Age

くわいのうす揚げ

This luxurious nibble is often served together with Deep-Fried Dried *Yuba* (page 195) and makes beautiful harmony with saké.

SNACK

fresh waterchestnuts, peeled (canned waterchestnuts are not a good substitute)
vegetable oil for deep-frying
salt

Cut waterchestnuts crosswise into thin slices and pat dry. Let stand 30 minutes, then pat dry again if necessary.

Heat oil to low temperature (320°F/160°C). Fry a few slices at a time until very light gold (thin chips will color more quickly than thicker ones). Drain on absorbent paper. Sprinkle with salt.

Best eaten hot, but also good at room temperature. Keeps 1 month in airtight container.

VARIATION: Deep-fry fresh waterchestnuts, either thinly sliced or cut in thirds or halves, until light gold. Do not salt.

Deep-Fried Waterchestnut and Nori Squares

Kuwai no Iso-Age

くわいの磯揚げ

Fresh waterchestnuts usually appear around the New Year in Japan. Though canned waterchestnuts can be used, fresh ones have a sweeter and deeper flavor, which is brought out by deep-frying. A creation of the Donke-in temple. Excellent as an hors d'oeuvre.

MAKES 16 PIECES

vegetable oil for deep-frying
4 Tbsps peeled and finely grated fresh waterchestnuts
1 sheet nori *seaweed, cut into sixteenths*
salt

Heat oil to medium temperature (340°F/170°C).

Drain (do not squeeze) liquid from grated waterchestnut pulp, if necessary. Spread a 1/8-inch (1/2-cm) layer of grated waterchestnut on each piece of *nori* seaweed and immediately slip into the hot oil, *nori* side down. Fry about 4–5 pieces at a time until each is light gold, turning pieces in oil as necessary. Drain on rack or absorbent paper. Salt lightly.

Best eaten hot. A temple portion is 3 pieces; but it probably will be hard to restrain yourself (and others) from eating more. Does not keep.

Piquant Waterchestnut Balls

Kuwai Dango no Ama-Kara-Ni

くわい団子の甘辛煮

Because waterchestnut dishes are very special and luxurious, they are generally limited to the temples where a princess-abbess was in residence. Such dishes are not encountered in traditional Japanese home cooking. Unflavored fried balls may be used in the Steamed Savory Cup (page 161) instead of oil or deep-fried *yuba.* An excellent hors d'oeuvre.

SERVES 4

5 Tbsps peeled and finely grated fresh waterchestnuts, some moisture lightly pressed out (or use canned waterchestnuts)
vegetable oil for deep-frying
FOR FLAVORING BALLS
2 Tbsps saké
2 Tbsps soy sauce
1 Tbsp sugar

Form finely grated waterchestnut into 12 walnut-sized balls. It might be tricky at first to make nicely shaped spheres, but you will soon get the knack.

Heat oil to medium temperature (340°F/170°C) and deep-fry a few balls at a time until light gold. Drain on rack or absorbent paper.

Mix flavoring ingredients in a small saucepan and bring to a boil over medium heat. Add fried waterchestnut balls and shake pan to coat them with flavoring liquid.

Serve 3 balls on each small dish. Eat hot or at room temperature. The flavor at room temperature is different from that when hot—both are good. Keeps 1 week refrigerated.

Sweet Simmered Kumquats

Kinkan no Satō-Ni

きんかんの砂糖煮

In the Kannon Sutra (*Kannon-Gyō*), one of the most important of Japanese Buddhist sutras, there is a list of treasures that translates ". . . gold, silver, lapis lazuli, nacre, agate, coral, amber, pearl . . ." (*kin, gin, ruri, shako, menō, sango, kohaku, shinju*). Kumquats are *kinkan* in Japanese, the *kin* (gold) of this treasure list. This is thus a festive dish in every sense. The salt enlivens and deepens the kumquats' flavor.

SERVES 4

12 kumquats, pricked 2–3 times with a bamboo skewer (this keeps fruit from splitting open and shriveling)

FOR SIMMERING

1 1/4 cups water
5 Tbsps sugar
1/3 tsp salt
2 Tbsps saké

Place kumquats in water to cover and simmer over medium heat for 10 minutes to remove any harshness and bitterness. Drain and discard water.

Place kumquats and simmering ingredients in a small saucepan, bring to a boil over medium heat, and simmer 30 minutes, uncovered. Cool and let rest in pot liquor overnight.

Serve at room temperature, 3 kumquats per portion with 1 Tbsp pot liquor spooned over them.

Karamono

からもの

The daikon often used in Kyoto is spherical, whereas the common daikon in Tokyo is a long cylinder. The Kyoto variety is somewhat sweeter and cooks more quickly than the Tokyo type. This Kyoto temple dish was originally made with the spherical daikon, but since the Sankō-in is in Tokyo, the local daikon (the most common kind now) is used, and the cooking is long and slow. Daikon is enhanced by a little oil, and this radish and thin deep-fried tofu are a classical combination (see also page 88).

SERVES 4

4 1-inch (2 1/2-cm) slices peeled daikon radish, each slice cut in half
2 4-inch (10-cm) squares konbu *kelp*
6 1/2 cups water
1 sheet thin deep-fried tofu (usuage)
FOR SIMMERING
1 Tbsp soy sauce
1 tsp salt
3 Tbsps saké
1 tsp sugar
seven-flavors spice

Place daikon and *konbu* in a large saucepan with 6 1/2 cups water, cover pan, and bring to a boil over high heat. Reduce heat to medium and simmer until very tender (test by pricking it with a toothpick)—about 1 hour.

While the daikon is simmering, prepare the *usuage* by first pouring boiling water over the sheet to eliminate excess oil, then cut it crosswise into 3/8-inch (1-cm) strips.

Add simmering ingredients and *usuage* strips to the daikon and its pot liquor and simmer, uncovered, over medium heat for 30 minutes.

Place daikon pieces and *usuage* strips in medium-sized dishes, spooning about 2 Tbsps of the pot liquor over each serving.

Serve hot. Garnish with a dash or two of seven-flavors spice in the middle of each daikon piece. May be cooled and reheated. Keeps 3 days.

Note: The pot liquor remaining may be mixed with *okara* (tofu lees) and eaten or used to simmer vegetables such as burdock and carrots. It is delicious and versatile—do not hesitate to invent new uses.

Bright and Crunchy Daikon Rolls

Hari-Hari Daikon no Sunomono

はりはり大根の酢のもの

This dish originated in the rural countryside of Japan. It was not guest food, perhaps because it is so good that the farm family kept it for their own pleasure. Adopted as a temple food, it is one of the few *shōjin* dishes that allow the sun to do most of the "cooking." For some reason, people who ordinarily do not like vegetables or vinegar find this delicious. If *yuzu* citron is not available, use other citrus peel or strips of fresh ginger.

MAKES ABOUT 50 ROLLS

6-inch (15-cm) length of daikon radish, unpeeled

1 large yuzu *citron (or 2–3 lemons, 1 orange, 1/2 grapefruit, or a large knob of ginger)*

SWEET VINEGAR

6 Tbsps rice vinegar

2 Tbsps sugar

1/2 tsp salt

1/2 tsp soy sauce

Cut daikon into thin rounds; to get 50 rounds, the slices should be slightly less than 1/8 inch (1/2 cm) thick. Spread rounds on a flat basket or screen and dry in the sun for 3 days. Obviously, continuous sunny weather is needed for this. A conventional or microwave oven may be used, but the result is not as good as sun drying.

Peel the *yuzu* (or lemon) with a sharp knife as you would an apple. The width of the peel should be about 3/4 inch (2 cm). Cut the peel into strips about 1/8 inch (1/2 cm) thick. If using ginger, peel, slice into 1/16-inch (1/4-cm) thick rounds, and cut into 1/8-inch (1/2-cm) thick strips.

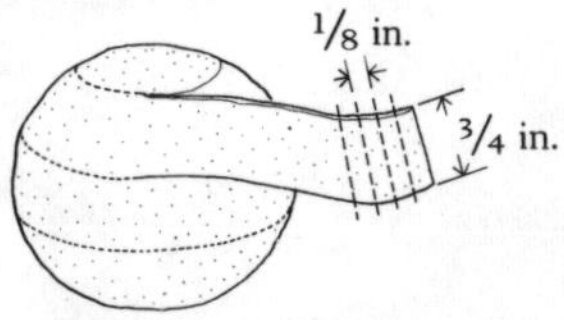

Place one strip of citrus peel (or ginger) on each daikon round near one edge and roll.

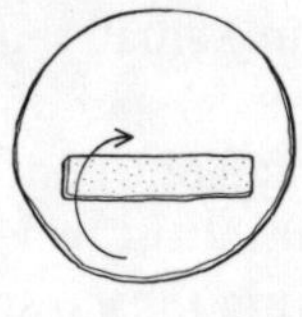

Thread a strong needle with white cotton thread (never use a synthetic fiber), tie both ends together so that the thread is double, and thread 7–8 rolls on each thread length so that the rolls do not open. Hang threaded rolls in sun and dry for 3 days.

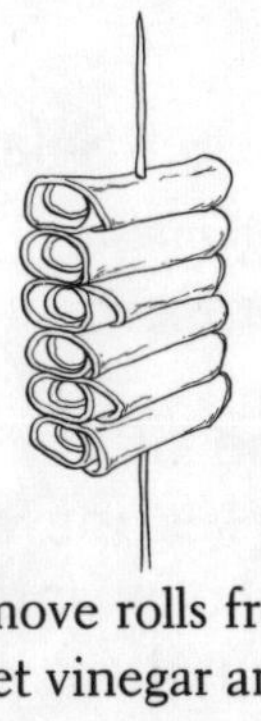

Mix the sweet vinegar. Remove rolls from thread, place in nonmetallic lidded container or jar. Add sweet vinegar and let stand overnight or 24 hours in a cold place or in refrigerator.

Serve 3 or 5 rolls per portion (or as many as you like—this is addictive food). Keeps 3 months refrigerated.

Daikon with Miso Sauce

Daikon Oden

大根おでん

This dish, made in temples and homes throughout Japan, is delicious, practical, simple, hot, and nourishing. In Kyoto the large turnip-shaped variety of daikon is traditional for this dish; in Tokyo, the long daikon. Best in winter, when daikon are plump and large.

SERVES 4

4 1 1/2-inch (4-cm) lengths of daikon radish, peeled

MISO SAUCE

4 Tbsps sweet white Kyoto (saikyō) *miso*
2 Tbsps saké
1 tsp sugar

Place daikon rounds in ample water (water from washing rice may be used), cover pot, and bring to boil over medium heat. Reduce heat to low and simmer until soft—about 20 minutes. Prick with toothpick to test for tenderness.

Blend miso sauce over low heat in a small saucepan. If daikon cools before serving, reheat it in its pot liquor.

Spread miso sauce on each hot daikon round and serve immediately. Optional garnishes are slivers of *yuzu* citron or lemon zest, a tiny sprinkle of sesame seeds or poppy seeds, a young *sanshō* sprig (*kinome*). Place garnishes in center of miso.

New Year Salad

Onamasu

おなます

This Donke-in version of one of the standard Japanese New Year's dishes is enriched by sesame and *shiitake* mushrooms. The dish also appears at Donke-in on November 24, during the special observances commemorating the death of the temple's founder.

SERVES 4

2 1 1/2-inch (4-cm) lengths daikon radish, peeled
1 tsp salt
1 1/2-inch (4-cm) length medium-sized carrot, scraped well
1/2 sheet thin deep-fried tofu (usuage; *pour boiling water over* usuage *before cutting in half lengthwise)*

FOR FLAVORING USUAGE
- *3 Tbsps* dashi *(see page 81)*
- *1 tsp sugar*
- *1 tsp soy sauce*

3 medium dried shiitake *mushrooms, reconstituted in tepid water and stems removed*

FOR FLAVORING SHIITAKE
- *2/3 tsp vegetable oil*
- *1 tsp sugar*
- *1 tsp soy sauce*

SESAME DRESSING
- *4 Tbsps white sesame seeds, toasted and ground (see page 65)*
- *1 Tbsp rice vinegar*
- *1/2 Tbsp soy sauce*
- *1 Tbsp sugar*

Cut daikon strips by first cutting pieces lengthwise into rectangles, then stacking rectangles and cutting into julienne strips (see page 62).

Place daikon strips in a bowl and toss with 1 tsp salt.

Cut carrot into julienne strips in the same manner as the daikon. You need about 2 Tbsps of carrot strips. More can be used, but the visual effect will suffer.

Add carrot strips to daikon and toss well.

Let stand about 10–15 minutes, until water appears in the bowl, then squeeze out moisture. Rinse away salt in cold water, then squeeze out water again.

While salted daikon-carrot mixture is emitting water, cut *usuage* crosswise into julienne strips about the same size as daikon strips. Place in small saucepan with its flavoring ingredients and simmer over medium heat for about 3 minutes, until liquid is almost all absorbed. Spread on plate to cool.

Cut *shiitake* mushrooms into julienne strips. Place in small saucepan or frypan with 2/3 tsp vegetable oil and stir-fry briefly. Add 1 tsp sugar and 1 tsp soy sauce and stir-fry until flavor is absorbed—about 2 minutes. Cool on plate.

Combine ground sesame, rice vinegar, soy sauce, and sugar and blend.

Add daikon-carrot mixture to sesame dressing and toss well. Add cooled *usuage* and *shiitake* mushroom and toss again.

Serve at room temperature in small individual dishes or family style. Keeps for 1 week to 10 days refrigerated. The flavor is best on the second or third day.

VARIATIONS: Snow peas, string beans, spinach stems, or stems of other greens, parboiled and cut into julienne strips, may be added.

Turnip and Apricot Salad

Kabura to Anzu no Sunomono

かぶらとあんずの酢のもの

Red and white (in combination) always signify a festive event in Japan. This Sankō-in original is guest food.

SERVES 4

1 Tbsp saké
4 large dried apricots, cut into fine julienne strips
2 medium-large (3 oz/90 gm) turnips, tops removed, peeled
½ tsp salt

SWEET VINEGAR
2 Tbsps rice vinegar
1 Tbsp sugar
generous pinch salt
1 Tbsp water

Pour 1 Tbsp saké over cut apricot and let stand 5 minutes.

Cut turnips in half lengthwise, slice them crosswise, then stack slices and cut into thin julienne strips, keeping the strips as long as possible.

Place turnip in a bowl and add ½ tsp salt. Toss to coat turnip strips with salt and let stand 5 minutes. Rinse well to remove salt and drain thoroughly. Return to bowl.

Mix sweet vinegar in a small bowl, making sure the sugar is dissolved.

With your fingers press out liquid from apricot against side of bowl and add apricot to turnip strips. (The apricot liquid is delicious—use it for something else or drink it.) Toss to mix.

Pour sweet vinegar over turnip-apricot mixture and toss well.

Can be eaten immediately, but best when flavor matures overnight. Serve chilled or at room temperature. Keeps 1 week.

Lotus Root in Plum Dressing

Renkon no Bainiku-Ae

れんこんの梅肉あえ

This original Sankō-in dish is another child of necessity—the sudden arrival of more guests than expected and no time to buy food. The kitchen was searched, and the narrow ends of the lotus root, which cannot be used in most dishes that utilize this vegetable, were sliced thinly and flavored with the pickled plums (*umeboshi*) that are always present in a Japanese larder. This recipe is based on one for lily root (*yuri-ne*) in plum dressing.

SERVES 4

1/4 lb (115 gm) medium lotus root (2 in/5 cm diameter), peeled and ends trimmed (place in lightly vinegared water to avoid discoloration)

FOR FLAVORING LOTUS ROOT

1 2/3 cups water

3 1/3 Tbsps rice vinegar

1 Tbsp pickled plum flesh (bainiku)

2 scant tsps sugar

1 tsp saké

Cut peeled lotus root in half lengthwise, then slice as thin as possible (less than 1/16 in/2 mm thick). Immediately put slices back in lightly vinegared water to avoid discoloration.

Place flavoring liquid in a medium-sized saucepan and bring to a boil quickly. Add lotus root slices and reduce heat to medium. Simmer, uncovered, until lotus root is just cooked but still crisp—about 5 minutes. Drain and cool.

Place the pickled plum flesh (pickled plums are *umeboshi*; the flesh is known as *bainiku*) in a *suribachi* grinding bowl or mortar and pound to a smooth puree with a pestle (or use food processor). Add sugar and saké, mixing well.

Add cooled lotus root slices to pickled plum puree and toss with a wooden spoon or other nonmetallic implement until all slices are coated. Serve in small dishes at room temperature. Keeps 3 days refrigerated.

VARIATION: *Enokidake* mushrooms, thick base cut off, parboiled for 4 minutes, then drained and cooled, make a good combination with plum dressing. About 6 ounces (180 gm; two standard Japanese packets) of *enokidake* make 4 servings as used in this book. See also Mountain Yam with Plum Dressing (page 138).

Lotus Root, Chrysanthemum Petal, and Raisin Salad

Renkon to Kigiku to Reizun no Sunomono

れんこんと黄菊とレーズンの酢のもの

The companionship of lotus root and vinegar is well demonstrated in this vinegared "salad," which is a pleasant meeting of East and West. Chrysanthemum petals are not mandatory—substitute nasturtium flowers, rose petals, or whatever will be attractive and enliven the dish.

SERVES 4

1/4 lb (115 gm) lotus root, peeled and ends trimmed (place in lightly vinegared water to avoid discoloration)
1/4 of 1/3-ounce (12-gm) package dried yellow chrysanthemum petals
1–2 Tbsps raisins (or other dried fruit, chopped)
DRESSING
3 Tbsps rice vinegar
1 Tbsp sugar
1/2 tsp salt
2 tsps saké
1 Tbsp water

Cut lotus root into very thin slices (cut root in half lengthwise if its diameter is large). Place lotus slices in a bowl and cover with ample boiling water. Let stand 1 minute. Drain and cool.

Reconstitute dried chrysanthemum petals in boiling water for 2–3 seconds. Plunge into cold water. Drain and gently squeeze out water.

Combine lotus root, chrysanthemum petals, and raisins (or chopped dried fruit) in a bowl.

Mix dressing, add to lotus root mixture, and toss well. The chrysanthemum petals may have a tendency to clump; the only solution for this is patient work with chopsticks and fingers to separate them.

Refrigerate overnight. Serve chilled or at room temperature in individual small dishes or family style in a single bowl. Keeps about 1 week refrigerated.

Sweet Bean-Stuffed Lotus Root

Renkon no Azuki-Zume

れんこんのあずき詰め

This sweet confection is possibly of Chinese origin. The sweet azuki bean paste (*anko*) filling complements the gentle flavor of the lightly vinegared lotus root. This temple guest dish is also used as a votive offering on the Buddhist altar.

SERVES 4

2 ½-inch (6 ½-cm) length of medium lotus root (2 in/5 cm diameter), peeled

FOR FLAVORING LOTUS ROOT

2 ½ cups water
2 Tbsps rice vinegar
3 Tbsps sugar
1 ½ tsps salt

1 cup boiled azuki beans (or use canned sweet bean paste [anko] *and eliminate sugar, salt, and the procedure for making the paste)*
1 cup sugar
½ tsp salt

Place lotus root and flavoring ingredients in a medium-sized saucepan and simmer, uncovered, over medium heat until lotus root is just cooked—about 15–20 minutes, depending on thickness of root.

Puree the boiled azuki beans in a blender, food processor, or through a sieve. Place puree in a small saucepan, add 1 cup sugar and ½ tsp salt, and simmer over low heat, stirring constantly (a wooden rice paddle is good) until liquid evaporates somewhat, the mixture becomes thicker, and it develops a deep sheen—about 10 minutes. The sweet bean paste will thicken more as it cools.

Place cooled bean paste on a plate or in a bowl. Place lotus root on the paste and push root into mixture repeatedly so that the bean paste is forced into and fills the holes in the root. Tap the root several times to eliminate air bubbles.

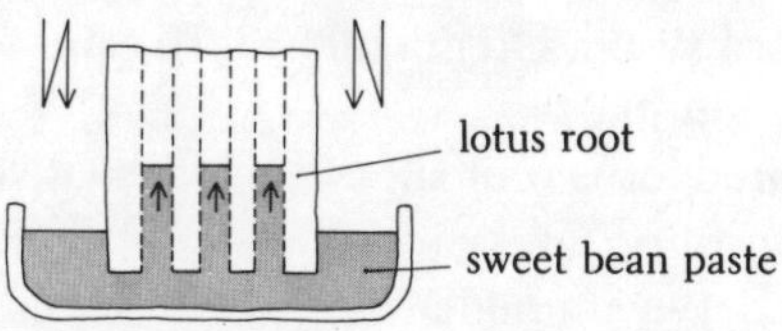

Refrigerate stuffed root 1 or 2 hours, then wipe or scrape off excess bean paste from ends of root. The sweet bean paste may emit some water.

Cut into 4 slices and serve each slice in a small dish. Keeps 2–3 days refrigerated.

Lotus Root with Lemon Syrup

Su-Renkon no Remon Shiropu-Kake

酢れんこんのレモンシロップかけ

The shape of the lotus root is shown to advantage in this dish. Sweet combines well with touches of sour here, and this subtle harmony is brightened by *yuzu* citron (or lemon or lime) zest.

SERVES 4

1/4 lb (115 gm) medium lotus root (2 in/5 cm diameter), peeled and ends trimmed (place in lightly vinegared water to avoid discoloration)

FOR FLAVORING LOTUS ROOT

1 2/3 cups water
3 1/3 Tbsps rice vinegar

SYRUP

3 1/2 Tbsps water
5 Tbsps sugar
1 Tbsp lemon juice

finely grated yuzu *citron (or lemon or lime) zest*

Slice lotus root into thin rounds. If root diameter is large, cut root in half lengthwise before slicing. Immediately place slices in lightly vinegared water to avoid discoloration.

Place flavoring ingredients in a medium-sized saucepan and bring to a boil quickly. Add lotus root slices and reduce heat to medium. Simmer, uncovered, until lotus root is just cooked but still crisp—about 5 minutes. Drain and cool.

Place water and sugar in a small saucepan and simmer until about the thickness of corn syrup. Do not allow it to caramelize. Remove from heat and add 1 Tbsp lemon juice.

Place vinegared lotus root slices on 4 small dishes, pour 1 Tbsp or so of hot syrup on each portion, and garnish with a dab of grated *yuzu* citron (or lemon or lime) zest. Serve immediately. Syrup keeps indefinitely, and vinegared lotus root keeps at least 3 days refrigerated—but *yuzu* (or lemon) zest should be freshly grated just before serving.

Spinach with Walnut Dressing

Hōrensō no Kurumi-Ae

ほうれん草のくるみあえ

Every year the Sankō-in temple receives large quantities of walnuts from a parishioner, and it was this gift that inspired the use of nuts instead of the conventional sesame in this type of dressing. Of course, other nuts besides walnuts may be used, and different kinds of nuts may be combined.

SERVES 4

½ lb (225 gm) spinach, washed and crowns (thick place where stems meet) cut off (and reserved—see following spinach crown recipes)

WALNUT DRESSING

4 large (or 6 small) whole walnuts
1 tsp sugar
4 tsps soy sauce
saké or water (or both)

Parboil spinach in lightly salted water until just tender. The time varies greatly with the age and size of the spinach—in all cases, the cooking time should be kept as short as possible.

Rinse spinach in cold water, squeeze out water gently but firmly, then cut both stems and leaves into 1-inch (2 ½-cm) lengths.

Crush walnuts in a *suribachi* or mortar, leaving small chunks of nut. Do not crush until smooth. Add sugar and soy sauce and mix well. If the flavor is a little dense, dilute dressing to taste with a little saké or water or both.

Add spinach and toss well to coat with dressing.

Serve at room temperature in small individual dishes or in one bowl family style. Keeps 1 day refrigerated.

Spinach Crowns with Sesame Dressing

Hōrensō no Ne no Goma-Ae

ほうれん草の根のごまあえ

The most delicious part of spinach is usually thrown away. This is the thick, rosy crown, where the stems come together and out of which the root descends. This dish from the Donke-in temple is yet another example of the Buddhist impulse to avoid waste. In keeping with this, 2 of the recipes following were created for this book.

SERVES 4

16 spinach crowns (about ⅓ lb/160 gm), washed well (see below)
sesame (or nut) dressing (see page 113 or preceding)

A degree of bother is necessary to rid the spinach crowns of dirt and grit. It might be best to soak them a bit and then use a toothpick or skewer to remove the dirt from between the stems.

Parboil crowns in lightly salted water over high heat for 4 minutes or until just barely cooked. Plunge into cold water to cool. Drain and cut crowns into slices lengthwise (cutting crosswise results in a mess). Small crowns may be used as is.

Make dressing, add spinach crowns, and toss to coat.

Serve at room temperature in small individual dishes or in a single bowl family style. Keeps 1 day refrigerated.

Spinach Crowns with Sesame-Vinegar Dressing

Hōrensō no Ne no Goma-Su

ほうれん草の根のごま酢

Spinach improves after the first frost, but this vegetable is best in midwinter. At that time the root crown is red and sweet. This dish is everyday fare at Kyoto temples and not considered guest food, but guests at an intimate dinner will be surprised and delighted by this "new" vegetable. The root crowns of some other leaf vegetables may be used in the same way as spinach crowns.

SERVES 4

4 large or 8 small (total about 3 oz/90 gm) spinach crowns, washed well (see previous recipe) and thinly sliced lengthwise

SESAME-VINEGAR DRESSING

4 tsps sesame paste
2 tsps soy sauce
2 tsps saké (optional)
2 tsps rice vinegar

Place sliced spinach crowns in small saucepan with a little water, cover tightly, and braise until cooked but still crisp. Large crowns will take about 8 minutes, but the timing will vary much with the size of the crown slices. Rinse in cold water and drain.

Blend the sesame-vinegar dressing in a small bowl. Add cooked spinach crown slices to dressing and toss well.

Serve at room temperature in small dishes or family style in one bowl. Eat immediately. Does not keep.

Spinach Crowns and Ginger Stir-Fry

Hōrensō no Ne no Shōga Itame

ほうれん草の根の生姜炒め

SERVES 4

1 Tbsp vegetable oil
6–7 thin slices fresh ginger, cut into julienne strips
1/3 lb (160 gm) spinach crowns, well washed (see page 177) and sliced lengthwise

Heat oil in frypan or wok over high heat, add ginger, and stir-fry for 20 seconds. Add spinach crown slices and stir-fry until just tender—about 3 minutes.

Transfer to individual serving dishes or a single bowl and season to taste with salt, soy sauce, and/or a squeeze of lemon juice. Best eaten hot, but all right at room temperature. Does not keep.

Saké-Braised Spinach Crowns

Hōrensō no Ne no Mushi-Ni

ほうれん草のむし煮

SERVES 4

1/3 lb (160 gm) spinach crowns, well washed (see page 177) and thinly sliced lengthwise
salt
1/4 cup saké

Place spinach crowns in medium-sized saucepan and sprinkle lightly with salt. Add saké, cover pan, and bring to a boil over medium heat. Braise until just tender—about 2–3 minutes. The liquid should evaporate.

Best eaten hot, but also all right at room temperature. Does not keep.

VARIATION: Add a blend of 4 tsps miso (any sweet miso) and 4 tsps saké to the hot, braised crowns and toss well.

Brussels Sprouts with Miso Sauce

Mekyabetsu no Kawari Nuta

芽キャベツのかわりぬた

This original recipe using a vegetable recently introduced to Japan is just home cooking and can be made in large quantities. The delicate mustard background flavor enlivens that of the Brussels sprouts.

SERVES 4

2/3 tsp basic Japanese mustard mix (see page 51)
piece orange or tangerine peel
20 Brussels sprouts, cleaned and bottoms scored in a cross

MISO SAUCE

4 Tbsps sweet white Kyoto (saikyō) *miso*
4 Tbsps saké

Dissolve mustard in about 1 cup water in small saucepan, add peel and Brussels sprouts. Bring to a boil, cover, and braise over high heat until tender-crisp and bright green. Do not overcook.

Blend miso sauce.

Spoon 2 Tbsps miso sauce over each portion of 5 Brussels sprouts. Serve hot or at room temperature. Keeps 1 day.

All Season

Dried-Frozen Tofu Mélange

Kōya-dōfu no Unohana Modoki

高野豆腐の卯の花もどき

This protein-rich food is part of daily temple fare and is eaten on top of rice.

SERVES 4

1 cake dried-frozen tofu (Kōya-dōfu)
1 tsp vegetable oil
2 fresh (or *reconstituted dried*) shiitake *mushrooms, stems removed, finely chopped*
1/2 tsp soy sauce
2 Tbsps finely chopped carrot

FOR FLAVORING CARROT

7 Tbsps water
2 tsps soy sauce
1/2 tsp saké

2 young green beans, parboiled in lightly salted water, rinsed in cold water, and finely diced

Reconstitute dried-frozen tofu by soaking it in lukewarm water until fully expanded and soft—about 5 minutes. Rinse in cold water, then gently but firmly squeeze between hands to expel milky liquid. Repeat squeezing and cold water rinse until milky liquid is no longer emitted. Press out almost all of the moisture.

Tear dried-frozen tofu into small pieces, place in a mortar or *suribachi* grinding bowl, and pound with a pestle until it resembles crumbled foam rubber (or use food processor). There should be no lumps. If too much moisture has been pressed out, the tofu will act like a sponge and be hard to pound. In that case add 1 Tbsp water.

Place a small saucepan over medium heat, add the vegetable oil and chopped mushroom and stir-fry about 30 seconds. Add 1/2 tsp soy sauce and stir-fry until all liquid is absorbed—about 1 minute. Set mushroom aside.

Place chopped carrot and carrot simmering ingredients in the same saucepan. Bring to a boil and simmer over medium heat until soft, then add mushroom and crumbled *Kōya-dōfu*. Using 4 (yes, 4) chopsticks, stir well over medium heat until most of the liquid is absorbed or disappears—about 4 minutes. The mixture should not be too dry—the consistency should be between dry scrambled eggs and mashed potatoes. Add chopped green beans and mix well.

Serve in small deep bowls, either hot or at room temperature. Keeps very well, but this depends on what ingredients are used.

VARIATIONS: Other finely chopped ingredients such as boiled ginkgo nuts, thin deep-fried tofu (*usuage*), boiled green soybeans (*edamame*), etc., may be added.

Not Exactly Hamburger

Kōya-dōfu no Unohana Modoki no Yakimono

高野豆腐の卯の花もどきの焼きもの

This variation of the preceding recipe is important enough to merit a special heading. These protein-rich patties successfully exploit the flavor of flour.

1 recipe Dried-Frozen Tofu Mélange (preceding recipe)
2 Tbsps flour
vegetable oil

Add 2 Tbsps flour to the preceding recipe and form small oval patties. Heat a small amount of vegetable oil in a frypan over medium heat and add patties. Sear both sides, then reduce heat to low, cover pan, and cook about 4 minutes. Keeps 1 week refrigerated.

Simmered Dried-Frozen Tofu

Kōya-dōfu no Fukume-ni

高野豆腐の含め煮

Since this inexpensive dish is almost pure protein, keeps well, and goes well with other foods, it is part of the daily temple—especially Zen—fare.

SERVES 4

1 cake dried-frozen tofu (Kōya-dōfu)

FOR SIMMERING

1 cup water
1 1/2 Tbsps sugar
1/2 tsp salt

Place *Kōya-dōfu* in lukewarm water until fully expanded and soft—about 5 minutes. Discard the soaking water and replace with cold water. Holding the tofu in one hand, gently and firmly press it with the palm of the other hand to expel the milky liquid. Repeat this process, changing the water every time, until no more milky liquid is emitted. Press out all water before continuing.

Cut tofu cake into eighths and place pieces in a small saucepan with ingredients for simmering. Bring to a boil quickly, reduce heat to medium, and simmer, uncovered, 5 minutes. Reduce heat to low and simmer 10 minutes more. The liquid will reduce greatly. The small pieces of *Kōya-dōfu* should be the consistency of fine wet bathsponge, and most of the liquid should be absorbed. *Do not overcook,* or tofu will fall apart.

Serve hot or at room temperature. If serving later, remove tofu pieces to a small plate so they will keep their shape. Serve 2 pieces in each small dish. Keeps well unrefrigerated—3 days in summer, 5 days in winter.

Dried-Frozen Tofu Tempura

Kōya-dōfu Fukume-ni no Tempura
高野豆腐含め煮の天ぷら

Like potatoes, *Kōya-dōfu* is a very versatile food and can be prepared in many ways—this being but one of the more elegant ones.

SERVES 4

vegetable oil for deep-frying
2 Tbsps flour
2 Tbsps water
pinch salt
1 recipe Simmered Dried-Frozen Tofu (preceding recipe)

Heat vegetable oil to medium temperature (340°F/170°C).

Mix tempura batter. Unlike batter for the fluffy type of tempura, this should be mixed until no lumps of flour remain.

Lightly press out about half of the liquid from the small pieces of simmered *Kōya-dōfu.*

Dip each piece of simmered *Kōya-dōfu* in the batter and coat evenly (chopsticks are the best tool for this), then deep-fry until the corners are lightly tinged with gold—about 3 minutes. Best eaten hot.

VARIATIONS: A pinch of finely chopped perilla (*shiso*) leaves, parsley, mint, or other fresh green herbs may be added to the batter, as may powdered green tea (*matcha*), crushed walnuts, etc.

Konnyaku in Miso Dressing

Konnyaku no Miso-Ae

こんにゃくの味噌あえ

In Japan this dish is said to have been served to the Śākyamuni Buddha when he descended from the mountain after attaining Enlightenment. It is traditionally served on Jōdō-e, December 8, the recognized date of this event, which is one of the great Buddhist observances, along with Buddha's birth (April 4) and his entering into Nirvana (February 15).

SERVES 4

1 cake (about 10 ounces/270 gm) konnyaku
1 tsp salt
2 2/3 Tbsps sweet white Kyoto (saikyō) *miso*
4 tsps saké
2 tsps ginger juice
pinch salt

Sprinkle *konnyaku* with about 1 tsp salt, rubbing salt into the entire surface, and knead vigorously. This makes the *konnyaku* firmer. Rinse well and pat dry.

Slice *konnyaku* into 40 slices (about 1/16 in/1/4 cm thick). Place in a dry medium-sized saucepan over high heat and stir (with chopsticks), taking care not to break slices. Water will be given off. Stir slices constantly until all water is expelled and the *konnyaku* sizzles loudly and begins to stick to the pan. Remove from heat and let cool.

Place miso in a bowl and blend with saké, ginger juice, and salt. Just before eating, add *konnyaku* slices and mix well to coat slices.

Place 10 miso-coated slices in a decoratively arranged mound in each small deep bowl. Serve at room temperature. Does not keep.

Konnyaku Lumps

Chigiri Konnyaku

ちぎりこんにゃく

In contrast to the careful slices in the previous recipe, this dish utilizes *konnyaku* in rough nuggets, highlighting how the shapes of food give us pleasure. The blandness of *konnyaku* is here offset by a spicy accent.

SERVES 4

1 cake (about 10 ounces/270 gm) konnyaku

4 tsps sugar
2 Tbsps soy sauce
1 Tbsp saké
black pepper (finest grind) or 7-flavors spice, or red pepper

Hold *konnyaku* cake with both hands at one end and whack it soundly against a clean surface 5 times; reverse ends and repeat process. Turn 4 times, making a total of 20 whacks—10 whacks for each end.

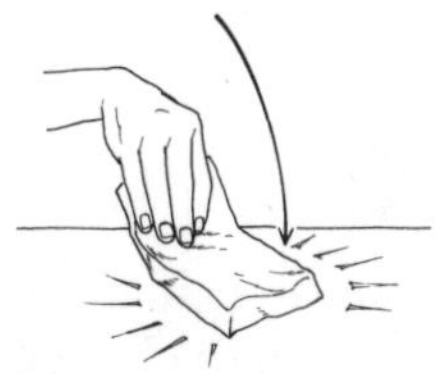

Dig your fingers into the *konnyaku* and twist, tearing off lumps about the diameter of a quarter (about 35–36 lumps total).

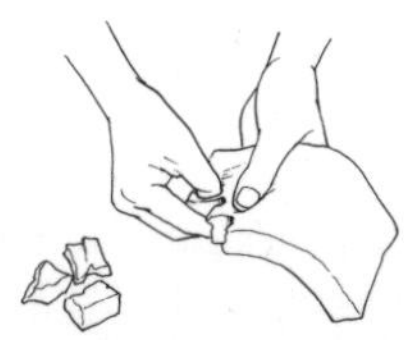

Place *konnyaku* lumps in a dry medium-sized saucepan over high heat and stir. Water will be given off. Continue stirring until all water is emitted and the *konnyaku* becomes a little milky, sizzles loudly, and begins to stick to the pan. Remove from heat.

Reduce heat to medium and add sugar, soy sauce, and saké to *konnyaku.* Cook, uncovered, stirring frequently, for 5 minutes. The liquid will disappear and the *konnyaku* will be colored a bit by the soy sauce. Remove from heat. Add 2–3 shakes of the finest grind of black pepper or Japanese 7-flavors spice (but be very cautious with red pepper) and mix well.

Serve hot or at room temperature in decorative mounds in small, deep bowls. Keeps about 1 day.

Konnyaku Tempura

Konnyaku no Tempura

こんにゃくの天ぷら

This is one of the elegant and simple variations of a basic Japanese food that has become popular with the people who have eaten at Sankō-in. An original of the Sankō-in, it is not found in Kyoto temples. Although it does not use seasonal ingredients, it is nonetheless associated with winter.

ALL SEASON

SERVES 4

vegetable oil for deep-frying
1 cake (10 ounces/270 gm) konnyaku
2 green perilla (shiso) *leaves, finely chopped*

BATTER

equal amounts of cake flour and water
pinch salt

MUSTARD-SOY SAUCE

1 tsp powdered Japanese mustard
few drops hot water
2 tsps soy sauce

Heat oil to medium-hot temperature (350°–360°F/175°–180°C).

Cut *konnyaku* into 1/4-inch (3/4-cm) thick slices.

Place finely chopped perilla in a cloth napkin or piece of cheesecloth, wash well while squeezing gently, then gently squeeze dry. This process eliminates any bitter or harsh flavor in the leaves.

Mix batter well. Add chopped perilla leaf and stir. Add *konnyaku* slices and coat with batter.

Place *konnyaku* in hot oil and deep-fry for about 2 minutes. They should remain white, not become golden.

Add enough water to powdered Japanese mustard to make a thick, smooth paste. Add soy sauce and mix well.

Dip one flat side of each *konnyaku* slice into mustard-soy sauce. Serve 3 slices per portion in small dishes. Should be eaten hot!

Konbu Puffs

Kizami Konbu no Agemono
刻み昆布の揚げもの

This recipe is included because it is a fantasy, using one of the rarest of Japanese ingredients. Traditionally, *kizami konbu* was only served to an imperial prince-abbot or princess-abbess of a Kyoto temple. Today it is sold in perhaps two or three places in Kyoto, and it is likely that this food will disappear in the near future. The little deep-fried balls of *kizami konbu* literally melt on your tongue.

SERVES 4

1 ounce (30 gm) kizami konbu
vegetable oil for deep-frying

Form 12 balls of *kizami konbu* filaments; each will be about 1 inch (2 1/2 cm) in diameter.

Heat oil to medium-high temperature (350°F/175°C). The oil temperature must be precise—too high, and the *kizami konbu* becomes bitter; too low, and it becomes soggy. Place balls of *kizami konbu* into oil one at a time with chopsticks, being careful to keep the ball shape. The filaments will expand slightly. The total deep-frying time is about 5–10 seconds.

Arrange 3 balls in each small saucer. Serve hot or at room temperature. Keeps 1 week, but do not refrigerate.

Fried Unohana

Iri Unohana

炒り卯の花

The mash or lees (*okara*) remaining from making tofu are inexpensive, plentiful, and nourishing—ideal everyday temple food. By itself *okara* is not interesting, but it is brought to life by the addition of a little oil and a few other ingredients. This dish is also part of standard Japanese home cooking—something the family eats, and not for guests.

SERVES 4

1/2 sheet thin deep-fried tofu (usuage)
1 tsp vegetable oil
1-inch (2 1/2-cm) length large carrot, scraped and very finely chopped
2 medium dried shiitake *mushrooms, reconstituted in tepid water, stems removed, and very finely chopped*
3/4 cup (100 gm) okara
4 tsps saké
4 tsps soy sauce

Pour boiling water over *usuage* to remove oil; drain, and chop very finely.

Place a medium-sized saucepan over low heat and add 1 tsp vegetable oil. Add finely chopped *usuage* and stir-fry about 30 seconds. Add carrot and *shiitake* and stir-fry about 1 minute. Add *okara* and continue to cook, stirring constantly and breaking all lumps in the *okara*.

After about 5 minutes, add 1 Tbsp saké and 1 Tbsp soy sauce. Continue stirring until all lumps in the *okara* are gone and the color is a light gold throughout—a total of about 15 minutes. The result is a mixture that looks like fine, dry, golden breadcrumbs.

Serve at room temperature in small dishes. This dish may also be sprinkled on rice or rice gruel (or, say, on salad or baked potato). Keeps about 5 days refrigerated.

Deep-Fried Millet Fu

Awa Fu no Iso-Age

粟麩の磯揚げ

It is unlikely that millet gluten bars will be available in the United States, but if they are, this simple dish is quite delicious. It is considered luxury food and has about a hundred-year history in Kyoto Zen temple cooking.

SERVES 4

4 3/4-inch (12-cm) length millet (awa) fu
potato starch (katakuriko) *or cornstarch*
1 sheet nori *seaweed, cut into quarters*
vegetable oil for deep-frying

GINGER-SOY SAUCE

1 tsp fresh ginger juice
1 Tbsp soy sauce

Cut millet *fu* into 8 1/2-inch (1 1/2-cm) lengths. (Millet *fu* comes in a standard-sized loaf or stick in Tokyo, measuring 4 1/2×2×21 cm). Dredge pieces in *katakuriko* or cornstarch.

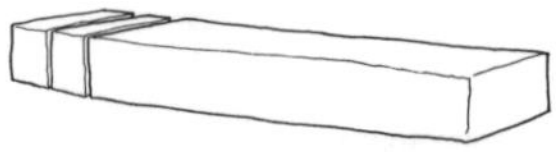

Stack quartered *nori* and cut longer side into thirds. Wrap 1 strip of *nori* around each piece of millet *fu*. *Nori* shrinks greatly when deep-fried, so it

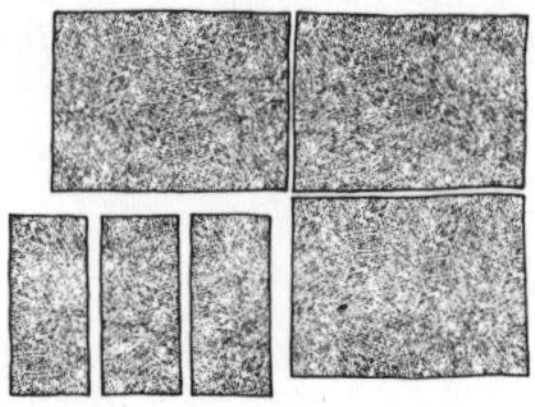

should be wrapped *very loosely* around the *fu*—just overlap the ends and seal by dampening one end with a wet fingertip. Do not worry if the result looks like a ten-year-old boy in daddy's trousers.

Heat oil for deep-frying to medium temperature (340°F/170°C). Fry 4 pieces at a time until the surface is crisp and light yellow (but not golden)—about 1 1/2 minutes. The *nori* band will contract to fit the *fu*.

Mix ginger-soy sauce.

Dip one side of each deep-fried piece in ginger-soy sauce and serve hot, 2 pieces per portion. Best eaten hot, but can be eaten at room temperature. Keeps 1–2 days.

Pouch Sushi

Inari-Zushi

いなりずし

The fact that commercial preparations of this stuffed-pouch sushi are mostly dull and flavorless has made many Japanese forget how delicious *inari-zushi* can be when made with a little care. The sushi rice in this version is brought alive with sesame seeds and a touch of aromatic *yuzu* citron zest in winter; in summer perilla—both the leaf and seeds—can be added. This is a plebeian food made to feed large groups in temples.

SERVES 4

1 2/3 cups short-grain rice
1 2/3 cups water
FOR FLAVORING RICE
3 Tbsps rice vinegar
1 Tbsp saké
1 Tbsp sugar
1 tsp salt
4 sheets thin deep-fried tofu (usuage)
FOR FLAVORING USUAGE
1 2/3 cups water
2 Tbsps soy sauce
2 Tbsps sugar
1 tsp salt
2 Tbsps saké
2 tsps black sesame seeds, toasted (see page 65)
1–2 pinches finely grated yuzu *citron (or lemon or lime) zest*

Cook rice in equal volume of water so that grains are firm, not mushy. Blend vinegar mixture for flavoring rice, taking care that the sugar is dissolved.

Place hot rice in a wide, shallow pan (see page 61). Add vinegar mixture gradually while tossing and fluffing rice with a wooden spatula or rice paddle, holding the paddle horizontally and working with a sidewise motion (avoid squashing or pushing down on the rice). When the vinegar mixture has been absorbed, spread rice over surface of container and let cool to room temperature.

Place the *usuage* in colander and pour on boiling water to remove excess oil. Drain briefly, pat with paper towels, then cut *usuage* sheets in half crosswise. Carefully tease open each half with fingers to form a pouch.

Place *usuage* pouches in medium-sized saucepan and add ingredients for flavoring *usuage*. Place lid ajar (so there is a 1-inch gap between lid and pan), bring just to a boil over high heat, remove lid, and reduce heat to low immediately. Simmer until pouches are soft and the pot liquor is reduced a bit—about 20 minutes. Do not overcook, or the pouches will fall apart. Remove pan from heat, but leave *usuage* pouches in pot liquor to cool to room temperature and absorb flavor. When cool, remove pouches from pot liquor and drain. Reserve pot liquor for other uses (see page 66).

Sprinkle toasted black sesame seeds over cooled rice and mix well. Add finely grated *yuzu* citron zest to rice, again mixing well. Toss the rice once more, taking care not to squash it.

Using your fingers, stuff pouches a little more than half-full of sushi rice. Do not overstuff. Fold over mouth of pouch and place fold side down on serving plate.

Two pouches form a satisfying snack or side dish; 7 pouches form a good meal, accompanied by tea. Keeps 2 days, but the flavor is best for the first 4 hours. Never refrigerate sushi for any length of time, because the rice hardens.

Grilled Usuage

Yaki Usuage

焼き薄揚げ

Very simple, cheap, and quite delicious. Good for lunch, snacks, and as an accompaniment to saké.

SERVES 4

4 sheets thin deep-fried tofu (usuage), *cut in half crosswise (do not rinse in boiling water)*
soy sauce
4 Tbsps finely grated daikon radish

Place *usuage* under broiler and grill until just browned and crisped on each side. Take care not to overbroil. Cut each half-sheet of *usuage* into thirds.

Place six pieces of grilled *usuage* on each small dish or serve family style in one bowl. Pour a bit of soy sauce over the *usuage* and serve with 1 Tbsp finely grated daikon per person. Eat hot or at room temperature. Keeps for about 1–2 days. Recrisp in oven if necessary.

Deep-Fried Usuage

Usuage no Agemono

薄揚げの揚げもの

Here is another good snack and saké accompaniment, involving the double-deep-frying of tofu.

SERVES 4

4 sheets thin deep-fried tofu (usuage)
vegetable oil for deep-frying
salt

Cut each *usuage* sheet into fourths crosswise, then cut each fourth once diagonally.

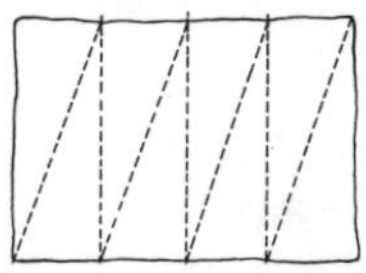

Heat oil to medium (340°F/170°C). Deep-fry *usuage* pieces until slightly puffed and quite crisp—about 3 minutes. Drain on absorbent paper and sprinkle with salt.

Serve hot. Keeps well; recrisp if necessary.

Golden Sushi Rolls

Usuage no Maki-Zushi
薄揚げの巻きずし

This version of rolled sushi is really almost the same as Pouch Sushi. The use of the inside face of thin deep-fried tofu on the outside of these rolls makes an interesting variation, and the addition of *nori* seaweed enlivens the flavor.

SERVES 4

4 sheets thin deep-fried tofu (usuage)
FOR FLAVORING USUAGE (OPTIONAL)
1 2/3 cups water
2 Tbsps soy sauce
2 Tbsps sugar
1 tsp salt
2 Tbsps saké
2 sheets nori *seaweed, cut in half crosswise*
3 1/2 cups prepared sushi rice (see page 189)

Trim off 3 sides of each *usuage* sheet, reserving trimmings. Either simmer *usuage* in the same manner as for Pouch Sushi (page 189) or just use as is. After simmering, open up one sheet and spread it out with the deep-fried side down.

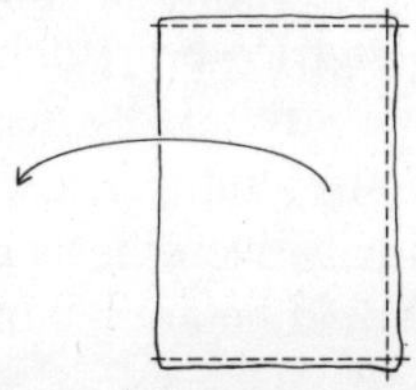

trim off 3 sides and open up *usuage*

Place half *nori* sheet on opened-up *usuage* and trim *usuage* to the same size as the *nori*, again reserving the trimmings. This is based on sizes of *usuage* in Tokyo and may demand some improvisation (such as overlapping 2 sheets) in the United States, where *usuage* sheets vary in size. The desired result is *usuage* overlaid by *nori* in a size convenient for rolling around a sushi rice core, which will then be cut into bite-sized slices.

Spread about 7/8 cup (loosely packed) prepared sushi rice on the *nori* sheet about 3/8 inch (1 cm) from near edge to 1 1/4 inches (3 cm) from far edge. Place a line of *usuage* trimmings across middle of rice (remember, there are 3 more *usuage* sheets to trim to the same size as the *nori*). Roll in the same manner as *nori-maki* (page 64) and cut into 3/4-inch (2-cm) lengths.

Serve decoratively to show off cut side, either in individual dishes or family style, on a plate. Keeps about 1 day, but the flavor is best within about 4 hours after making. Do not refrigerate because the rice will harden.

Rōbai

ろうばい

This is an original dish of the Sankō-in and is one of the stars of this book and of the food served at the temple. Fresh wheat gluten is available at only one place even in Tokyo, so you probably will have to make it for yourself (see page 66). However, the crisp-fried version below freezes well, and it is as easy to make a lot as a little, so a half-dozen rounds or so can be stocked in the freezer. *Rōbai* can also be combined with vegetables and used in other dishes (see following recipe and page 110).

SERVES 4

I. CRISP FRIED

1/4 lb (115 gm) fresh wheat gluten (nama fu)*—a piece about the size of a small fist*

vegetable oil for deep-frying

MUSTARD-SOY SAUCE

small amount of basic Japanese mustard mix (page 51) blended with 2–3 Tbsps soy sauce to taste

Heat oil to medium temperature (340°F/170°C).

With your hands, stretch the wheat gluten until it is about the size of a small dinner plate and is about 1/8 inch (1/2 cm) thick. Do not worry if there are some holes in the round. Place the stretched wheat gluten in hot oil. It will shrink immediately, so continue stretching it, using chopsticks or perhaps two forks. The elasticity will gradually decrease as it deep-fries, and the holes will fry crisp. Ideally, the result should be an 8–9 inch (20–23 cm) round, but do not be concerned if the shape is irregular, because it will be cut into bite-sized pieces. When one side is crisp and light gold, turn the round over and deep-fry the other side to the same degree. You may find it necessary to flip the round over once again. Drain briefly on a rack or on absorbent paper. (If you are making additional rounds, repeat the process, using 1/4 pound of fresh wheat gluten for each round.)

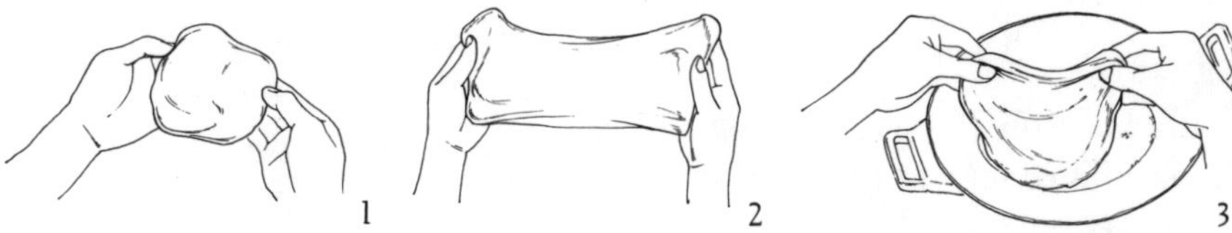

1, 2. stretch fist-sized lump of gluten   3. place in hot oil

4, 5. stretch with chopsticks while deep-frying   6. turn over once or twice

Mix mustard-soy sauce.

Cut deep-fried round into 3/4-inch (2-cm) squares or pieces. Divide pieces into 4 portions and serve hot on small dishes, accompanied by a dip of mustard-soy sauce.

II. DEEP-FRIED AND SIMMERED

1 round of crisp-fried Rōbai *(see preceding)*

FOR FLAVORING RŌBAI

2 cups water

6 Tbsps soy sauce

3–4 Tbsps saké

1/2 tsp basic Japanese mustard mix (see page 51)

Put flavoring liquid in a medium-sized saucepan over medium heat, add 1 round of crisp-fried *Rōbai,* cover pan, and boil 3 minutes. Remove lid, reduce heat to medium-low, and simmer for 2 minutes more. Cook just long enough for flavor to penetrate. Do not overcook, or wheat gluten will disintegrate. Remove round (now quite soft) to a chopping board and cut into 3/4-inch (2-cm) pieces. (Reserve pot liquor for other uses—see page 66.) Place the cut *Rōbai* in a bowl and add 1/2 tsp basic Japanese mustard mix. Do not use a Western mustard mixed with vinegar. Add a *bit* more mustard if you think it necessary, but take care that the mustard remains a background flavor and does not dominate.

Divide into four portions. Best served hot, but also good served at room temperature. Keeps 2–3 days refrigerated.

Anything Goes Roll, with Sauce

Rōbai to Yasai no Makimono

ろうばいと野菜の巻きもの

An informal concoction, simple and inelegant, like a hamburger. Without the sauce, this is finger food; with sauce, it becomes the equivalent of a French-dip sandwich.

SERVES 8

1 round of Rōbai I *(see preceding recipe)*

⅓ medium carrot, cut into thin slices lengthwise

FOR FLAVORING CARROT

1 Tbsp sweet white Kyoto (saikyō) *miso*

1 Tbsp saké

3 fresh shiitake *mushrooms, stems removed and cut into thick julienne strips*

FOR FLAVORING MUSHROOM

1 tsp vegetable oil

2 tsps sugar

2 tsps soy sauce

1 Tbsp saké

8 young green beans, parboiled in lightly salted water and plunged into cold water

3–4 leaves butterhead lettuce

2 Tbsps nattō *(optional)*

MUSTARD-SOY SAUCE DIP

small amount of basic Japanese mustard mix (page 51) in soy sauce to taste

SAUCE

7 Tbsps water

3 Tbsps soy sauce

1 or 2 Tbsps sugar, depending on how sweet you like it

2 Tbsps potato starch (katakuriko) *dissolved in 2 Tbsps water*

basic Japanese mustard (page 51) or wasabi *horseradish mix (page 57)*

Simmer carrot slices in ample water over medium heat for 3 minutes. Discard water. Add 1 Tbsp sweet white Kyoto miso and 1 Tbsp saké to carrot in saucepan and simmer over low heat 2 minutes (water is not necessary). Let cool in miso.

Place 1 tsp oil in saucepan and stir-fry mushroom about 1 minute. Add sugar, soy sauce, and saké and simmer over medium heat until liquid is gone.

Cut parboiled green beans into thick strips on the diagonal.

Tear lettuce into strips.

Place *Rōbai* round on plastic wrap. Spread carrot, mushroom, green beans, lettuce, and *nattō* in a band 2 inches (5 cm) wide across round about 3/8 inch (1 cm) from near edge. Roll, using plastic wrap to keep the roll as firm as possible.

Trim messy edges from roll, then cut roll in half and each half into four pieces.

Place one slice, cut side up, in each dish. If eaten without sauce, the roll may be dipped in mustard-soy sauce; or . . .

Bring all sauce ingredients except potato starch to a boil over medium heat in a small saucepan. Add potato starch, making sure it is well dissolved in water, and stir constantly until thickened.

Spoon about 2 Tbsps sauce over each portion. Garnish with a dab of basic Japanese mustard mix or *wasabi* horseradish in the middle of each sauce-covered slice. Serve immediately and eat hot. Mix well before eating. Does not keep.

Deep-Fried Dried Yuba

Hoshi-Yuba no Kara-Age

干し湯葉のから揚げ

This Kyoto temple food is a good snack and a marvelous saké accompaniment. It is also used as an ingredient in soups and steamed dishes.

SNACK

vegetable oil for deep-frying
dried yuba
salt

Heat oil to medium temperature (340°F/170°C).

With scissors, cut dried *yuba* sheets into 1 1/2×2-inch (4×5-cm) pieces. Drop pieces of *yuba* into hot oil one at a time. They will expand suddenly—frying time is about 1 second. Remove immediately, drain on absorbent paper, and salt lightly.

Keeps well in an airtight container. Recrisp in oven if necessary.

VARIATIONS: Working very fast with chopsticks, fold or crease the *yuba* pieces as soon as they are in the hot oil. Or, use about 1/3 of a dried *yuba* sheet and quickly fold the *yuba* twice as it expands, using chopsticks and pushing the *yuba* against the side of the pan. This is slightly tricky at first, but do not worry about making neat folds—attractively messy folds are what you want. Drain and salt lightly.

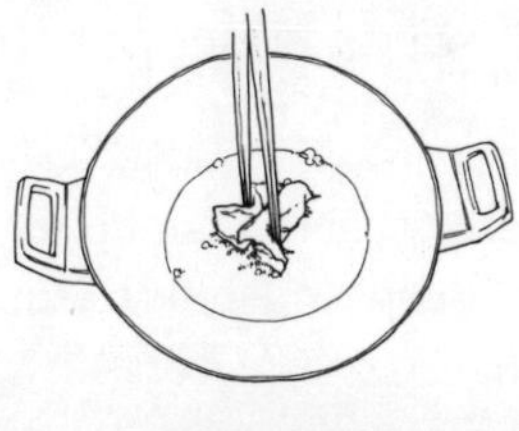

Fried and Simmered Dried Yuba

Hoshi-Yuba no Age-Ni

干し湯葉の揚げ煮

Yuba was a luxury food, and *yuba* dishes were part of the cuisine of the temples housing an imperial princess-abbess. If possible, fresh *yuba* was used, but because this goes bad quickly in Japan's humid summer, dried *yuba* dishes became part of the summer fare.

SERVES 4

vegetable oil for deep-frying
2 sheets dried yuba, *cut in half crosswise (with scissors)*
FOR SIMMERING
- *3/4 cup water*
- *2 tsps soy sauce*
- *1/4 tsp salt*
- *1 tsp sugar*
- *1 Tbsp saké*

Heat oil to medium temperature (340°F/170°C) and deep-fry *yuba* as in the preceding recipe. Soak fried *yuba* in a small bowl of hot water until soft—about 3 minutes. Discard water.

Place simmering ingredients and the softened deep-fried *yuba* in a small saucepan and simmer 3 minutes over medium heat.

Place 1 piece of *yuba* in each small dish and spoon over a bit of pot liquor. Serve hot or at room temperature. Keeps 2–3 days, but do not refrigerate. Reheat before eating.

Sesame "Tofu"

Goma-Dōfu

ごま豆腐

This dish is not tofu at all, but a nonsweet, delicately flavored pudding, cut into clean rectangles resembling tofu cakes. Sesame tofu is the ultimate in rich guest food and is representative of all *shōjin* cooking, regardless of Buddhist sect. This variation, which is made at the Donke-in, uses untoasted sesame seeds. The same dish made with toasted seeds is deeper in color.

SERVES 4

special equipment: any square-cornered container that is about 1 1/2 inches (4 cm) deep and holds 1 cup of liquid

½ cup white sesame seeds
1 cup water
¼ cup (50 gm) potato starch (katakuriko) *or* kuzu *starch*
(cornstarch is not a substitute)
basic wasabi *horseradish mix (see page 57)*

Place sesame seeds and water in a blender and blend until seeds are as fine as possible—about 5 minutes. Strain the liquid through a fine sieve or 3 layers of cheesecloth into a large, heavy saucepan. Squeeze out all liquid from pulp and discard pulp or find some creative use for it (see end of recipe). This should leave about 1 ⅔ cups sesame milk.

Add the potato (or *kuzu*) starch and mix thoroughly with your hand. A spoon is not the right tool for this job; your hand can feel and eliminate lumps in the starch most efficiently (or whirr in a blender or food processor).

Place on medium-high heat and stir vigorously and constantly with a sturdy wooden paddle or wooden spoon. At first the mixture will be very stiff and lumpy. It becomes softer as you stir, but you may need someone to hold the pot on the heat. The advantage of a large saucepan becomes clear as you stir this mixture. Keep stirring vigorously until the mixture develops a sheen and large, elastic bubbles appear (about 10 minutes). Remove from heat and stir vigorously an additional 2 minutes. A certain amount of the thickened mixture will adhere to and form a coating on the pan. (See end of recipe for an idea of how to use this coating; it is a shame to waste it.)

Rinse rectangular container with water and do not dry. Pour in sesame mixture, and bounce or tap container on work surface, then pat the top of it with the back of your hand or a large spoon to eliminate air bubbles. Place container on two disposable chopsticks in a large shallow pan and circulate water around container to force-cool sesame mixture. Do not refrigerate to cool; the mixture will harden. The cooling sesame mixture will not be harmed if it gets a little wet. When cool, run your finger around edge of container and turn out the sesame "tofu" into a shallow, water-filled pan. Cut into 6 pieces in the water.

Serve each piece of sesame "tofu" in a small, deep bowl garnished with a dab of prepared *wasabi* horseradish in the middle and ½ tsp soy sauce spooned into the bottom of the bowl (not over the "tofu"). The type of starch used determines how long this will keep. *Kuzu* keeps longer than *katakuriko*; the latter will give off liquid. There are even various qualities of *kuzu*. On an average, sesame "tofu" keeps about 1 day. If it is refrigerated, use plastic wrap or a protective container.

Pulp—The sesame pulp may be mixed with a little saké and soy sauce that has been cooked briefly over medium heat and then used as a dressing; it may be combined with crushed nuts of some kind for another type of dressing; or it may be used in the same manner as *okara*.

Coating on saucepan—Put some water in the saucepan and allow the starchy lining to loosen from the pan. It may come off in a single piece. This is good cut in pieces and served with a thin syrup of saké and sugar, with a bit of sugar sprinkled on top and a dab of finely grated *yuzu* (or lemon or lime) zest as garnish. A little experimentation should turn up some creative ways to use this coating.

Sesame "Tofu" in Broth

Goma-Dōfu no Kuzutoji no Tsuyu

ごま豆腐の葛とじのつゆ

Sesame "tofu" is the *sashimi* of *shōjin* cooking. Here is an adaptation for winter, a way to make sesame "tofu" a hot dish. But take care—heat applied directly to this "tofu" will result in a mess. A lightly thickened broth holds heat while gently warming the "tofu."

SERVES 4

3 1/3 *cups* konbu dashi *(see page 81)*
4 *fresh* shiitake *mushrooms, wiped and stems removed*
1 *tsp salt*
1 *tsp soy sauce*
1 *tsp saké*
1 *Tbsp potato starch* (katakuriko) *dissolved in 1 Tbsp water (cornstarch is not a substitute)*
4 *portions sesame "tofu" (see preceding recipe)*
4 *sprigs chrysanthemum leaves, spinach, trefoil, or any other tender leafy green*
4 *slivers* yuzu *citron (or lemon) zest*

Place *dashi* and *shiitake* mushrooms in a medium-sized saucepan. Cover and bring to a simmer over medium heat.

Add salt, soy sauce, saké, and dissolved potato starch. Stir until thickened.

Add sesame "tofu" pieces to hot thickened broth and remove from heat immediately or sesame "tofu" will melt. Let stand 2–3 minutes, until "tofu" pieces are warmed through.

Parboil chrysanthemum leaves (or other greens) in lightly salted water and plunge into cold water to set color and stop cooking.

Place 1 piece of sesame "tofu," 1 *shiitake* mushroom, and 1 sprig of parboiled green in each deep soup bowl (lacquer bowls are best). Carefully ladle broth into bowl. Garnish each bowl with a sliver of *yuzu* citron (or lemon) zest.

Sesame "Tofu" with Thick Sauce

Goma-Dōfu no Ankake

ごま豆腐のあんかけ

Another way to heat sesame "tofu." This is a luxurious, hearty food for blustery winter days.

SERVES 4

THICK SAUCE

1/2 cup konbu dashi *(see page 81)*
1 generous Tbsp sugar
1 1/2 Tbsps soy sauce
1 Tbsp potato starch (katakuriko) *dissolved in 1 Tbsp water (cornstarch is not a substitute)*

finely grated ginger (optional)
4 portions sesame "tofu" (see page 196)

Place thick sauce ingredients in a small saucepan over medium heat. Stir until thickened and remove from heat.

Bring an ample amount of water to a boil in a small saucepan and remove from heat. Add 4 sesame "tofu" pieces and let stand until "tofu" is thoroughly warm—about 5 minutes.

Place each piece of warmed sesame "tofu" in a medium-sized dish, taking care to keep the shape intact. Top each piece with one-fourth of the thick sauce and garnish with a dab of finely grated ginger.

Eat hot. Does not keep.

Five-Color "Tofu"

Goshiki-Dōfu

五色豆腐

Nontofu tofu is an invention of Zen temple cooking. The variations below are based on Sesame "Tofu" (page 196), but are firmer and denser in flavor, so that portions are smaller. The *konbu* kelp confection is part of traditional *shōjin* cooking, but the raw sugar, carrot, beet, tangerine, and almond "tofu" were created for this book in order to explore this recipe idea and to provide entertaining flavor and color contrasts. There are, in fact, six variations (two orange-colored ones). Serve an arrangement of small slices on individual decorative dishes. Keeps 3–4 days refrigerated.

ALL SEASON

Konbu Kelp "Tofu"

Konbu-Dōfu

昆布豆腐

Here is a good example of the use of leftovers—always important in temple cooking. Use the *konbu* kelp remaining from making *dashi* and some well-flavored pot liquor, such as the pot liquor from *Rōbai* (page 196). Cut the *konbu* into 1-inch (2 1/2-cm) squares and simmer in flavored liquid (sparked, if you like, with a bit of red pepper, *sansho*, or black pepper) for about 10 minutes.

SERVES 4–6

special equipment: a rectangular container with a depth of about 1 1/2 inches (4 cm), holding about 1 cup of liquid

1/4 lb (115 gm) flavor-simmered konbu *kelp (as described above)*
1 cup water
7 Tbsps (50 gm) potato starch (katakuriko) *or* kuzu *starch*
MUSTARD-SOY SAUCE
dab of basic Japanese mustard mix (page 51) in 1 Tbsp soy sauce

Place *konbu* and water in a blender or food processor and whirr until well blended. The mixture will contain small spots of *konbu*. Add the starch and whirr until dissolved.

Place mixture in a medium-sized saucepan over medium heat and, stirring constantly (a sturdy rice paddle is good for this), cook until thick, elastic, and the mixture develops a sheen. You cannot stir this too much, and it will take a small amount of muscle. The process is the same as in Sesame "Tofu."

Wash 1-cup capacity container mentioned above in cold water and do not dry. Pour in hot *konbu* mixture and shake and bounce the container on a flat surface to eliminate air bubbles.

Make a water bath as described in the Sesame "Tofu" recipe and let water circulate around container for about 1 hour.

Run your finger around edge of container, then invert "tofu" into a shallow, water-filled pan. Cut into 4 or 6 pieces.

Serve with a dip of mustard-soy sauce.

Savory Raw Sugar "Tofu"

Kurozato Dōfu

黒砂糖豆腐

1 cup raw brown sugar (use true raw sugar or something close to it; "brown sugar" is not a substitute)

1 cup water
⅓ tsp basic Japanese mustard mix (see page 51)
½ tsp finely grated yuzu *citron (or lemon) zest*
7 Tbsps (50 gm) potato starch (katakuriko) *or* kuzu *starch*

Dissolve sugar in water. Add remaining ingredients and mix well. Follow steps as in preceding recipe, but cut firm "tofu" on a damp cutting board rather than in water.

Carrot "Tofu"

Ninjin Tōfu

人参豆腐

¼ lb (115 gm) carrots, scraped well
¼ cup saké
1 Tbsp sugar
½ cup saké
½ tsp salt
water
7 Tbsps (50 gm) potato starch (katakuriko) *or* kuzu *starch*

Cut carrot in 1-inch (2 ½-cm) rounds. Simmer carrots in ¼ cup saké and enough water to cover in covered saucepan until just cooked—about 15 minutes. Mix sugar, ½ cup saké, salt, and enough water to make 1 cup of liquid. Puree cooked carrots in blender or food processor (or with mortar and pestle and sieve if you like labor) together with this liquid and potato starch. Proceed as in *Konbu* Kelp "Tofu" above.

Beet "Tofu"

ビート豆腐

¼ lb (115 gm) raw beets (or equal amount canned beets, see below), peeled and sliced or chopped
2 tsps fresh ginger juice
2 tsps lemon juice
2 Tbsps sugar
¾ tsp salt
pinch pepper
¼ cup saké
water
1 scant tsp basic Japanese mustard mix (see page 51)
7 Tbsps (50 gm) potato starch (katakuriko) *or* kuzu *starch*

Place raw beets, ginger juice, lemon juice, sugar, salt, pepper, and saké with enough water to cover in a saucepan and simmer until cooked. Remove beets from pot liquor and add enough water to make 1 cup of liquid.

If you use canned beets, combine all these ingredients and add enough liquid from the can to make 1 cup of liquid.

Puree beets in blender or food processor (or with mortar and pestle and sieve) with 1 cup of liquid, 1 tsp basic Japanese mustard mix, and potato starch. Proceed as in *Konbu* Kelp "Tofu" above.

Tangerine "Tofu"

Mikan Dōfu

みかん豆腐

2 tangerines or mandarin oranges, or 1 small orange
1 cup water
2 Tbsps sugar
½ tsp salt
2 Tbsps saké
7 Tbsps (50 gm) potato starch (katakuriko) *or* kuzu *starch*

Wash citrus fruit well to remove as much wax or other preservatives as possible. Remove and discard half of the peel. Slice fruit (including remaining half of peel) and remove seeds.

Place all ingredients in a small saucepan and simmer over medium heat until peel becomes soft—about 3–5 minutes for tangerine, longer for orange. Puree in blender or processor (forget the mortar and pestle for this one), add potato starch, and whirr until well mixed. Proceed as in *Konbu* Kelp "Tofu" above.

Almond "Tofu"

アーモンド豆腐

⅔ cup raw almonds
½ cup water
2 tsps sugar
¼ tsp salt
1 Tbsp saké
almond extract (optional)
7 Tbsps (50 gm) potato starch (katakuriko) *or* kuzu *starch*

Blanch almonds and immediately whirr in food processor or blender until as fine as possible, adding liquid a little at a time. It might be best to add the freshly blanched almonds slowly to the machine rather than trying to "liquefy" them all at once.

At this point you may sieve the mixture through two layers of cheesecloth, squeezing out all the liquid possible and using the almond pulp for something else, or simply use the mixture as is, with small granules of almond in it. If you remove the pulp, replace with equal volume of water and a few drops of almond extract. You might want to use almond extract anyway.

Combine all ingredients and whirr until well mixed. Proceed as in *Konbu* Kelp "Tofu."

Vinegared Shaved Konbu

Tororo Konbu no Sanbaizu

とろろ昆布の三杯酢

Tororo konbu, a form of thinly shaved *konbu* kelp, was used in everyday food at the Donke-in in Kyoto. This dish from the Sankō-in is eaten in very small quantities and is an excellent accompaniment to saké.

SERVES 4

4 generous Tbsps shaved (tororo) konbu *kelp*

SWEET VINEGAR

- *3 Tbsps rice vinegar*
- *1 Tbsp sugar*
- *1 Tbsp soy sauce*
- *1/6 tsp salt*

Break up and shred the *tororo konbu* with your fingers.

Mix the sweet vinegar ingredients in a small bowl, making sure the sugar is dissolved.

Spoon 2 Tbsps sweet vinegar over the *tororo konbu* and mix well. The sweet vinegar keeps well; you will soon find good use for the amount remaining, or you might use it to make more of this dish!

VARIATION: Mix this dish with an equal quantity of thin cucumber slices or shreds.

Salt-Grilled Tofu

Shioyaki-Dōfu

塩焼き豆腐

Centuries ago, this startlingly simple way of making tofu delicious was a plebeian dish popular in Naniwa (now Osaka). It seems to have entered Kyoto temple cuisine sometime before the early seventeenth century, for it is recorded in a diary of that time, describing temple experience.

SERVES 4

salt
1 cake regular tofu cut into 2 1/2×1 1/4×3/8-inch (6 1/2×3×1-cm) pieces
vegetable oil
1/4 cup saké, simmered briefly over low heat to remove alcohol
lemon juice
soy sauce

Wet the tips of the middle and index fingers of one hand, dip these fingertips into salt, and rub all surfaces of one tofu piece to salt it. Repeat with remaining pieces. The amount of salt is small—dip your fingers in salt *once only* for each piece.

Lightly oil a fine grill in a broiler or a piece of aluminum foil. Place tofu pieces on oiled grill or foil close to broiler heat. (Or use a lightly oiled frypan.) Broil (or fry) until tofu begins to turn gold and lightly brown in places—about 7 minutes. (While tofu is broiling, simmer saké in a small saucepan.) Turn tofu over carefully to prevent crumbling and broil other side until it begins to develop brown spots—this time about 3 1/2 minutes.

Add tofu pieces one-by-one to simmering saké and heat until each is just warmed through.

Remove from heat and serve immediately in small dishes with a squeeze of lemon juice and a dash of soy sauce. Eat hot!

Sōmen Noodle Nori Roll

Sōmen no Nori-Maki

そうめんの海苔巻き

Buckwheat noodles (*soba*) are used in the popular version of this dish. This refined noodle roll also appears as part of offerings on Buddhist altars.

SERVES 4–5

2 bundles thin ("hand stretched" or tenobe*)* sōmen *noodles*
2 sheets nori *seaweed*

DIP

2 Tbsps soy sauce
1 Tbsp saké
basic wasabi *horseradish mix (see page 57)*

Tie each bundle of *sōmen* noodles firmly with sturdy cotton thread or trussing string (using about 5 turns of string) 3/8 inch (1 cm) from one end. Do not tie both bundle ends. Place bundles in ample boiling water over medium heat and boil until just cooked—about 2 1/2 minutes.

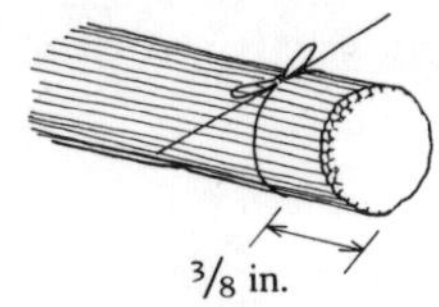

Cut each bundle next to string and discard uncooked portion. Spread noodles on a clean towel to drain, taking care to keep them parallel. Keep bundles separated.

Lay a sheet of *nori* seaweed (wide side toward you) on a clean, dry towel, and spread 1 bunch of noodles across *nori,* leaving a 3/8-inch (1-cm) margin nearest you and a 1 1/4-inch (3-cm) margin on the far side.

Roll firmly, using kitchen towel to help make the roll taut. Repeat this process for other *nori* sheet. Cut both rolls in half and each half into quarters.

One portion is 3 pieces. Serve on small plates with cut face of roll up. Mix dip of soy sauce and saké, place in tiny dishes, and add a dab of prepared *wasabi* horseradish to each dip. Mix well. Eat within 1 hour of making or *nori* will become limp and messy.

Rice Patties

Gohan no Yaki-Mochi

ご飯の焼き餅

This rice "hamburger" is country and temple food, not a dish that a sophisticated city dweller would invent. It is a good example of flour enhancing the taste of rice and is a very convenient dish for leftover cooked rice.

SERVES 4

1 2/3 cups cooked short-grain rice
1/2 tsp salt
4 tsps flour
vegetable oil

Mix cooked rice, salt, and flour in a bowl. (Optional—refrigerate rice mixture overnight or 1/2 day in an airtight container. The flavor will improve.)

Divide rice into fourths and form each into an oblong patty.

Pour just enough vegetable oil into frying pan to form a film. Heat over low heat, add rice patties, and fry each side slowly until golden.

Serve hot or at room temperature. Keeps 2–3 days. Do not refrigerate.

Steamed Tofu Loaf

Mushi-Dōfu

むし豆腐

This is one of the more sophisticated ways to prepare tofu as food for guests.

SERVES 4

1 cake regular or "silk" tofu
½ Tbsp flour
½ tsp salt
1 Tbsp sugar
1 tsp saké
soy sauce or wasabi *horseradish-soy sauce*

Place tofu on a chopping board (with a chopstick under end of board) and press under 2 dinner plates for 3 hours or under a 2-pound (1-kg) weight for 1 hour.

Place pressed tofu in a bowl and mash until about the consistency of oatmeal. It should not be too smooth.

Add flour, salt, sugar, and saké and mix well.

Moisten a kitchen towel or double thickness of cheesecloth. Place tofu mixture on towel (or cheesecloth), form into a bar about 2×1 inches (5×2 ½ cm) in cross-section and as long as your steamer can hold—you can steam the entire amount of tofu at once if the steamer is large enough. Roll tofu in the cloth.

Place cloth-wrapped tofu bar in preheated steamer and steam 15 minutes. (Longer steaming time is needed if you steam all the tofu at once.) Repeat process for remaining tofu.

Remove from steamer and cool without unwrapping. Unwrap cooled tofu bar and cut into 1-inch (2 ½-cm) slices. Messy ends may be cut away.

Serve 2 slices per portion at room temperature with a bit of soy sauce or *wasabi* horseradish-soy sauce (see page 205) as a dip. Keeps 1 day refrigerated.

Salad with White Dressing

Shira Ae

白あえ

This is an unusual version of a dish that is well-known in Japanese cuisine. It is a festive food that is representative of temple cooking, regardless of sect. The variations possible are endless. Do not hesitate to use your favorite and appropriate vegetables.

SERVES 4

½ cake regular or "silk" tofu
⅙ cup (25 gm) carrot cut into julienne strips
FOR FLAVORING CARROT
½ cup water or dashi *(see page 81)*
⅙ tsp salt
1 Tbsp saké
2 large dried shiitake *mushrooms, reconstituted in tepid water (reserve soaking water), stems removed, and cut into julienne strips (or use fresh* shiitake*)*
FOR FLAVORING SHIITAKE
½ cup water or soaking water from shiitake
2 Tbsps soy sauce
1 Tbsp sugar
1 Tbsp saké
2 tsps sugar
⅓ tsp salt
¼ cup (20 gm) snow peas, parboiled in lightly salted water, plunged into cold water, and cut diagonally into julienne strips

Place tofu in water to cover in a saucepan. Bring to a boil over medium heat and simmer 5 minutes.

Wrap tofu in a clean kitchen towel, place on a cutting board, and press under a dinner plate or flat lid weighted with about 1 pound (450 gm) for 1 hour. A water-filled bowl or pan makes a convenient weight.

Simmer carrot in flavoring liquid until just tender. Drain and cool.

Simmer *shiitake* mushroom in its flavoring liquid (making sure sugar is dissolved) for 5 minutes over medium heat. Drain and cool, reserving pot liquor for other purposes.

Place pressed tofu in a bowl and mash well with a pestle (or use a food processor). Add 2 tsps sugar and ⅓ tsp salt and blend until smooth. (The consistency of the tofu is a matter of taste. Some like it a little lumpy; others, creamy smooth.)

Combine tofu, carrot, *shiitake* mushrooms, and snow peas and toss until mixed.

Serve at room temperature in individual dishes or family style in one dish. Keeps about ½ day.

VARIATIONS: Almost any vegetable can be used in this dish. Some classical ingredients are green beans, *konnyaku* filaments (*shirataki*), *hijiki* seaweed, wood-ear mushrooms, sea greens (*wakame*), and lotus root.

Steamed Tofu Cup

Otōfu no Chawan Mushi

豆腐の茶碗むし

The steamed cup (*chawan mushi*) dish known throughout Japan is made with egg. This version from the Donke-in temple uses tofu and is often offered to guests. A remarkable variation using grated turnips and rice is found on page 161.

SERVES 4

special equipment: cylindrical, handleless Japanese teacups (or *chawan mushi* set)

2 cakes regular or "silk" tofu
1 2/3 cups konbu dashi *(see page 81)*
1 Tbsp soy sauce
1 tsp salt
2 Tbsps saké
1 sheet dried yuba, *cut in quarters*
vegetable oil for deep-frying
12 "petals" lily root (optional), parboiled
8 ginkgo nuts, shelled, parboiled, and peeled
12 small rectangles carrot, parboiled
either 8 stalks trefoil, each tied into a knot or all 8 stalks cut into 3/4-inch (2-cm) lengths, or 4 medium (or 8 tiny) snow peas
1 large fresh shiitake *mushroom, stem removed, cut into 8 wedges*
basic wasabi *horseradish mix (see page 57)*

Blend tofu with *dashi* until smooth in a bowl, food processor, or blender. Add soy sauce, salt, and saké and mix.

Deep-fry *yuba* (see page 195).

Place 1 piece of *yuba*, 3 "petals" of lily root (optional), 2 ginkgo nuts, 3 carrot rectangles, either trefoil (2 stalks tied into a knot or 5 cut pieces) or 1 medium (or 2 tiny) snow peas, and 2 wedges of *shiitake* mushroom in the bottom of each cylindrical cup. Pour 1/4 of the tofu mixture into each cup.

Heat steamer and place cups with tofu mixture in it. Lay a clean kitchen towel over cups and steam 7–8 minutes.

Remove towel and place a dab of prepared *wasabi* horseradish in the middle of the cooked tofu mixture.

Serve hot! Mix well before eating—with spoon or chopsticks. The mixture is looser than egg custard.

Deep-Fried Tofu in Thick Sauce

Otōfu no Ankake

お豆腐のあんかけ

This dish is for every season but summer. It is a typical *shōjin* dish and has volume yet is subtle in flavor.

SERVES 4

1 cake regular tofu

THICK SAUCE

- *1 cup water*
- *2 Tbsps potato starch* (katakuriko) *(or 3 Tbsps cornstarch)*
- *3 1/2 Tbsps soy sauce*
- *2 1/2 Tbsps sugar*

vegetable oil for deep-frying

4 tsps ginger juice

Drain water from tofu by wrapping it in a clean kitchen towel and placing it on a chopping board, one end of which has been raised about 1 inch. Let stand about 10 minutes. Cut drained tofu into quarters.

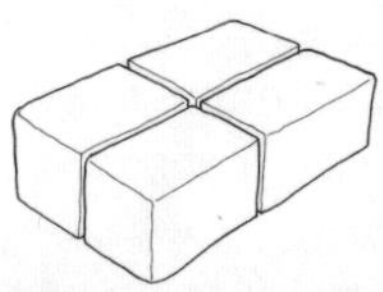

Put all thick sauce ingredients in a small saucepan and mix well to dissolve sugar. Place over medium heat and stir constantly until thick—about 2–3 minutes.

Heat oil to medium temperature (340°F/170°C). Place 2 or 3 tofu pieces in hot oil. This will cause much bubbling. Keep tofu moving so pieces do not stick together, turning them after 30 seconds. Total deep-frying time is about 1 minute or until very pale gold.

Place 1 piece of deep-fried tofu in each medium-sized dish. Top with 1/4 of thick sauce and pour 1 tsp ginger juice on each serving.

Serve hot! May be eaten with spoon or chopsticks.

Zenzai and Pearls

Shiratama no Zenzai

白玉のぜんざい

This ever-popular sweet originally was eaten at the moon-viewing observances in autumn. *Shiratamako,* convenient and inexpensive starch granules made from glutinous rice, is much used at Donke-in for making dumplings for soups, confections, etc. This dish may be flavored in many ways—vanilla, rum, brandy, fruit jam, and the like.

SERVES 4

6 Tbsps (40 gm) shiratamako
2 Tbsps boiling water
1/2 cup sweet azuki bean paste (anko), *either chunky or pureed (see page 44)*

Mix *shiratamako* with boiling water until the mixture is about the texture of your earlobe. This will entail a little muscle work.

Bring ample water to a boil and reduce heat to medium.

Make 8 balls with *shiratamako* mixture. Put each ball on the palm of your hand, flatten it slightly, and press a small dimple in the middle with your finger.

Drop 2–3 "pearls" into the simmering water and cook until they float to the surface. Remove from simmering water with a slotted spoon and drop into cold water.

Heat bean paste, place 2 heaping Tbsps in each small dish, and arrange 2 "pearls" on top.

Eat hot or chilled.

VARIATIONS: A thinner, almost souplike consistency of hot bean paste with "pearls" is called *oshiruko.* Toasted *mochi* is often used with *zenzai* and *oshiruko* instead of *shiratamako.*

Zenzai may be eaten hot, at room temperature, chilled, or on shaved ice, and may be made with whole azuki beans, partially crushed beans, or azuki puree.

Walnut Relish

Kurumi no Iri-Ni
くるみの炒り煮

The produce of the Shinshū region west of Tokyo finds its way to the capital in the same way that the prevailing winds blow the ash from eruptions of Mt. Asama. Walnuts are one such product. In this case, again, the walnuts are a gift from a Sankō-in parishioner, and the generosity of this gift over the years has stimulated culinary creativity.

SERVES 4

2/3 cup crumbled walnuts
2 Tbsps saké

2 Tbsps soy sauce
1 Tbsp sugar (optional)

Combine all ingredients in a small saucepan and simmer over medium heat for about 3 minutes. The sugar is not necessary, but it may even be increased if a sweeter result is desired.

Cool and serve in small individual dishes or family style in one bowl. Eat as a snack, relish, or garnish for rice, vegetables, tofu, etc. The flavor is strong, so small servings are sufficient. Keeps indefinitely refrigerated.

Burdock Relish

Gobō no Tsukudani
ごぼうのつくだ煮

The "head" and "tail" of the burdock root, which are not used for elegant burdock dishes, are sliced and used for this dish. This relish goes well with rice.

SERVES 4

6-inch (16-cm) length of burdock root, scrubbed with a stiff brush
3 Tbsps soy sauce
3 Tbsps saké

Cut burdock into 4 1 ½-inch (4-cm) lengths, and split each piece in half lengthwise. Cut each half into fifths lengthwise, so that each 1 ½-inch (4-cm) length yields 10 pieces.

Place burdock in a medium-sized saucepan with ample water and bring to a boil. Reduce heat to medium and simmer 10 minutes. Drain.

Simmer cooked burdock, soy sauce, and saké over low heat in a small, partially covered saucepan for 20 minutes. Cool.

Serve in small amounts. Keeps 1 month refrigerated.

Golden Shred Sushi

Hoshi-Yuba no Gomoku Chirashi-Zushi
干し湯葉の五目ちらしずし

Mixed sushi rice topped with various crumbled or finely chopped ingredients is eaten throughout Japan. This version is from the Donke-in temple, where it is made in large quantities and served over the following 2 days. This is guest food, appears at lunches, and also has a place among Buddhist altar offerings.

SERVES 4

8 sheets dried yuba, *reconstituted in hot water (about 10 seconds submersion) and drained*

FOR FLAVORING YUBA

- *7 Tbsps* dashi *(see page 81)*
- *1 tsp saké*
- *1 tsp soy sauce*
- *1/6 tsp salt*

4 medium dried shiitake *mushrooms, reconstituted in tepid water (reserve soaking water) and stems removed*

FOR FLAVORING SHIITAKE

- *3/4 cup water from soaking* shiitake
- *1 1/2 Tbsps soy sauce*
- *1 1/2 Tbsps sugar*

1 1/2-inch (4-cm) length medium carrot, scraped

FOR FLAVORING CARROT

- *3 Tbsps water*
- *2 tsps sugar*
- *1/6 tsp salt*

2 ounces (60 gm) lotus root, peeled (place in water to avoid discoloration)

FOR FLAVORING LOTUS ROOT

- *3/4 cup water*
- *1 Tbsp vinegar*
- *1 Tbsp sugar*
- *1/6 tsp salt*

12 snow peas, parboiled in lightly salted water and plunged into cold water

1 sheet nori *seaweed, cut in half*

6 2/3 cups prepared sushi rice (see page 189)

Cut reconstituted *yuba* sheets into 1-inch (2 1/2-cm) widths then stack these and cut into julienne strips. Place in small pot with flavoring liquid and simmer over low heat for 2 minutes. Drain.

Cut reconstituted *shiitake* mushrooms into thin julienne strips. Simmer *shiitake* and its flavoring ingredients in small saucepan over medium heat until liquid is absorbed—about 10 minutes.

Cut carrot into fine julienne strips (first cut lengthwise then crosswise), then simmer over medium heat with its flavoring ingredients until just cooked.

Thinly slice lotus root crosswise. If root is large, cut slices into thirds; cut slices of small root in half. Simmer in its flavoring ingredients until just barely cooked and still crisp—about 3 minutes. Keep in pot liquor until use.

Cut parboiled snow peas into thick julienne strips on the diagonal.

Crumble 1/2 *nori* sheet into small bits. Cut remaining half *nori* sheet into fine shreds.

Toss together everything except *yuba,* snow peas, and fine *nori* shreds.

One portion is 1 2/3 cups. Carefully arrange a mound of sushi on each individual dish, then sprinkle with *yuba,* snow pea strips, and *nori* shreds.

Keeps 2 days, but *do not* refrigerate. This sushi can be steamed if you wish to eat it hot, but in that case sprinkle the *nori* shreds on after steaming.

Tofu Sauté

Yaki-Dōfu no Atsuyaki

焼き豆腐の厚焼き

SERVES 4

2 Tbsps vegetable oil
1 cake grilled tofu (yaki-dōfu), *cut in quarters crosswise*
2 tsps saké
4 tsps soy sauce

Heat oil in frying pan over medium heat. Add 1 piece of tofu and fry until golden on both sides.

Mix saké and soy sauce. When both sides of the tofu have browned, pour 1 tsp soy sauce mixture over tofu in pan and fry about 30 seconds. Turn over and fry the other side 30 seconds.

Clean frying pan and repeat process for remaining 3 pieces of tofu.

Serve hot! A garnish of a dab of Japanese mustard (page 51) in the middle of each piece of tofu is also delicious.

Apricot and Agar-Agar Salad

Hoshi-Anzu to Kanten no Sunomono

干しあんずと寒天の酢のもの

This attractive Sankō-in original is good all year round, but especially in summer, when the sparkling agar-agar seems particularly cool and refreshing. Dried persimmons are used in Japan.

SERVES 4

1 1/3 ounces (40 gm) dried apricots (or peaches)
2 Tbsps saké

1 bar agar-agar (powder, granules, and twig forms cannot be used here)
$1/6$ tsp salt
1 Tbsp rice vinegar
$1/2$ tsp ginger juice

Cut dried fruit into thick julienne strips. Place in a small bowl and soak in 2 Tbsps saké (or a little more, if necessary) until soft.

Soak agar-agar in water for 10 minutes. Squeeze out water, then tear into penny-sized pieces.

Mix agar-agar and softened fruit. Add salt, rice vinegar, and ginger juice and mix well.

Serve small amounts at room temperature. Keeps well refrigerated.

Deep-Fried Konbu

Age Konbu
揚げ昆布

The word *konbu* is also pronounced *kobu,* which evokes the verb *yorokobu*—"to take pleasure in, to be happy, to enjoy, to be joyful." *Age,* "fry," is a homonym for the word meaning "to ascend, go up." This simple dish is thus both symbolic and delicious. It appears at special, festive temple meals and is included in altar offerings.

SERVES 4

$2/3$ ounce (20 gm) the best and thickest dried konbu *kelp available (do not buy thin, wrinkled* konbu)
vegetable oil for deep-frying

Dry *konbu* in the sun for one week. The *konbu* should be brittle and break easily when fully dried. Oven drying is also possible, but be careful not to scorch it.

Cut *konbu* in 1×2-inch (2 ½×5-cm) pieces (or break it, for an informal effect).

Heat oil to medium-high temperature (350°F/175°C). Test a sliver of *konbu* in the oil. It should fry immediately and not be bitter. The oil temperature is delicate and may need some adjustment and care.

Deep-fry one piece of *konbu* at a time for roughly 10 seconds, turning once in oil. Drain on absorbent paper or rack.

Serve as an hors d'oeuvre or snack in a small mound on each dish. Marvelous with saké. Keeps 1 week in an airtight container.

Bean Flowers

Nattō no Mochi Gurumi

納豆の餅ちぐるみ

This is a variation of the Flower Petals recipe on page 72, using fermented beans (*nattō*) instead of burdock. The cheeselike flavor of *nattō* blends well with that of the *mochi* in this favorite dish of an abbess of the Donkē-in temple. Good for lunch or tea time.

SERVES 4

4 Tbsps nattō
2 tsps soy sauce
½ tsp basic Japanese mustard mix (see page 51)
4 round or square pieces mochi *(about 2½ in/6½ cm in diameter)*

Mix *nattō* with soy sauce and mustard. Moisten and wring out a cloth napkin.

Grill a piece of *mochi* on one side only just until soft throughout. (Be careful it does not puff up too much and get hard to handle.) Place soft *mochi* on damp cloth and spread with fingers until half again as large.

Place 1 Tbsp *nattō* in middle of *mochi*, fold, and serve.

Eat immediately! Does not keep.

Buckwheat Gruel

Soba Gayu

そばがゆ

Though most Japanese are very familiar with buckwheat noodles, uses of whole kasha (buckwheat groats) are rare. Here is one.

Simmer 1 part kasha in 5 or 7 parts water (depending on how you like it) until a soft gruel is formed. Timing will depend on whether a toasted or untoasted buckwheat is used. Add salt to taste.

Eat hot. Keeps well and can be reheated as desired.

Buckwheat-Miso Topping

Soba Miso

そば味噌

Whole kasha appears in the diet of a few isolated areas and in temple food, perhaps as a holdover from the diet of earlier times.

This relishlike mixture is good on rice or sprinkled on parboiled vegetables, tofu, or *konnyaku.*

MAKES ABOUT 2/3 CUP

4 Tbsps miso (any kind)

4 Tbsps saké

½ cup kasha (buckwheat groats)

Blend miso and saké. Toast kasha in a dry frying pan until browned and aromatic.

Combine hot kasha and miso mixture and mix well. Cool.

Keeps very well.

Miso Mayonnaise

味噌マヨネーズ

The sweet white Kyoto (*saikyō*) miso used so much in the cooking of Zen nunneries forms a marvelous base for a mayonnaise containing only vegetable products. This can have as many variations as there are people to create them, so only a basic outline is given here. A food processor is fast and efficient, but a wire whisk does not entail much effort.

Use about half as much liquid as the amount of sweet white Kyoto miso. This can vary somewhat, depending on density and flavor of liquid.

Some liquids are:
- *water*
- dashi
- *tomato juice or sauce*
- *green vegetable puree*
- *saké*

Blend liquid and miso, adding small amounts of any such seasonings as:
- *salt*
- *vinegar*
- *lemon juice*
- *basic Japanese mustard mix (see page 51)*
- *ginger juice*
- *finely chopped perilla* (shiso) *leaves or other herbs*

Mashed fresh *yuba* or tofu may be whipped into the miso mixture at this point. Finely grated daikon radish is also good.

Finally, use ½ to ⅔ as much vegetable oil as original amount of miso. While whisking or processing miso mixture, slowly add oil as you would when making mayonnaise, continuing until the mixture is stiff and the flavor is rich enough. Adjust seasoning if necessary.

Generally keeps very well refrigerated, but this depends on what you put into it.

Cabbage with Tomato-Miso Mayonnaise
キャベツのトマト味噌マヨネーズあえ

1 head cabbage, cored
⅓ cup tomato-miso mayonnaise

Cut cabbage in fourths. Steam 3 of the fourths until tender-crisp. Cool.

Tear steamed cabbage into salad-sized pieces, then do the same with the raw quarter cabbage and toss together. Add tomato-miso mayonnaise and toss well. This is a wet salad; add more mayonnaise if you desire.

Keeps 2 days. The flavor is best the day after making. A little water will be emitted.

INDEX

定価3,500円
in Japan